COPS AND REBELS

A STUDY OF PROVOCATION

End of exit ramp from West Side Highway, 125th Street, Manhattan, where Alfred Cain, Jr.,

COPS

AND

REBELS

A STUDY
OF PROVOCATION

PAUL CHEVIGNY

PANTHEON BOOKS

A DIVISION OF RANDOM HOUSE

NEW YORK

Library of Congress Cataloging in Publication Data
Chevigny, Paul.   Cops and Rebels.
Bibliography: pp. 329–32
1.   Negroes—Social conditions—1964–
2.   New York (City)—Police.   3.   Trials (Conspiracy)
—New York (City)   4.   Black Panther Party.   I.   Title
E185.86.C44   301.45′1′9607307471   72–570
ISBN 0–394–47218–7

Design by Fran Gazze

Manufactured in the United States of America
by The Book Press, Brattleboro, Vermont

FIRST EDITION

This book is dedicated to

Bell,

Katy,

and Blue

ACKNOWLEDGMENTS

My thanks are due to the Board of Directors and the staff of the New York Civil Liberties Union, who backed me in taking the conspiracy case around which this book is centered, and patiently sat by while I wrote the book, when they could just as easily have told me to stick to my general docket of cases.

Particular thanks are due to Mike, Florence, and Loren Siegel, who threw the best of all fund-raising parties, and to Mel Lewis and Jimmy Knepper, who did us all the honor of coming to play the gig.

The people whose names appear in these pages, witnesses, judges, and lawyers, but especially the Cain family, Conrad Lynn, and Elliot Taikeff, have contributed time and ideas to this book. Arthur Eisenberg, Mary Morgan, Joan Temko, Seu-Wen Wei, and Sharon Coleman also worked on the case.

The study of *agents provocateurs* in Chapter 10 depended on the advice of a myriad of people. Norman Rush, with his encyclopedic knowledge of the literature, started me off in the labyrinth, and among many others who pointed the way are William Kunstler, Paul Jacobs, Jack Nelson, Norman Siegel, Charles Morgan, Frank Donner, George Fischer, Maximilien Rubel, Henry Schwarzchild, Gerald Lefcourt, Elizabeth Holtzmann, Eric Hobsbawm,

Bernard Fischman, Robert Fogelson, Aryeh Neier, and Steve Krugman.

Sara Blackburn and Lewis Cole suggested concepts which I have used.

Seu-Wen Wei, Toby Jo Platt, and Chris McDonald all helped prepare the manuscript.

André Schiffrin, Eve Cary, and my wife, Bell, all read and criticized the manuscript. Some of their suggestions I grandly rejected, and I am responsible for the consequences.

CONTENTS

INTRODUCTION

I did not read the newspapers on Sunday, August 17, 1969.
If I had, I would have found that two people I knew and
had once represented in criminal misdemeanor cases, Alfred Cain, Jr., and Ricardo De Leon, had been arrested the
day before while driving off the West Side Highway with
two other people whom I did not know, Wilbert Thomas
and Jerome West. They were said to be members of the
Black Panther Party, and it was claimed that they had been
caught just in time to prevent an act of political banditry
against the New Dunston Hotel in Harlem. They were
charged with extremely serious crimes, including attempted
murder of a policeman. Even if I had read the newspapers
that Sunday, I would not have had any idea that I would
become involved in the case.

I first began to think about writing this book in the midst
of the criminal conspiracy case which came out of that
arrest and is at the heart of this book. Because I had known
two of the defendants before, my initial purpose was to
trace the way these men came to political radicalism and
then into conflict with the law. I knew I could do no more
than sketch those origins for Ricardo De Leon, because I
was only slightly acquainted with him; but the life of Alfred
Cain, Jr., who was my client, I thought I could follow more
closely.

The first part of this book is concerned with the lives of
Alfred and his brother Anthony, as young black men in
Brooklyn. I had defended them in a criminal case, minor by
the standards of the criminal courts but major in their lives.
I was prepared to describe this, but I wanted to go to them
and to their family and find out what other influences had
shaped them. In January 1971, after the trials of the conspiracy case were over, I drove to the Cain home in the
Bushwick district of Brooklyn with a tape recorder to tran-
scribe memories and opinions from the Cain brothers and
their parents. I heard not only about the cases I had worked
on, but about schools, the police, racism, and military
service.

The Cain brothers, like Ricardo De Leon and Jerome
West, were not famous men. They were not national leaders
of the Black Panther Party, and the first part of the book
thus traces the background and views of men in the street
who adhered to the Black Panther Party. This is not to say
that the people in this book are "ordinary," as people; they
are not. But it is important to know how rank-and-file Black
Panthers came into the party, how they came by their convictions, and how they defend them. Other people who
knew all the principals in the conspiracy case appear here
as well; one of those interviewed was indicted separately
from Cain, De Leon, and West, in a related case. While the
narrative of any one of the principals, taken by itself, may
not clearly reveal his character, all the people in the book
reflect and comment upon one another. All the narratives
taken together make a portrait, I believe, of the lives of
young black radicals, and throw some light on what there
was in the family, in the state, and in recent history which
led them to their position. A tragic sense of life is possible
for some of these men, as it is for every black man who
chooses to resist his condition: they recognize the odds
against them from the state, the risks they must take, and
they take those risks because they see no alternative.

While Part One is largely a personal and political record, through narrative, trial transcripts, and the ideas of contemporaries and predecessors, Part Two is in a more public voice, being an account, chiefly through trial records, of the conspiracy trials of Cain, De Leon, and West. At its simplest level, Part Two is a detailed study of the jury trial at work in a political case. The words of Part One will not be forgotten by the reader, however, just as the lawyers never forgot what they learned about the defendants and witnesses outside the courtroom; that knowledge will bring special light to some otherwise veiled points in the testimony at the trial.

The conspiracy case was the crossroads between the lives of the three defendants and Wilbert Thomas, the black undercover policeman who joined the Black Panther Party in February 1969 and ultimately testified against the three after their arrest in August 1969. If this were a novel, it might trace the life of Wilbert Thomas in the same detail as that of the Cain brothers, showing how young black men of similar backgrounds (that much is clear from the little we do know) came to be on a collision course; but it is not a novel, and I can at best suggest the similarities and differences. We know much about Wilbert Thomas's character from his behavior before witnesses and at the conspiracy trials, but there is much in him which remains unexplained. His lonely ambition, his contempt for the lives of poor black people, his distorted views about his radical companions are all here, but the ultimate sources—both in himself and, in a broader sense, in the orders of his superiors—for his acts of provocation can only be hinted at.

After I began work on Parts One and Two—an account of lives and antecedents culminating in a criminal case with a political dimension—I realized that this was not enough. The conspiracy case was a paradigm for modern political trials. The police claimed, on the one hand, that it was an instance of what historians call "social banditry"—a holdup to obtain funds for a revolutionary group. On the other hand, it was apparent on the face of the case—as will become more evident in the chapters which follow—that there were strong elements of official provocation in it. As it turned out, this was evidently not a case of social banditry. There were ideas or theories about social banditry among the defendants which were combined (and perhaps molded) by the police into a conspiracy to commit a crime of violence. The case was a kind of hybrid, a juncture between political crime and political provocation. It represents the extreme edge of radicalism, and of official reaction against that radicalism.

Social banditry and official provocation are each classic problems of politics during times of social unrest, and I have sought in this book to outline the historical traditions into which fall the actions and ideas both of the defendants and of the police. The modern urban phase of the history of the Robin Hood impulse has yet to be written, but some of what is known is sketched in Chapter 4. Part Three deals with the entire problem of political provocation by government agents, from the vantage points of history and law. In Chapter 10, I have tried to collect the major cases, including older ones from France, Russia, Great Britain, Germany, and Italy, and contemporary ones from the United States. As far as I can tell, a synthesis of all the political provocation cases has never been done before, and I originally undertook it because I suspected that the methods and personalities of *provocateurs* must be so similar from one time and place to another that patterns of police methods would emerge. The most striking pattern that emerges in the end has little to do with police work: it is the repetition of official motives behind the provocations. Chapter 11 considers legal remedies for the problems of provocation, together with the enormous difficulty of inducing anyone to adopt new remedies, or even to stop abolishing the existing ones. The concluding chapter brings all the abstractions, the legalisms, back to the people in Part One.

This book is not about the Black Panther Party—as I think the party would be the first to claim. The principals were, for the most part, somewhat on the outs with the party, and the party repudiated them after their arrest in 1969. The book does not, except tangentially, deal with the evolution of Panther party ideas, but with the evolution of people into Black Panthers—what it was about those ideas that fitted the experience of the men who appear in this book. It is about how black people become revolutionaries, and how the police and the rest of society deal with them.

The chapters which follow assume some slight familiarity with the Black Panther Party, as well as with the police. The split in the party ranks after 1970 is largely irrelevant to this book, and the philosophy and special stance of the party in 1969 and 1970 is not easy to put into a few words. The party is Marxist-Leninist—dedicated to a socialist revolution, by violence if necessary, of which it is the vanguard. Although it favors coalition with other groups, it views black people in America as a colony. It holds that poor and jobless black people, part of the *Lumpenproletariat* of classical Marxism, are a revolutionary force. It believes that black and other minority people in the United States must prepare for the struggle by arming and defending themselves against oppression, especially by the police. The party is expected to "exemplify revolutionary defiance" by showing that acts of resistance can be successful, and at the same time to serve and educate the people in community programs.

The police are accustomed to being obeyed. When they tell a man, usually a member of some outcast group, to move along, they expect him to do it. The refusal to obey a command, whether it is legally enforceable or not, is considered a threat to good order and may lead to an arrest, for in the street arrests are a means of enforcing police authority as well as law. Sometimes a man, by his mere status or opinions, constitutes a threat to police authority, and such a man tends to provoke harassment and arrest.

The ideas about the police in the preceding paragraph could have been derived from my earlier book, *Police Power*. The police actions and trial testimony described in Chapter 2 can be explained by those ideas. There are things about relations between police and such determined radicals as the Black Panthers, however, which are not in that book and could not have been predicted from reading it (or writing it, for that matter). Most individuals who are harassed by the police do not, and do not intend to, present any real threat to police authority. The Black Panthers, however, mounted vociferous and physical opposition to the police. They must have seemed to many policemen like the incarnation of a nightmare: black people who made it their business to defy the police, and were willing to back up their defiance with guns. The police were willing not only to harass the Panthers but also to take creative action to fit them into a theory of conspiracy. That requires infiltration and provocation; but beyond simple infiltration, the political arm of the police, for ideological reasons of their own or working with others, have tried to get the Panthers to fit a pattern of criminality that suits them. As a political development, police provocation is important because it represents an attempt by the authorities to make their opposition fulfill a public image of violence, and to engineer consent for the repression of that opposition.

I should say a few words about method. All the trial records are derived from the official transcripts, except for the *voir dire* of the jury in Chapter 7, which is drawn from my notes because the minutes have not been transcribed. All the tape-recorded narratives and conversations are from interviews held in 1971. Every word set down is from the speakers, except where an occasional explanatory word or phrase is inserted in brackets. The order of the parts of this recorded material, of course, is often not as it was on the tapes—such conversations tend to ramble—but I have at most restrung ideas like beads on a necklace. I used this method for several reasons. One of them is that this is a book by a white man chiefly about black men and the ideas of black men; I subscribe in part to the view that there is a limit to the ability of a white man to interpret or criticize the ideas of black people. Furthermore, at this stage in our knowledge, ideas directly from the participants are more interesting than an interpretation of them by anyone. Finally, an extended dialogue, such as a tape can record, is the only forum in which basic questions of tactics can be discussed. The Cain brothers and other Black Panthers have come to grips with fundamental issues about economics, politics, and repression. The police are coming to grips with those issues as well, in heretofore secret ways which I hope this book will help to reveal.

PART ONE

BROOKLYN

If you saw the neighborhood I used to live
in, Brownsville, you'd think that the revolution had been here and gone.

ALFRED CAIN, JR.

1

HOME

Brownsville is low yellow-brick buildings, and most of them look as though the neighborhood had been taken by storm, block by block, in hand-to-hand fighting. In the three years before 1970, perhaps thirty percent of its apartments had been abandoned, and they were then being casually burned, by vandals and by chance.

Park Place, where the Cain family lived in 1969, is a short street on the border between Brownsville and its slightly less ghostly neighbor, Bedford-Stuyvesant. The block where the Cains lived is a brave exception to the surrounding dilapidation. Houses are carefully plastered and painted, windows have new awnings, and garden plots are planted in front. So much defiance is needed to maintain the standard that hortatory signs are posted along the block, one with the words "Respect Others," and another advertising the local block association. In the very next street, a little park has been turned into an impromptu automobile graveyard.

I knew from experience that Alfred Cain's dramatic words were true of Brownsville, before I ever saw his old block on Park Place. I was surprised to find that block; it expresses a standard of integrity in the face of the city that the Cain family itself has. Everyone notices that integrity: judges, probation officers, jurors—everyone, in fact, except assistant district attorneys and undercover agents. At the same time, it is characteristic of Alfred Cain that he would not mention the neat block. He would prefer to emphasize his solidarity with his companions and his ghetto neighborhood, rather than his difference from them.

The Park Place address figures in a later chapter of this story, when Alfred and Anthony Cain were members of the Black Panther Party. The narrative that immediately follows is largely centered around an earlier address, on Marcy Avenue in Bedford-Stuyvesant. That house—run down, with a littered front stoop—reflects less prosperity than the one on Park Place. It is just around the corner from neighborhoods indistinguishable from the Park Place block; on the side streets there are scrupulously kept houses, once again with monitory signs in the front yards. The house is down the avenue from Boys' High School, which both brothers attended, a handsome Victorian brick building with fancy ironwork.

During January 1971, the two oldest Cain brothers, Alfred and Anthony, and their mother and father sat down in the living room of their apartment and told their story from the beginning, before I knew them.

Alfred Cain, Jr., in his middle twenties, is the oldest son. He adds to the Cain family habit of reserve in personal matters a now inveterate cynicism about the power of the printed word to make any difference in the issues that concern him. He is, moreover, a little impatient with the events of his life before he became a Black Panther, because he knows so much more now than he did then. He is short and dark, with somewhat pockmarked skin which was later to figure peripherally in his conspiracy case. He wears brass-rimmed glasses, a bushy "natural" haircut, and sometimes a startling remnant of his army uniform: a green dress coat, with a small lacquer medal of the face of Mao on the left pocket, where the marksmanship award is usually pinned.

ALFRED CAIN, JR.:

I had quit school just before the time I graduated. I just couldn't relate to it; for some reason, I had always rebelled.

I remember one particular incident in economics class where we had this teacher who was into a thing about capitalism and the necessity for what they call a middleman. What she was talking about was the necessity to eliminate the middleman, and to consolidate the functions connected with manufacturing goods. She was saying that this would allow the consumers to buy goods at a cheaper price.

At that time I had read about one-half of the *Communist Manifesto*. Now, I didn't understand it systematically, but for some reason I just wanted to interject certain points; I didn't want to agree with her. We got into a long thing, and she became fairly emotional behind it, you know, and a lot of people in the class—it was an honors class—they understood where I was coming from.

I was running down a thing where I felt that if you did eliminate the middleman, that what would happen would be that the money would be concentrated in whoever it was that was manufacturing, or whoever it was that was at the higher echelons; according to the *Manifesto*, Marx had predicted that because of the nature of capitalism, the bigger pigs would push the smaller pigs out of existence.

Being an avowed capitalist like she was, she just couldn't even see running this particular thing down. She was telling me, "Well, what do you believe that these people do with the money? They don't just take the money and hide it in a vault; they take it and reinvest it and build the economy." Actually, I didn't understand the analysis that I had been getting into and trying to project. I had been basically doing it because I didn't want to be there.

We had another punk teacher at Boys' High. I remember that he told me, on one occasion, that it was his opinion that the only way the problem of black people could be solved in this country was if black people, through a process of attrition, like, they intermarried with the majority of the white people and just disappeared. I remember this really turned me off!

I did graduate. But just before that I had made my mind up that I was going to go out and work and get some money together, and besides the fact that as I said, I just couldn't relate to school at that time. I was working the Garment Center, pushing a hand truck, and that almost flipped me out. What happened was, as I say, I had quit school and I was making some time up at night to get that diploma—just because you're supposed to have it. I became a new slave, because when I finished working I didn't have the energy to do anything else. I wasn't making any money, but that was the only thing I could do at that time. I did that for a while, then I went off to other factory-type jobs.

I had thought that I wanted to go to college. I had made an appointment to go to Howard sometime during my junior year. Just later on, I didn't relate to school, so, after I had made the appointment, even though I did want to go to college . . . well, we also weren't able to financially afford it at that time.

All the high school seniors, at the beginning of the term, take a test, a Regents' scholarship test to determine what level they're at, and on the basis of the test, I was given one of those scholarships.

But, the two scholarships I had didn't apply to Howard University. The first scholarship I got was a National Negro Scholarship fund, which couldn't be used for Howard University. And the other scholarship, the Regents' scholarship, was just for New York State.

Another reason was, I had had a contradiction with the teacher at the time who was supposed to be counseling us in college, and I didn't get a lot of counseling at that time because he felt that I was a hoodlum. You see, there was a thing in Brooklyn at that time, a lot of people were jitter-bugging—gang fighting—and at one point I had told him that I had been involved in that whole scene of gang fight-ing. I don't know exactly how it went down, but I think he came to the conclusion that I still was. Of course, he didn't relate to me in terms of being capable or motivated or what-ever his criteria were, to be able to deal with college work. Somebody from the school had recommended me for some financial aid from the school, a partial scholarship, and he vetoed that, he wasn't for that.

About the jitterbugging, to an extent you could say I was jiving him, because I had been involved in it, like everybody out there in the area. We moved out to Marcy Avenue, in Bedford-Stuyvesant, around '58 or '59. I would have been fourteen, I believe. They had what they called the Chap-lains and Buccaneers. Actually, you had some young bloods out there still jitterbugging in '63 and '64. I had come to the conclusion that this didn't make no sense, you know, so I had cut it loose; not that I was ever enthusiastic about it —what happens is, in order to survive, you have to belong to an organized group out there. I chose the Chaplains, be-cause of the fact that when I first showed out there, the Buccaneers were chasing me home, and they were very serious about what they were doing. It wasn't, as I say, something that I really dug. Even at that time I could see that brothers killing brothers didn't make any sense.

There were a lot of other reasons . . . My mother had a little bit of college education, and my father had related to some form of higher education, and they were still doing bad. I could see that the people whom you saw in the com-munity who were really like making it, or seemed to be mak-ing it, were not people who had a whole lot of education, but people who was out there and was taking what they wanted—hustlers of one form or another. These were the only people that you had to identify with in terms of success.

At that time I hadn't been doing what you would call objective political study. I had been on to some things that Malcolm had done, and I had been involved in some school boycotts that this dude Reverend Galamison had done. We were into that for a couple of months and it didn't work out. But I was developing a certain political consciousness, though I hadn't done a lot of studying. I still felt there was a possibility for making it in the system, you know.

I would work for a while, then I would cut loose and I would gamble. I was shooting a little craps at that time, and I was playing a little cards. In fact, that's how I first got busted. I was shooting craps with this dude down in the subway, and the pigs showed on the set. The pig said, "Give me your fucking name," or something like that, so myself and the pig, we went into a thing. I didn't dig the way he had addressed me, so—I don't remember verbatim what I said, but I said something to the effect, "Well, I don't have a fucking name," like that. We got into an argument, and the pig said, "All right, I'm taking you down to the station house," so he did, and he busted us for disorderly conduct behind that.

Pigs were constantly stopping my brother and me, harassing us, pigs going in my pockets. One day I had a small baling hook in my pocket and the pig stopped me. Actually, it was my brother's coat; he was working for some grocery store at that time, and he used a small baling hook in his work. I happened to put his coat on, because I was walking some people back from where I lived. It was out in Bensonhurst, I think—you didn't have too many black people living there at that time. So, like right away he wants to know what we're doing out there. Then he goes in my pocket and he finds the hook and asks me what's it for and I tell him, "Well, I use it on the job," and so on and so on. We got into a thing where he called up to find out whether anyone had just been stuck with a baling hook, you know, and to find out whether or not any crimes had been committed. Eventually he let us go, but I think he kept the baling hook. There's just a series of incidents in which we were constantly being harassed by the pigs. So, I never related to the pigs.

I took the test for a job at the post office. It was supposed to be paying more money than I had been used to making at that time. I was only in the post office about two months before I got drafted. And before that I had been relating to, you know, jive gigs, factory gigs. I had worked for the Internal Revenue for a couple of months. I had five or six jobs during the time.

I didn't dig the draft. What happened was, I hadn't registered at the time I was supposed to, because I didn't relate to that military thing, and when I did, I had to register because of the fact that I wanted to go get some jive job and I had to have a draft card in order to do that. Then what I did was, I filed as a conscientious objector. I told them I didn't believe in that madness about killing people for this country and all of that. It was behind the religion thing I had had a little bit earlier. The family had related for a period of time to the Jehovah's Witnesses.

I knew that if it came to the point where my survival was at stake, I would kill. I realized that when I went to apply, because I had been in situations where it was either me hurt someone else or they were gonna hurt me, and this is what you come up through, being in the streets. [But] I had been listening to Malcolm for a while, and I had come to the conclusion that this country wasn't really serving black people. I knew that the war was wrong, you know, in the sense that these people hadn't done anything to me, and I didn't dig going over there and shooting them up. I just didn't want to go in the army. That was to me the quickest way of dealing with that, and as I say, it was some aftereffects of the religion thing. Couple months after that, they sent me my draft notice. You know, they never had any hearing on the conscientious-objector thing; they just ignored that.

When I first went in the army, I hadn't dealt with it objectively, because of the kind of beliefs that I had at that time and because I felt that they just would not keep me in the army. I thought that they would kick me out. I told them I was a CO, you know, and I went through a thing that I was supposed to be crazy. They had asked me several questions that I answered affirmatively on their mental-health thing that made them think that I must be nuts. I guess intentionally I didn't want to relate to that madness. You know, like I wanted to get out of the army. I hadn't reached the point where I was ready to risk going to jail. So I just figured, from the things that I do, they are going to cut me loose, but they never did.

As I say, at that time I had been working in the post office. I was making a few dollars. I was making twice as much as I was making before and I figured, well, it's a half-ass job, and that was one of the reasons why I went into the war in the first place—I said that I'll keep that job, so I went in. I didn't believe that they were going to keep me in the army, and I said, Well, I'll just come on out and try to get that money together and get out here and do the best that I can for myself.

They sent me to Fort Bliss, Texas, and put me in an automatic-weapons unit. This was 40-millimeter cannons, on a truck, and what they call a quad-50, which is four 50-caliber machine guns. I took that and I took some additional things on automatic-weapons mechanics.

They had us going through a lot of madness. See, right after we came out of the heavy-weapons training, they sent us out in the desert to train with the special forces. That was supposed to be antiguerrilla training. I can't clearly define why I allowed myself to go through these changes; in a sense I would rather be out in a desert than staying in a post, because you had a whole different thing from the regimentation. So I just went out there and I related to it. Soon after that, they formed our units up.

I had been going through so many changes in Fort Bliss; the people I had been running with, one of them had got put in the stockade, and one of them had deserted. I had got busted down to the lowest rank I could get busted to, because I was AWOL for about two or three weeks. What they had done was, they had sent our units home for Christmas leave for fifteen days. But after the fifteen days, we were supposed to come back and lay up in Texas for another month and a half, two months before going to Vietnam, and usually when a person leaves to go to Vietnam they get a thirty-day leave, and being that we didn't have a thirty-day leave, most of the brothers in the unit made their mind up that they weren't coming back on time. When time came for us to report in, a lot of the battalion was AWOL. They busted most of the brothers in the unit right after that.

They sent my battalion to Vietnam, but they left me back, because I was supposed to be crazy. I had "some touches of paranoia." A lot of the blacks, they didn't go. In our company, I think eight brothers were left behind for various reasons. You know, they had just concluded that most of us should be getting mental help. They were asking me questions to the effect, did I feel that people were picking on me. So I told them I believed someone was picking on me— that's right, that's correct. Because it was true! Because the army itself, society, was attacking me, was constantly committing aggression against me.

What happened next was that they said, Well, we need some bodies in Vietnam. One battalion that had left for Fort Myers had specialized in automatic weapons, and had taken a lot of casualties with the marines. They were ready to take crazy people then. So when I had the choice, I said, all right, I'll go. Because, see, I felt at that time, if I go to

Vietnam, then I'd be able to get out about three or four
months early. [But] I had to stay until way after Christmas.

My friends in the army were conscious of being black
and oppressed, but they didn't have a clearly defined direction. Things that we would do at that time were like resisting spontaneously. Then we'd fall back in, and then, it
would get to be too much again and we would just go off,
but like I say, it wasn't anything like we had real direction
at that time—we didn't.

You see, what happened is, during the time I was in
Vietnam, I realized that there were certain people who are
not going to respect you, and the only way you can deal
with them is through force. In Vietnam, it's a thing where
nobody messes with you—you got that M-16, you got that
machine gun. We were able to get that respect—not because of the fact that people wanted to give it but because
of the fact that they were scared. We didn't mess with
nobody, and nobody messed with us—I mean white
people, and some brainwashed NCOs who were reasonable
facsimiles of black people, Negroes, lifers. We were constantly being moved on in the army, and we realized there
was no hope of dealing with the whole thing peacefully.
There was no hope in saying that we could go through legal
channels.

I became conscious of a lot of things after I went to Vietnam. When I went into it, I realized from the beginning that
it was wrong, but I said, Well, I'm going to just go ahead
and slide through, come on back home, and pick up this
job I got and make some money.

I was a machine gunner, quad-50—actually four machine
guns. We were going through shooting up people's villages, tearing down people's houses, digging up crops. We
were supposed to be destroying enemy bases—a search-
and-destroy-type thing, and also pulling reconnaissance on
roads. To me, those people, all they wanted to do was grow
some rice. I realized that even then. Then I realized this

whole thing, shooting up people and getting shot at, you can't do that—just can't go out there and say, Well, I'm going to make some money and that's it. Because in 1967 we had the Detroit rebellion; we had the Newark rebellion. You know, we read accounts in the paper. During this time I dug that I was doing the same thing in Vietnam that they were doing here in Detroit and Newark—they were shooting up my people's villages.

It is not a thing that you can pinpoint to say that on this particular day and that particular incident caused you to realize all this was wrong, that the society was pulling aggression against you. What happened was that I had always realized this; at the same time I hadn't seen any method of dealing with it. And through that thing in Vietnam, I began to realize that Malcolm was correct, that you have to defend yourself; you don't have any foundation unless you have a foundation in your people—that you have to relate to one another. We were forced to do this in Vietnam, the brothers, and it came to a point where, through having to deal with what I was dealing with there—you know, shooting up people's villages—and reading in the paper about people shooting up black communities here, and reading about young brothers fourteen and fifteen years old dealing with the pigs, and me realizing that I was the one that was supposed to be back there dealing with the pigs rather than over here in Vietnam, I came back with the attitude then that we have to get ourselves together. If the Man is geared in such a way that he just commits systematic aggression against you, because of the fact that he feels as though he has the authority to do this, the only way you can stop him from doing this is either to eliminate him or to be able to control him.

After I came back, when I started working for the post office, I couldn't even relate to it any more. . . .

———

More bashful than his older brother, Anthony Cain is the most laconic of men. He at first refused to be interviewed, saying, through his brother, that he had "nothing to contribute." When he did consent, I had to cross-examine him to get at the details.

ANTHONY CAIN:

As far back as junior high school, I had difficulty just going along with the course. My attitude wasn't on the level where I could just sit there and go along with what the teacher was doing. I would go off on something else—talk with some other students. I was labeled as being disruptive. What they did, this particular problem, they took it out on my aptitude marks. I found coming through junior high school and going into high school, I had a lower average which wasn't reflecting my aptitude. It was the teachers' reflection on me.

In school they have certain standards. You have to be disciplined where you can sit down and more or less pay attention to what the particular instructor is dealing with. Homework is supposed to be geared to helping you solve problems which if they came easy to you, there was no necessity in doing. Then I didn't see the relevance in homework—it was quite easy. This was the particular attitude I had.

This particular school that I was going to, it wasn't one of the better schools. It was one of the tougher schools in Brooklyn. I think we had the highest number of gangs there. In junior high, I had one particular teacher who had been in the war; he lost a leg. He was very heavy on discipline. I had him for two periods. This English teacher, if something was going down that he didn't particularly dig, especially on the part of the brothers in the class, he would excuse the sisters to another class and have the brothers stand up for two periods, which was an hour and a half. Things like this created a certain antagonism.

I went to Boys' High, the same as Alfred, and I left the last year. They recommended that I leave. They didn't want to put me out of school. What they said was that I have a particular attendance as well as, they said, a behavior problem, and they didn't want to put me out of school because that would make it bad as far as getting into another high school, them having thrown me out of school. What they recommended was that I should leave school and come back when I felt my behavior and attendance could be kept on a level with their standards.

I was out of work at the time. I was out of high school and out of work both. I was about nineteen when I enrolled in a program, the year following my departure from high school. It was a manpower-training program, a new program supposed to create some type of employment for people who are unskilled. There was quite a lot of talk of black people not having substantial jobs and being key factors in the system as far as unemployment because of the fact that they were unskilled. I had started this manpower program that offered various technical skills. I attended two different manpower centers. At the first center, this was on Nostrand Avenue in Bedford-Stuyvesant, I started out working with a woodworking machine. At this particular time I had this thing—I drew fairly well as far as sketching goes. They felt that my particular academic skills warranted not so much me going into woodworking or working with machines. They thought that I had the capabilities to work better with my mind, and they recommended this draftsman course which I eventually took. It was a one-year course and I completed it. The program is divided into the technical skills or whatever various courses you desire to take. You get a specific amount of training in this, say, like half a day or three hours, plus you get three hours academic skills—mathematics, reading, and things in this line. We also had group counseling—a guidance counselor, you know, who would talk to you about things on the job, appearance and so forth. It was the guidance counselor who recommended me, who told me they have a draftsmanship program.

The drafting field is a well-paying job and it's a relatively easy job. The last drafting job I had, I was working in a well-established company. It was a well-paying job, and it would have been a long-standing job if I had stayed and geared myself to it. I would be making two hundred dollars a week. The type of work I was doing was work on armaments and weapons systems and things like that. The company does a lot of research stuff—work on the F-111 jet. They are very security-conscious, and you have to be bondable for one hundred thousand dollars. I had been arrested twice before, and I wasn't supposed to be bondable, especially doing work of that nature. Everyone there was supposed to have been security-cleared. I might have got the job because I went to an agency and paid for it.

I would like to go back into drafting eventually.

Melvina Cain is the vivacious and dramatic member of the family. She makes her points strongly, backing her sons to the limit.

MELVINA CAIN:

I was born in South Carolina. My father tried, say, to lift me by the bootstraps, to send me to college to do what black people there could do, either teach or become a nurse. The idea was that he wanted to lift the stigma that was put on the black people there. I went two years to college, Benedict, in Columbia, South Carolina.

At that time I was more or less brainwashed. Being brainwashed, you can't see any further than the eye will let you see. And the eye let me see that I was in the position that I was, and that was all. I remember certain things that happened in my life, and at the time I didn't say anything about it. I came from a black high school. (They didn't have black-and-white schools then.) We were trying to get a bus for the football players. We had tickets to sell, and I stopped and asked this white policeman if he would buy one of the tickets. He said, "Move on, nigger." That is what we got there—"girl" or "boy" or "nigger." At that time, you were not to tangle with the white man; I just went along. I just moved.

And I grew up working for them. During this time, they didn't have these political minds that they have today. My thought was to get the education to move on up that step, as my father put it, so that I wouldn't have to empty the slop jar, or be a chambermaid, and I did get myself to that position. I didn't reach the level that he wanted me to then, but I was better able to understand what my children . . . to say, "Go on, go on higher."

When I met my husband, he was in the service in Fort Jackson, South Carolina. That was during World War II. They shipped him through—Fort Jackson was one of the dropping-off points before they sent him to another base in Gadsden, Alabama. I met him in town; I was going to college. He had been to New York and was drafted from New York. After I married him, he got out of the service, and we came to New York.

I had minor jobs—I worked as a counter girl, I worked in a factory in the Garment Center, and when I started having children, I pursued the housewife-and-mother role. Mr. Cain has been working in the post office more or less since the end of the war.

Basically, I haven't been going to church since I have

been in New York for twenty-seven years, but there are religious groups that have come to me. My children were brought up very religious in the manner of the Witnesses— the Jehovah's Witnesses. Some ten years ago I was in the Jehovah's Witnesses.

The greatest demand now is to educate the masses— not to educate along society's thought—people have been educated enough. The youth of today has learned and they are moving from what they have learned about society, they are moving against society. That is why the government and the society say that a minority has begun to disrupt. They have taught youth what hypocrites they are, and what youth must do about it. You look back at how they have done the Indians. They have taken away the land of the Indians and pushed them back so that they are not even citizens any more. And they did it through violence. And yet when youth brings violence upon them today, it is a sin, it is not supposed to be. Youth takes what it has been taught and uses it, puts it in motion, and it is wrong. They take these young boys when they are eighteen years old and just beginning to live—eighteen, nineteen, and twenty—they put them into the army, they inject them with the idea of kill, kill, kill, for what? What are they killing for? They send them over there to destroy lands of other people, their homes, their livelihoods and everything. And when they bring them back to these shores, they say You cannot kill any more, you're becoming a civilian. They have leaflets out how to become a soldier, how to be a GI, and when you come back, how to be a civilian. How can you be a civilian any more? Say, you take an animal who has tasted blood, his lust is for blood. The youth that has gone over there and killed, and has been taught to kill, his first instinct when anything strikes out is to kill. And that is what he knows now, that is to kill. He must fight for his life. He must fight the injustices that have been done to him. And that's where we are morally wrong in saying that you can kill somebody else, but when you come back, you try to fight for your rights, we're going to jail you. And that is what the youth of today is fighting against: hypocrisy.

I think it goes deeper back than that, say, what my parents tried to do for me. They tried to educate me to better myself in a different way. But I saw what was happening to the boys through incidents that happened to them, and how the police had come into communities, how they had drawn guns representing the law, representing order, and came in and used the blacks and Puerto Ricans in any manner they wanted. And take this, my son Alfred he went overseas when he went into the army. He came back with a beautiful thought of how the government is literally destroying the lives and livelihood of these people over there, and turning them against each other, and calls it justice. And when you get back here you have to fight for what you went over there supposedly to fight for. And they talk about justice, he had to fight for his job to get his status when he was working at the post office before he went into the service. After he came out, he had to fight to get his job back.

[Here Alfred Junior interrupted: "I want to mention something. You got that part wrong about the job. You know I couldn't dig the job."

"I know that you quit it," said Mrs. Cain.

Alfred went on: "At the time I wasn't geared this way any more. They made it like they were doing you a favor working for them—how lucky you are, how fortunate you are, not being skilled in anything, making that much money. That's submissive, so that was why I cut it loose. These people were not doing me any favor. They made money off my labor. If they weren't, they wouldn't be hiring me, that's the nature of the capitalist system. I couldn't care less about that."]

I was hoping that Alfred would go to—in fact I hoped that all of my children would have gone to college. But he wasn't able and we didn't have the money to say, "Here, go to college." Mr. Cain was working at this time, but we having seven children, that was a big responsibility. At that particular time, on Marcy, we were paying one hundred seventy-some dollars for seven rooms, and then we had the overhead of the light and gas and all the other incidentals. One hospital bill right after the other, you know. We just never had the money to save. If he had gone, he might have worked at a different angle than what he finally ended in. He could have gotten with a political-minded group—organizations within the educational structure itself, educating the people as to what has to be done.

Having come up in these conditions—lack of money, lack of proper food, lack of proper dental health, lack of decent housing—makes my sons more liberal, more willing to fight for a better condition. As Alfred says, rather than let the younger generation inherit it, we'd rather go on to fight for it now. If I had had this mind, if I had had this knowledge, say, when I was coming along, maybe it would have been a different world, it might have been a little easier for these boys in these groups that are coming along now.

———

Alfred Cain, Sr., has been a postman for more than twenty years. Usually as laconic as Anthony, he too avoided the interview at first. Once he sat down to talk, however, his epic talents as a storyteller completely drowned his reluctance. The events of his life, with the police, in the army, even in relation to weapons and to crime, foreshadow his oldest son's story in the strange way that a father's life sometimes does.

ALFRED CAIN, SR.:

In Winston-Salem, North Carolina, I used to work for a tobacco company. We used to put up Prince Albert tobacco, we used to make that in cans. You did everything, wherever they needed you: pack the tobacco, and then sometimes they had tobacco coming off the machine, you had to pack it up as fast as it came. There definitely was no future. You were inside and you inhaled that stuff all day. We were getting eighteen cents an hour until Roosevelt came in; when he was made president, they raised it to twenty cents. Mother used to tell me, she said, "That's the way of life here." I said, "Yes, but I got to find me something better. I can't go through life like this."

My mother, she was a cook all her life. She had to adjust herself to that, but I just couldn't take it. If you go on the street, you want to go to the bathroom, you had to wait till you found a black bathroom. You know what I mean, you see more bathrooms with "White" on than "Black." For example, my brother was hit by a car, and he had a fractured skull. The guy who hit him was white. He got a white ambulance for my brother; otherwise my brother wouldn't have got one. And he rushed him to the hospital; otherwise my brother would probably have died. Because the neighborhood he was in—the blacks were over the other side of town.

Anyway, I was doing very good at school. I felt that the first opportunity I got I was going to leave. You know—I don't know if you have been to the South—they tell you to pray and take care of yourself. I felt that if opportunity presented itself, I could make it.

My grandmother was black and my grandfather was a Cherokee. He said that if the Indians had been together, they would never have lost the country, but they were so busy fighting among themselves, the white man took over. When they realized what a mistake they made, it was too late! He would always tell me, "Son, whatever you do, always remember, no matter where you are, try to get the black people together." And he says, "Don't trust the white man. Maybe you wonder sometimes why I drink like I do" —my grandfather up to the time he was eighty-nine years old, when he was killed by a streetcar, he used to drink a quart a day. I think he used to make it himself.

It was around 1936 I left Winston-Salem. I was about twenty years old at that time. I had never caught a freight train before in my life. I went over to Greensboro—that was where the train used to leave straight for Washington— I caught the train, and came into Washington. As I recall it, I met a few guys, mostly white, on the train, and at that time Joe Louis had just lost to Max Schmeling. Boy, they were kidding me, telling me, "Look at Joe Louis, he's riding a freight train."

When I went into Washington, I think I had fifteen or sixteen dollars in my pocket. I said, the first thing I got to do, I got to try to find me a place to stay, and try to find me something to do. So I went to a place called the Boston Buffet, and asked them if they needed a dishwasher, mop floors—anything. So they said, "Yes, we could use a dishwasher." At that time I think they were paying me a buck and a half a day. I worked there for about ten hours a day. I did get my meals—it was a restaurant—so that helped a little. I was happy when they took me, there were so many guys coming in every day looking for a job. Things were really bad at that time.

At night I looked around, I found me a car parked that was open, and I slept in the car. And I would go around in the park in the morning, and find me a place to wash up and clean up. I got me a locker in the station, and I put my clean clothes in there. When I got ready to change, I would take them into the park and change my clothes and go to work.

I was there for about four or five days. One morning I go in and they tell me I could have off, because they wanted me to work Sunday. So I went out to sit in the park, and there were a couple of blacks there that were drinking wine. The guy offered me a drink. I told him that I didn't drink wine, so he said come on drink wine. So I sat there and he drank, he consumed practically the whole bottle. And all of a sudden he goes *boom* on the bench—passed out. I am sitting there, I am writing a letter home to my mother. A cop came on over to me, he says to me, "Nigger, come on and help me pick up this nigger here." So I turned around and looked at him, I didn't think he was talking to me at first, because I'm minding my own business, I'm not doing anything—I'm writing a letter to my mother. Then he takes his stick and he says, "You." You know, in Washington they had this little place where you stand to get the streetcar, he wanted me to pull him out there so when the wagon come all he had to do was to put him in the wagon. He says to me, "Are you going to help me pick this nigger up or not?" So I say, "I am not paid to pick up this man." So right after I refused to pull the man out there, he called, "You, nigger, you come over here." So another guy came over to him, and they drag the guy out. Then he came back to me—he had his hand on the gun then—he took the stick and he pushed me with the stick right here. And he says, "Nigger, if I ever catch you in this park again, I am going to put you in jail." I looked at him, and said, Well, the guy's got a gun. If he had not had a gun I would have tried him. Because I wasn't doing anything, I was writing a letter to my mother. [Here Alfred Junior muttered, "You were realizing the importance of weapons."]

So I said, "Well, this is not the place for me—I am going to leave here right away." So I go back to the Boston Buffet and tell the guy that I just got a letter telling me that my mother is sick—I have to go. He said, "Why are you going? I was just going to put you on steady."

So I go out to where the trains were. I just got up on this electric train—I was on the ladder—it started off so fast I was scared to death. I got off in Jersey, and there was no problem, I got a ride to New York. First thing I did, I said, Well, I look so bad, I got to get a haircut. I had heard so much about the North being so different, and when you came to the North, things would be different. I still had my pay from Washington, approximately forty dollars. I go into a barber shop, and the guy says to me, "What do you want here?" I say, "I want to get a haircut." He said, "Don't you see we're all white folks? We don't cut no nigger hair here." So I said, Damn! This place is just as bad as Washington. I knew my grandmother had moved to Detroit— maybe I should go to Detroit. Then I thought, Maybe I'll hang around here and see if everything is so bad around here, because I had heard many stories about how New York was a great place to live and everything.

At the foot of Grand Street and East River Drive, there was a big parking lot with approximately a hundred and fifty cars. I speak to the guy, "Could you use an extra guy here?" He said, "Do you stay sober?" I say, "Sure." He says, "Can you read and write good?" I say, "Yes, I just finished high school." So he says, "You must be kidding." I say, "No, I can give you the address of the school, you can get in touch with them." He says, "I am going to give you a chance. You will get fifteen dollars a week. You work seven days a week, twelve hours a day." I say, "No day off?" He says, "We cannot afford to have any days off, because things are bad."

I worked from eight o'clock at night to eight o'clock in the morning—all the cops from the neighborhood used to come and sleep in the place at night, and I would wake them up for the call box. And they would bring me food and cake. Anyway, during the time I was there I didn't do too bad for the time that I put in.

We had one cop, I forget his name, but he used to come in every night and go to sleep. He would tell me, "Be sure to wake me up because I got to go to the call box." He was drinking every night. I went over to him one night—I know that he was pretty loaded when he came in—I wanted to wake him up ten minutes before time for him to hit the call box. When I woke him up, he grabbed for his gun, and when he grabbed for his gun, I grabbed him. I was trying to talk to him, tell him who I was. What he did, he tried to hit my arm away, so I said, I don't know what's wrong with this guy; I can't take a chance. So I hit him in the back of the head, and he dropped his gun. Then I took him to the office and washed his face. He was so apologetic. Every time he came around, he would tell me how sorry he was. He would bring me extra stuff and everything. Eventually, he lost his job; he drank.

I had a chance to meet all types of people. Down on Delancey Street, they had anything you wanted to buy— jewelry—anything you wanted to buy there. By me working there, I became known around the neighborhood. I went in a jewel place and bought me a watch, bought me a ring. That night a fellow I was working with, one of the mechanics in the garage where I worked, he said to me— he was Polish—said to me, "Would you have a drink with us?" I said, "Sure, I don't mind." I wasn't drinking much at that time. He had about three of his friends—all white. I had a few drinks with them. When they thought that I was drunk, they hit me in the head and took my watch, and left me bleeding. And I worked with him every day. I spoke to the boss about it, and the boss told him—the boss was Jewish—that if they didn't get my stuff back he is going to fire them all. So next day when I went in, he had my stuff on the table. But you see this scar on my head?

After that, I said, Well, in this neighborhood I have to do something to protect myself. Because I found out the cops, they would look away with anything like that. If you were black in the neighborhood, the only time they would be friendly to you was after they got in trouble. I mean most of the guys, for punishment, would be sent to Harlem. They tell me, come to Harlem, let the blacks see me with them, so nothing would happen to them, because in Harlem at that time, the people would drop something from the roof.

I think I stayed on that job for about one year and a half. I put my money in the Bowery Savings Bank on Grand Street and the Bowery. I figured that I would go on to Detroit and find out what things were in Detroit. I went to Detroit and I came into the same problems. Detroit is a place that's all alleys. I had people there, but I didn't know exactly where they were, and I was trying to find them. What really hurt me is everyone you see would say, "Nigger, where are you going?" Nigger this, and nigger that. I mean like you are an animal. Hate began to grow inside of me. I took up with some guys there—they were telling me that we could get along, and they know places where we could make extra money. So I went back with this fellow. He said that he was going to California. We went to Saginaw, Michigan, and that night he says to me, "You wait here, I am going to catch someone." So I say, "Catch who?" he says, "You *are* stupid—I'm going to rob somebody." So I say, "What are you gonna rob for?" He says, "You want some money?" I say, "I don't want any money like that." That night after eight o'clock, he found this elderly guy—the guy must have been between sixty-five and seventy—so he says, "I am going to hit him in the head." I say, "No, you are not. Not with me. I am going." He says, "I am not gonna do it." I say, "Why do you want to hit an old man like that?" So he says, "All right, if this is the way you feel about it."

The next day we went up to Dearborn, Michigan; that

was where they made up the trains. We were getting ready to get on a train there to go to California. He got on the train, he says, "Come on, come on," because when the train got a certain amount of speed you couldn't jump on it. So I told him, "I am coming, I am coming." I ran alongside the train, and when the train got up enough speed that he couldn't get off, I waved at him.

So then I got back on the freight, and I came back to Jersey City. And I came on back to the city [New York]. I was pretty fortunate—I found me a job in a garage because I had quite a bit of experience in it.

When the war was declared in December 1941, I was called. I was sent to Camp Upton, that was a place in Long Island. Most of the fellows that I was with in the service, they wanted to go with the cavalry, because Joe Louis was in the cavalry. I always wanted to go in the air corps. There were about six hundred guys who left at once. Quite a few of my friends, you know, said that if we go below Washington, we will be missing. About sixty-five to seventy guys left. And then they turned the names over to the FBI.

At that time, we were eating steak and chops, and we had a band playing when we left Camp Upton. Steak, chops, and chicken. We had a pullman. It was the first time I rode a pullman in my life! We were four days going to Florida. First thing I heard the guy say was [Southern accent], "My God, ain't this a damn shame, we was only expecting about two hundred people and we got all these people here; what are we going to do for food?" I said, "Oh, hell."

Then they started calling all the whites. They had two camps there in the air base. We had been sleeping together, eating together all the way down there, you know. So when they got to Tampa, Florida, they pulled the whites over to another camp and left us in this camp. The boys said that this is a little too much.

Anyway, for about two weeks they were feeding us stuff that even pigs wouldn't eat, because they said that the food didn't come in. So we decided that we were tired of this; we say if they don't give us some food, we are going to tear up the place. That morning we were getting ready, we had everything planned up to wreck the place. One of the boys had ratted to the CO, and they had the MPs out there with the guns.

After that I said, "Well, I am going to try to put my heart in this, but it is not easy." If you are going to fight, you know you may lose your life, you say, "What the hell am I fighting for?" Most officers were Southern officers, they treat you like you're an animal or something. But I said, "Well, I am going to try."

We stayed there for quite a while. Before we left, we went out to where the air base was. The water was so beautiful and clear there that you could see the fish all the way to the bottom. There must have been about twenty-five or thirty of us went out there looking at the water. Two carloads of white soldiers came along. They started calling us black no-tail bears. So the boys started to say that we may have us a little war right here.

What they would do, they'd give us guns, but wouldn't give us any ammunition. So what we would do, we knew where the ammunition was, we'd get ammunition, and we'd stick it in our boots. The word got around that a bunch of the boys had ammunition. So they checked up everything to see if the guys had it. What happened, our first sergeant found out about that, so he told us, and we hid it.

We left after a few months, and we went to Alabama. That was the worst place that I was ever in, in my life! Florida was a heaven compared to Alabama. You know when we first went to Alabama, if they would see us on the street and they were with their women, they'd tell us, "Get in the street, nigger, you know you ain't supposed to walk on the sidewalk." After this started, the blacks started going into groups and they started carrying guns. A few incidents, that's all, and the whole thing began to get a little better.

I know that none of us is perfect; as my old man used to say, we all have our imperfections. I know my kids. They are not too bad—average boys. I have did everything I possibly could to keep them happy. I know I never want them to go through what I have been through. I have been through hell, believe me. I am happy that all of them were born here in the city. I figured that they would have a lot better chance here than in the South. But now you would be surprised how the South is changing—changing quite a bit.

If the cops today would just try to understand the blacks a little bit more, I don't think they would—I mean you'd be surprised what I've seen. Back in 1962, I was going to work. I don't know what had happened, but a black came out of a house. He must have been sixteen or seventeen years old—maybe eighteen years old at the most. A radio car came over. There were two white cops and one black cop. When he came out of the house, they ran over to him. He swung, and they taken him and put him across the front of the car. The black cop walked away. And they beat him so that he was crying for his mother. They beat him. I told them, "Man, why don't you kill the guy?" So they told me, "You better go ahead, before we arrest you." When I walked over to him, right away he grabbed his gun. What hurt me so was that the black cop walked away. He didn't participate in it at all. He walked away, he walked down the street. After beating him—he was bloody and laying down—they picked him up and threw him in the car. When they threw him in the car, then the black cop came back, they all drove off together. That has been going on so long. I tell you the truth—I mean something will have to be done.

Things are changing today, but I mean they got to realize this thing: the kids that are coming along today, they don't mind dying. I remember years ago in my home state, they used to have the KKK march; everybody was scared of the

KKK. But people are not scared any more. Today, these kids coming along today, they don't give a damn what they got on—sheet or whatever. Now if the KKK comes around, they blow their heads off. You understand? There is a difference today, there is a difference.

Well, I don't know, maybe I said too much . . .

The Cain family narrative tells us that their response to the problems which confronted them was practical and level-headed. The Cain brothers met plenty of harassment, but they were strong people, sprung from and supported by strong people; they understood what was happening to them, and they coped with it. Much of the harassment came from the state: the school, the police, the army. But some help in coping came from the state as well: post office jobs and training programs. On balance, in 1967, where this part of the narrative leaves off, the society confronting the family, however arbitrary, does not seem totally unviable. With some reason, the younger Alfred Cain says that he still thought "there was a possibility for making it in the system." Much later, after Alfred Cain's trials, a juror—a black social worker—was to say, "He's no street guy. I know him; he had a chance just like me." This observation, while not entirely right, was an acute response to Alfred's obvious intelligence and ability to "deal with it." Both of the brothers were on the ragged edge, but ready to come to grips with the world as it was in 1967. They stood where the brook and the river meet.

2

MAGISTRATE'S COURT

When I first heard of Alfred and Anthony Cain, in May of 1967, I knew so little about them that I could not spell their last name. At that time, I was finishing up my work in the Police Practices Projects of the New York Civil Liberties Union, and the *Cain* case was one of a flood of cases painfully like it.

It began with an angry telephone call from a printer, Charles Campbell. He told a story of three young black men having been arrested on the subway and roughed up by the transit police, as he was returning home from work. As far as Mr. Campbell could see, the men had not been disorderly, but the police had ordered one of them to sit down and then to leave the train. When he refused, a brawl ensued.

That sort of arrest is depressingly common in the streets, but it is, if possible, an even more ordinary occurrence in the subway. The New York City Transit Authority's regulations contain a multitude of niggling prohibitions, against everything from playing music to carrying large objects. These are usually enforced by ejection from the subway, and if a person refuses to be ejected, as occasionally happens late at night, when the trains do not run often, an arrest usually follows. In my work on police problems, I had found that a transit policeman was no different from any other policeman: if a citizen refused his order, whether he was right or wrong that citizen was asking to be arrested, because it was

31

of paramount importance for the policeman to maintain his authority.

The unusual thing about the case was not its facts but the presence of a witness like Charles Campbell. The case had come to me, not through its black victims, but through a middle-aged white man who was a mere observer. More than that, he had gone to the precinct and found out the defendants' names. That in itself was an accomplishment; I had heard complaints about arrests of strangers in the street, but the observer usually had no idea which of the thousands of names on the court calendars might be the right ones. The police often refuse to give the name of a person arrested to a witness, virtuously protecting the defendant's right to privacy (although they do not hesitate to trumpet his name, address, and previous criminal record to the press when it suits their purpose). In this instance, however, perhaps because the arrest was made by the subway police rather than precinct officers, the station had given Mr. Campbell the names.

I began to try to investigate the case from the sparse facts Mr. Campbell had given me. According to my notes, two of the defendants were named "Kane"; I began to check the jails by telephone, but of course I could not find them.

Mr. Campbell was not one to trust the fate of others to a harassed lawyer. Some time later, he called me from Brooklyn Criminal Court with the correct spelling of their names and a list of the charges: disorderly conduct and resisting arrest. They were about to be bailed; would I take their case? I would if they asked me to, but I could not accept the case through Mr. Campbell, because he scarcely knew them.

A few days later, Alfred Cain, Jr., came into my office. He was wearing a white shirt and tie and his hair was cut short —very clean-cut. He was then in the army, during that short leave he has described, before being sent to Vietnam. Like me, Alfred was not surprised by the facts of the case. He and his brother had been going home with a friend to Brooklyn from a party in Manhattan, and they had been talking and laughing in the subway. A policeman had challenged them, argued with them, and ordered them off the train. When they refused, they had been arrested with some roughness. Again like me, Alfred was impressed only by the interest of Charles Campbell. He was mystified to the point where he seemed almost suspicious: "Why does a white man want to get into this thing, go down to court, spend time?" I was only slightly less surprised than he; I told him I had seen plenty of white people incensed at the treatment of blacks, but few with the determination of Mr. Campbell. Alfred shook his head, saying, "I guess I'm getting cynical." When I asked him in 1971 about his racial views at that time, he said, "I had never related to white people, not on a social basis, not for a long time, since junior high school, except for teachers and, you know, pigs I had been working for."

On several adjourned days of the case, the Cain parents came to court. At that time there was nothing in the least political or militant in the family's speech or appearance. The brothers wore suits, and they all had their hair cut short. So I came to know the Cains slightly, in a professional way. Anthony was then a draftsman, and Alfred had returned to his army unit. Instead of adjourning their case indefinitely, the court put out a warrant against Alfred, and William Smith, the third defendant, disappeared for good. The warrant made Alfred angry, as he later told me, and he wrote the mayor to complain; the result was a complaint investigation by the Transit Authority Police Department, which did not, in the end, help the defense.

At the time the Cain brothers came to trial, they were entitled to a trial by three judges of the criminal court, but not by a jury. Disorderly conduct was a mere "offense," not even carrying the stigma of a crime, but resisting an officer was a misdemeanor, bearing the maximum penalty of a year in jail. Even so, state law reserved the jury trial in New York

City for felonies, crimes with possible penalties greater
than a year. At that time, the State of Louisiana and the
City of New York were the only jurisdictions in the country
which permitted a penalty as severe as a year to be imposed
without a jury trial. The Louisiana practice was declared
unconstitutional just a few months after the Cain brothers
were tried, in 1968, but the New York City courts adhered
to their practice, although it now seems to have been pat-
ently unconstitutional, for two more years. The declaration
that the New York practice was a denial of due process of
law has never effectively been made retroactive, and it does
not help anyone tried before 1970.

In supporting the practice of trial by judge in New York
City, the district attorneys argued before the United
States Supreme Court, in the case of *Baldwin v. New
York*, that such a trial was just as "fair" as a jury trial.
The Court did not entirely agree.

> [T]he primary purpose of the jury is to prevent the possi-
> bility of oppression by the Government; the jury interposes
> between the accused and his accuser the judgment of laymen
> who are less tutored perhaps than a judge or panel of judges,
> but who at the same time are less likely to function or appear
> as but another arm of the Government which has proceeded
> against him.

The first Cain case perhaps throws some light on who was
right in that controversy—that is, whether a judge trial in
fact is as fair as a jury trial.

The criminal court in Brooklyn is a sad old building.
Thronged with defendants, witnesses, and lawyers, it is now
too small to handle the traffic. Courtrooms are sometimes so
jammed that latecomers, even defendants, cannot get in,
and it is not unusual to have to wait ten or fifteen minutes
for space on an elevator going upstairs.

By the time Alfred had returned from Vietnam, the minor

case of *People v. Cain* was nearly a year old, and we were forced to a trial as soon as the case appeared on the calendar. The trial was held in an overheated room on the sixth floor, before the three indifferent magistrates assigned to such trials in Kings County for the month. I knew them by reputation, and they did not inspire confidence; if I had been able, I might have contrived an adjournment, but I could not. Our witness, Charles Campbell, was present, and we went forward.

The charges had been brought by a young white transit patrolman. He was visibly shaken by the fact that a civilian complaint had somehow been made against him, and he relied on the support of older officers; an "investigator" of complaints for the transit police was in court supporting his boys. At a much earlier stage, on one of the adjourned dates, while the warrant was outstanding on Alfred Cain, the officer had even confided in me that he did not like his police job. As soon as this case was over, he said, he was going to California.

The disorderly-conduct charge recited that the Cain brothers and the missing William Smith

> while acting together in concert with each other did while on said train act in a loud and boisterous manner all to annoyance of persons in said train and when asked to desist and leave said train the defendants did refuse to do so, continued to act loud and boisterous, used vile and indecent language, and necessary force had to be used to remove them from train.

The resisting-arrest charge simply said that the three had resisted the arrest for that offense. The section of the New York disorderly-conduct statute under which the three were charged required at least the threat of a "disturbance of the peace," that is, a *public* disturbance. Cases had repeatedly held that a purely private argument, even between a policeman and a citizen, did not make out a public disturbance; there had to be others present to be disturbed by the abuse or obscenities. As usual, the shape of the law had some influence on the arresting officer's testimony. He introduced into his story a white passenger who was supposedly annoyed by the militant conduct of the defendants, but whose presence was, as later testimony would show, almost a physical impossibility.

A. Two of the defendants, Mr. Anthony Cain and Mr. William Smith, were seated on one side of the aisle with a male Caucasian passenger in between, and Mr. Alfred Cain was seated directly across. . . . [The seats] run parallel with the train.

Q. Now, were there any other passengers in the car at this time?

A. Yes, there were about at least 50 passengers.

Q. Now, what if anything did you observe about the defendants?

A. Well, as I entered the car, I heard William Smith state, "Hey, man, here comes a blue robot. Let's show this blue robot like we showed them in Watts." Whereas he extended his hand to Mr. Anthony Cain, who extended his hand and they slapped each other's hand saying "Cool, man, cool." Mr. Anthony Cain stated then, "Hey, man, we'll show Whitey, yeah, we'll show Whitey like we showed them in Harlem, yeah, man." And he extended his hand and Mr. Smith extended his hand and they slapped each other's hand saying "Cool, man, cool." However, this time, they hit the male passenger sitting in between them. Mr. Smith then stated, "That's nothing, man, we'll show them like we showed them in Chicago." And he extended his hand and Anthony Cain extended his hand, and they slapped each other's hand, and then Mr. Smith hit the male passenger, whereas the male passenger got up from the seat, went past me into the next car, and took a seat. . . .

Then Anthony Cain stated, "Hey, man, look at Whitey go. Boy, they're afraid of us now." And two more passengers who were sitting next to Mr. Anthony Cain got up from their seats and went further down into the car. I then went over to the defendants, I asked them to be quiet, to ease your voice, and stop disturbing other passengers. Alfred Cain, who was sitting behind me at this time, jumped up and he says, he stated, "Hey, man, you can't tell me what to do. We know our civil rights." I stated to them, "I wasn't referring to you, I was referring to these two gentlemen here, asking them to be quiet and stop disturbing the other passengers." He says, "That's my brother, and that's my friend, and you can't tell any of us what to do." And then William Smith and Anthony Cain stated, "Yeah, we know our civil rights. Don't bother telling us anything." I then stated to them, Alfred, I asked Alfred Cain to sit down and for the all three of them to be quiet and stop disturbing other passengers or otherwise I'll have to order them off the train. Alfred Cain then stated, "Man, you can't tell me what to do. I'm not going to listen to you. I'm not going to sit down. I'm not going to get off the train." So we entered Newkirk Avenue station at this time. I signalled for the patrolman on the station to respond. Patrolman K—— responded. He tried to talk to them for about five minutes, asking them to leave.

Q. What did he say?
A. He asked them, "Will you come with me," and, "Will you wait for the next train. Let's be men about this. You're holding up everybody. Everybody wants to go home. It's late at night." They refused to do so. Instead they became louder and more boisterous.

The officer next described the resisting arrest as a confused act of violence.

As I went to place Alfred Cain into, take him into custody, I went to grab him, he started swinging. We turned, went on the floor, we rolled out onto the platform.

The officer who came to assist, a black policeman, supported the young white policeman, asking all three of the young men to leave the train. He testified that they refused and cursed him out. The young policeman then formally arrested them all, and the black officer took into custody Anthony Cain, who resisted arrest simply by pushing him away with his hands.

A third policeman, who saw the train stalled and ran to help, had seized the third defendant, William Smith. He said that Smith resisted arrest by grabbing a support pole in the center of the car.

All the policemen's stories fitted together fairly well. The men did not purport to corroborate one another except on a few points, and thus they were difficult to cross-examine. Their stories were rather general, and there were no complex fact sequences or documents to go over. In the effort to find something to work with, I asked one of the officers for his memorandum book of the occasion. He did not have it, and my motion to strike his testimony unless I was given an opportunity to see it was denied. The subway police had, in a general way, made out a case, and it would stick unless we refuted it. The fact that there were three policemen in court to testify was in itself damaging, because it was a sign to the judges that the Transit Authority had some strong reason to want to win.

Our defense witness, Charles Campbell, testified that he had finished work early in the morning and got on the subway train at Times Square. In his account, there was no fighting, no racist patter, and no white man being harassed by the three.

A. When we get to Prospect Park, that is, when I say we, the train, got to Prospect Park, there were three young men who got on the car. They were in the front part of the car. There were about 12 or 13 men in the back part of the car. Everybody reading newspapers. . . . The rear door opened, and the officer came into the car, and he walked through the car. . . . He got a few feet past the three young men, and he turned around and came back, and said something to the one who was standing up.

Q. Did you hear what he said?

A. No, but he said it, he waited a moment, and then he pointed a finger at him. He says, "I told you to sit down." So the, I could hear it, and the young man turned to him, and said,

"Oh, all right, I'll sit down." . . . The young man did sit down, and the officer stood there for a moment and then he said, "I want you to get off at the next stop and wait for the next train." And the young man said, "I like this train. I'm going to stay on this train. I'm on my way home. I'm going to stay here." . . . As the doors opened at Newkirk Avenue, the police officer stepped to the door, he held himself against the door so the conductor couldn't close it, and then rapped his stick against the side of the car. Another officer came running down the platform, and they both came in the car, and they bent over, and they were talking to one of the young men, and the young man kept shaking his head.

Q. You didn't hear this?

A. No. . . . They continued to talk to him, and he kept shaking his head. Suddenly, they both grabbed him, lifted him off the seat, and started to push him toward the door. He got ahold of one of the handles, one of the bars in the middle of the car, and he held on. They pulled at him, and, but he held on real tight. But they finally got his hands disengaged from the bar, and they got him out on the platform, they forced him face down on the platform, and put handcuffs on him and then one of the officers hit him over the head with his club. . . . The motorman started to blow his whistle and two more patrolmen came running down the platform, which one patrolman held the first man on the platform, the other officers came in, grabbed the other two men, and forced them through the door and they forced them down, face down on the platform, and put handcuffs on them. . . .

[ASSOCIATE JUDGE]. What were the other two doing while the two officers took the—you say you think it's Alfred or Smith —onto the platform. What were the other two men doing?

THE WITNESS. They were just sitting.

[ASSOCIATE JUDGE]. Just sitting?

THE WITNESS. That's right. They didn't move.

[PRESIDING JUDGE]. Did you stay or remain on the train after the doors closed?

A. I did. When I got home, I felt so indignant about it, I phoned the Coney Island Police Station, and asked for the precinct closest to Newkirk Avenue, which they gave me, and I phoned and luckily, I hit the—I got the station. I asked if three men had been brought in and had been placed under arrest from a subway station. I was told yes. I said, where will they be booked. They said in night court in Manhattan. Well, there was nothing I could do. That was 3:30 in the morning, nothing I could do until morning. In the morning, I phoned Legal Aid.

The judges took over the questioning of Mr. Campbell even during his direct examination, but they went to extraordinary lengths in the cross-examination. One judge asked:

Q. Didn't you say that the only—that they were the only ones sitting in the front of the car?
A. Yes.
Q. Why was it that two of them sat on one side, and the other one sat on the opposite side?
A. I don't know, but I said it was only a few seconds that one got up and went over.
Q. Why was it necessary for this one?
A. I wouldn't know.
Q. Isn't it a fact that there was somebody else sitting there?
A. There was not anybody sitting there, no, sir.

At the very end, the presiding judge put these questions:

Q. Mr. Campbell, how long did this occurrence take, while you say, it was taking the defendants out of the car, and onto the platform? And somebody was striking one of them with a club, the whole thing?
A. The whole thing, about ten minutes. . . .
Q. And, you say you and the other passengers were looking out the windows at what was going on?
A. That's true.
Q. Did you or any of the others remonstrate with these officers?
A. No.
Q. You said nothing?

A. Not a word.
Q. You watched a boy being beaten, according to your testimony, and you did nothing?
A. That's right.

Despite all this, Mr. Campbell stuck to his story, without variation. At one point, he did accidentally introduce an important fact. He referred to the subway car as one of "the new trains," and Alfred Cain whispered to me that the new cars did not have seats for three at the ends of the car. That was in fact the case: at either end there is a seat for two along the wall, facing, across the aisle, a motorman's cabin and a single seat. As I called Anthony Cain to testify, I began to see the annoyed white passenger disappearing from the case.

Anthony finally explained the misunderstanding that had led to the arrest.

[M]e and defendant William Smith were sitting right beside each other, and my brother was sitting across, directly across the car from us. And, he was laying down as if he was sleeping and, me, I was telling jokes about my brother to Smith, and we were laughing and my brother happened to look up, and he saw that we were laughing, and we were looking at him. So he got up and he came over, and he was standing over us, and he said, "What's the matter," and, this, I said that I told him that I told Smith that he looked like a robot, you know, when he was marching, you know, back and forth during the service and me and Smith started laughing more, and he was, he was laughing. . . .

So, as he was standing above us, this officer right here. . . . He was coming to the train at the time, and my brother was still standing over us at the time, and we were still laughing, so the officer, he walked by, and he stopped, and he turned around and he told my brother to sit down. And my brother had turned around and he started looking at him. So, the officer hollered at him, and told him to sit down. So my brother said, All right, he'll sit down. So my brother had sat down, and the officer went and walked about four more feet, and he stood by a subway train door, almost directly in front of us, and me and Smith were still laughing, and my brother started in laughing, and he came back over, he walked from the doors, came back in front of us. . . .

So, he said that one of us was going to have to get off the train. And he was standing in front of William Smith at the time. So Smith, he asked him why that he was going to have to get off the train and, he said, "You're just going to have to get off the train," or something to that effect. So the train was pulling into the station at this time, and he said, "All right, are you going to get off?" And Smith said no, he's not going to get off. So, he went, he went like he was going to go out of the train, and he took his stick and he started banging on the outside of the car door, and a whistle started blowing, a train whistle. . . .

What had happened was now perfectly plain. The officer, new to the job, had tried to assert his authority against some black youths he thought were making fun of him. When they refused to obey, he felt obliged to arrest them, and they were clubbed in the process. Afraid that his false arrest would not stand up in court, the officer had made up a story about racial conflict. The court, however, was not so much interested in an explanation as in cross-examination.

The same judge who had conducted much of the questioning of Mr. Campbell again intervened.

Q. Did you hear Mr. Campbell tell us that the one who was holding onto the pole was your brother?

THE WITNESS. I heard that he said it might have been him or William Smith.

Q. Yes, but he didn't know which one was standing up at the time. But it was the one standing up at the time that held onto the pole and wouldn't get out. And you're telling us that the one who was standing up at the time on the strap was your brother. So therefore, he said that it was your brother who was holding onto the pole. Did you hear him say that?

A. I had commented before that he, the officer sitting here, had

told my brother to sit down and he said all right, he would
sit down. At which time he did sit down.

[PRESIDING JUDGE]. All right.

Alfred Cain followed his brother to the stand, and told
substantially the same story, except that he made a point of
the layout of the seats on the "new train."

We sat down on the seats where there—the seats at the end
of the car where there's only space for two people. Now, my
brother and Mr. Smith sat down in one of those seats and I
sat down at the opposite end of the car. Then, my brother
happened to say something to Mr. Smith that I couldn't hear.
So I got up.

During the cross-examination, there was more from the
same judge who had so frequently interfered.

Q. You say you saw the conductor there?
A. I believe I did, yes.
Q. Where was that?
A. He was on the platform. Well, I saw him either on the train
   or on the platform. . . .
Q. Did you see the conductor when you were all on the train?
A. No, I did not.
Q. Now, when you were on the platform—
[ASSOCIATE JUDGE]. Didn't you just say a minute ago you didn't
   know whether you saw him on the train or on the platform?
A. I didn't say that. I said I didn't know whether the conductor
   was standing on the train where they open the doors or
   whether he was standing on the platform. . . .
Q. All right. I remember she asked you the question did you see
   him while you were on the train and you said no.
A. I did not say while I was on the train. See, I was on the platform.
Q. From the platform you may have seen him standing on the
   train. Is that what you mean?
A. Yes.

That was the end of the defense case—or it would have
been, except that the associate judge of his own accord

called Charles Campbell out of the audience to assume the stand again, and began a further cross-examination covering pages and pages of the record. The questioning was all concerned with the fact that the printer generally took the same train at the same time and tended to see the same people, that in fact he knew two of the people because he worked with them, yet none of those people had been brought into court to testify.

The prosecution then called the conductor of the subway train. He was intended to be a "rebuttal" witness, but he actually helped the defense.

Q. And what, if anything, did you see when you stepped into the train?

A. Well, what I saw was that the officer was asking the gentlemen to leave the train, to come off the train, to get off the train.

Q. Did you hear anything else?

A. Well, they said "We know our rights."

[PRESIDING JUDGE]. Who said that?

A. Who said it?

Q. Yes. Put your hand down. Who said that?

A. Well, I cannot be exactly, I cannot point exactly to the fellow, the one that said it. But I know it was the two fellows with their faces pointing toward the platform, sitting with their back that way; and they were sitting—saying, get the officer's number, because we know our rights. And then I walked back to my operating position so that I would be in position to close the doors and proceed when the officer gave me the signal that everything was cleared.

This tended to establish that the defendants were not loud nor were they cursing, and that there was no sign of violence. The judge who was so proud of his cross-examining talents extracted an even more important fact.

Q. Where were they seated when you saw them?

A. Well, I didn't—I said this now. I did not give—there were three fellows, and I know there was two sitting in the back

and I think, I may not be correct on this, there was another
one sitting facing them on the other side on the end seat, like.

Q. Is that the sort of seats where only two can sit in one seat?

A. That is correct.

This statement alone should have disposed of the disorderly-conduct case. The extraordinary fact is that this question was put by the same judge who had earlier asked Mr. Campbell—in an effort to find out whether the white passenger was present—why it was necessary for the three to sit on opposite sides of the train. It was virtually impossible for that judge to have missed the point.

Both sides then rested. I moved to dismiss the charges, and after the briefest deliberation the judges found both brothers guilty on both counts.

Reading the record, some years and many cases later, I am still astonished at the brazen unfairness of this trial. The most striking abuse, of course, is the total imbalance in the examination of the witnesses. The judges questioned defense witnesses exhaustively, and police witnesses not at all. Not only that, but they actually prevented the defense attorney from obtaining the one really useful tool of cross-examination in a small case like this: the memorandum book. It was quite plain that they took the police testimony at face value, but assumed they had to find a hole in the defense testimony.

Appeals courts do frown on judges interfering in the examination of witnesses, but they will not generally reverse a decision for that reason in a case that is not tried before a jury. The theory is that hostile questioning has a very adverse effect on the mind of an inexperienced layman, whereas a judge can exclude the prejudice from his mind. The questioning in this case shows how wrong that assumption is. These judges revealed through their own questioning that they were unable to listen and analyze the evidence. Questions they put to Anthony and Alfred Cain showed that in their indecent eagerness to catch the defendants in a contradiction, they were actually unable to keep the testimony straight. The truth is that the average New York jury could have heard the evidence much more dispassionately than these judges.

Despite the fog of prejudice cast over the trial, the evidence that did come out should have been enough for an acquittal. There was no getting around the fact that the judges were confronted in Charles Campbell with a credible eyewitness who had no conceivable motive, either from personal friendship or supposed racial solidarity, to distort the facts. That he had known two other persons on the train was technically a defect in his story, because witnesses not called are presumed to be unfavorable. However, that is an unworkable rule in misdemeanor cases based on police testimony; as the judges perfectly well knew, it is hard enough to get even one independent witness in such a case. Nothing brought out by the district attorney really showed that Mr. Campbell was mistaken or had any motive to lie, and no one who had wanted to see the truth of the situation could have seriously doubted his story.

There was a doubt right on the face of the prosecution's case for disorderly conduct, when it came to the mythical white man slapped by the defendants. The testimony of the conductor established that this "phantom passenger," as we came to call him in the appeal briefs, could hardly have existed. Without him, there was no disturbance of the public, because the only authentic member of the public produced was Mr. Campbell, and he positively was not disturbed by anyone but the police. This particular point makes the conviction especially shocking. If there was no disturbance of the peace, then there should not have been a conviction *on any count, even if all the rest of the prosecution story was true*. If there was no disorderly conduct, then the police had no right to tell the three young men to leave the train; and even if they had cursed out the officers and had resisted arrest, as the policemen said they did, they could not have been lawfully convicted of a crime. It was and is the law that a man cannot be convicted of an offense for disobeying an unlawful police order, nor for a disturbance of the public peace that is a result of arguing with a policeman over an unlawful order. And it was the law at that time in New York that a man had a right to resist an unlawful arrest. If the judges found that there was no disturbance of the peace, then they were obliged to acquit on all counts, and they could not rationally have found that there was a disturbance of the peace, because one of the judges, in his own questioning of a prosecution witness, had established that the offended white passenger was a phantom.

Could any proceeding have been worse than the trial? The sentencing was. The little policeman who had arrested the defendants disappeared, but left his brand on them. That was uncharacteristic of patrolmen in my experience; however rough they are with people they arrest, at least they rarely bear them a grudge when they get to court. But this one told a vindictive story to the probation department about how he was resigning from the transit police to go to California because he had been injured by the defendants and "feared for his life." At the time of the sentencing, the judges retailed that story to me; stunned, I replied that the officer had told me back near the beginning of the case that he wanted to resign and go to California because he did not like his job. It was to no avail. Both brothers received sentences of nine months, and Alfred's was suspended because of his clean record and his military service.

This case cannot be explained away as an aberration by saying, for example, that these were exceptionally bad judges; I am sorry to have to say that they were not. They were appointed through the same system as many of their colleagues. Two of them, a man and a woman, had been lawyers married to Democratic district leaders. The third, that eager judge who questioned all the defense witnesses, had been a Republican assistant United States attorney whom Mayor John Lindsay had recently rewarded.

Then, at least, the trial itself was exceptionally unfair? Sad to report, it was not even exceptional enough to command a reversal on appeal. The issue of the "phantom passenger," although it went to the heart of the case, was not the clearest one for appeal, because it raised the question of the credibility of witnesses, which appellate courts do not like to review. The strongest point on appeal, as it turned out, was the failure to require the police witness to produce the memorandum book. Recent law had established an absolute right to have the notes and reports of a prosecution witness for cross-examination. Furthermore, I thought our position was substantially strengthened by the imbalance in the examination of witnesses. The court at the first level of appeal, the appellate term of the State Supreme Court, wrote these words, and only these words, about the case:

> While it was error to deny defendants' request to inspect the memorandum book of one of the three patrolmen who testified at the trial (*People v. Persico*, 24 N.Y.2d 758; *People v. Malinsky*, 15 N.Y.2d 86), we are of the opinion that the error was harmless in view of the cumulative nature of this officer's testimony and the overwhelming proof of guilt.

Had this not been so outrageous, it might have been laughable.

I applied for leave to appeal to the Court of Appeals, the state's highest court. But that court does not consent to review every error; it tries to hear cases which present novel issues of wide application. The right to the background reports had been so recently affirmed that the judge who heard the application saw no reason to take the *Cain* case.

It was the end of the line. I could not contrive a respectable reason to apply to the Supreme Court. The Cain brothers were bound to do nine months for a crime that I believed, an eyewitness believed, and they knew they had not committed.

Did the brothers Cain understand what had happened to them? They can best convince you of that themselves.

ALFRED CAIN, JR.:

The first thing that bugged me was the fact that they dropped that bench warrant on me; knowing I was in Vietnam fighting for these pigs, they still dropped the bench warrant on me. I wrote to Lindsay and I told him to investigate, because a superliberal of that type, he's supposed to be shaping up the Police Department, and like, he's supposed to be dealing with police brutality. Being I was supposed to be a serviceman, defending and all of that, I figured that they would investigate and they would just go ahead and squash that case because we hadn't done anything. I figured if they ever contacted the witness who contacted you, if Lindsay would send some of his aides down to talk to him, they would just go ahead and cut that loose. What happened was Lindsay, his office, they referred that to the TA, the Transit Department. I guess they sent it to the transit police, and I guess what they decided was they had to get a conviction, so they kept the case going because they felt that I was going to sue the city, because of the fact I had written Lindsay.

That had been my first experience where a pig had taken the stand and told a series of lies. Plus, that had really been my first contact with judges. Even though I had been arrested before that, they didn't do anything more than, say, after I'd spent about a week, nine–ten days in jail, they had turned me loose and put me on probation for a while. I felt those judges would be able to see the contradictions in the case, see the cops was lying, and we'd get cut loose because we hadn't done anything. We just figured it was so obvious that there was no way that they could convict us and just *do* it in front of the public, in the face of the people, like they did. We didn't believe this was possible.

The way they proceeded with that afterwards showed me that they move according to their interests, and I realized that if their interests are opposed to your interests they will do *anything* to you. I mean anything. I had realized they had their machinery rigged up. But I figured they would still stay within the outlines of, say, their own law. I had seen brothers get jammed up before, but when you go through that experience with them, you realize that you can't afford to go to these people for *any* justice because of the fact that they don't deal in those terms. They just use the courts as an instrument to keep you down. I became aware of that after that time. There's no way that any person who has the ability to think could say we were guilty. What happened is the judges were covering up for the city.

When they took us off that train, we hadn't been doing anything, we didn't attack the pigs, we didn't physically resist them. We just refused to get off the train. And they handcuffed us and they took us out on the platform and laid us out, and started stomping on us. For them to stomp us up and then get into court and tell lies about us, that just showed me, like, there's nothing happening, with these pigs, with these people that manipulate these pigs—these judges. So from that point on I said, if it's going to be this way, if it's going to be aggression, I'm not going to go out funny—I'm going to defend myself to the best of my ability, and I realized that the only way you can do this is by being organized. I had realized this from the time we were jitterbugging, I realized this at the time we were in the army.

ANTHONY CAIN:

At this particular time, I had been arrested twice before. As far back as the first time I was busted, I saw in what manner the courts were moving. This particular arrest, I had been hopeful, because of the fact that there was a witness involved, that we possibly could be acquitted of this. The witness, you might say, was part of the established order, in the fact that he was white and he was part and parcel of the same people that we were dealing with, and for him to voluntarily come out and say what he did, to come out and volunteer his services, I definitely felt that this was grounds in itself. The conviction just heightened the contradiction, showed clearer, rather, that black people just weren't going to get any justice as far as the courts were concerned. Particularly, looking back at the case, I saw that the judges just moved on the witness in such a manner as to totally discredit him. I had not been involved in a case where there were witnesses before. I was very much surprised that white judges would move on a white witness. This was a contradiction in itself. Another thing that happened, there was a black pig involved, and to see the way that he was manipulated into lying, into going along with their program, is another example of the type of injustice that black people are subjected to.

I think behind that sentence, that nine months I had gotten for the case, I was out of work for eleven days—I was waiting for bail to get out on appeal. I had given the people some nonsense story on the job, but the desire to draft—to function in that capacity—I didn't have it at that particular time. I became aware of things. At that particular time in the position I was in, money was no obstacle. I was living fairly well. At the same time, I was moving in circles where I would be in the hard-core oppressed areas—the particular area, it was Brownsville at that time. I realized a lot of things that were going on behind the court system and behind the arrest. I began to see more the conditions that black people were subjected to. What was happening was, it was creating a profound dislike for white people, you see. At this particular job I was working at, in my department, I was the only black person there. It was creating a strain in my relationship to white people. I had always had a dislike for white people, which stems from incidents that I have had. This case heightened this particular attitude I had about white people.

3

BLACK PANTHERS IN BROOKLYN

The Cain brothers were still not quite ready to join the Black Panther Party. People are extraordinarily resilient, and most of them don't like to let themselves in for conflict with the authorities, especially just after they have been released from the army. The brothers were still willing to play along.

ALFRED CAIN, JR.:

My brother and I are less than two years apart; we've always been tight. Right after we were convicted on that case, we had been working, we got some bread together, we had just bought a car—a Cadillac. It wasn't a new Cadillac, but we thought we were going to get out there, deal with the women, we were going to keep some money, go out there and stay high, myself and my brother, just do our thing—party. See, what happened was that right after we got the car the pigs tried to stop us one day. They felt as though no young nigger should be driving a Cadillac. They stopped us and put us through a lot of changes. The car at that time was not in my name—I was still in the process of paying and there were a couple hundred dollars due. So I hadn't got the registration transferred over to my name. When they stopped us, they asked for a registration and I showed it, but it wasn't

in my name. So they said, "Well, we're going to have to investigate this." They said they have to take me down to the
precinct, to see whether or not the car was stolen. Plus they
were running down a lot of madness. My brother could talk
more about that.

———————

The brothers' reaction to their run-in with the police this
time was harder, more intransigent than it had been the
last time.

ANTHONY CAIN:

We didn't stop immediately when the police officers had
wanted us to stop. When we were stopped, a pig jumps
out of the car, he sticks his gun in the window close by.
I didn't particularly like this fool sticking that gun by my
head.

We went down to the precinct after waiting awhile for
Alfred. We wanted to get some information, find out just
what was happening with him. When we entered the station, we were told to get out of the precinct. We tried to
tell them that we were there to find out what was happening
with him. I was with another brother who was in the car at
the time when they stopped us. One pig asked the sergeant
that was behind the desk at the time, should he arrest us,
too, and he said go ahead. Like we had some words. They
jumped on us, and we had some static. They whipped us up
pretty well there. We were eventually arrested and put on
some bullshit charges.

ALFRED CAIN, SR.:

Things like that—so many of these things—stick in you.
I believe—my son, that anything he would have decided to
do, he could have probably done it. But after the cops beat

him and worked my other son over, I think it did something to him. They beat Anthony and they threw him in jail. If I had been along, I would have been dead . . . somebody would have been dead, because I couldn't see the cops beat my child like that.

At the time the Black Panther Party took root in Brooklyn, in 1968, it had been working on the West Coast for a year and a half. Started in Oakland in the fall of 1966 by Huey Newton and Bobby Seale, the party had gained great notoriety in a series of startling confrontations. In one, Black Panthers, protecting the widow of Malcolm X, stood off the police in front of the *Ramparts* office in San Francisco, while Huey Newton faced down a policeman, daring him to draw his gun.[1] Their most famous political act was to march into the California legislature with loaded guns, dressed in their customary berets and dark jackets, to protest the passage of a bill which made it illegal to carry a loaded weapon in an "incorporated area."[2] The bill became law (and made confrontations such as Huey Newton's stand-off in San Francisco legally almost impossible), but the protest, which was the most clear-cut possible act of defiance against legislative repression of the Panthers, captured the imagination of young black people all over the country. The Cain brothers were to remember it as the first act which attracted them to the party, long before it was active in New York.

In October 1967, Huey Newton, himself seriously wounded, was arrested and charged with the killing of an Oakland police officer. Partly in an effort to mobilize support for Newton in the spring of 1968, the Panthers had a membership drive, centering in New York, where hundreds were recruited during and after the month of June.[3] The drive reached its peak after spring at Long Island University, and brought the party to the attention of young people.

The Panthers were interested in attracting men who had been in the army, because, as Bobby Seale said, they were "cats from off the block," and they understood weapons. Substantially all the people involved in the narrative portions of this book came into the party at that time.

There was bound to be confusion in organizing a New York branch of the Oakland-based Panthers, if for no other reason than that the gun laws in New York were so much more restrictive than those in California. "Picking up the gun" is usually an offense in itself in New York. There was some conflict between the Brooklyn and Manhattan offices, and Panthers from the West Coast often criticized and ultimately imposed direct control over the Brooklyn chapter.

During the winter of 1968–69, the Panthers expanded their programs for serving the people, particularly the free breakfast program for children and the medical clinic program. At the same time, the party tried to eliminate those members whom Bobby Seale collectively refers to as "jackanapes, renegades, and *agents provocateurs*,"[4] meaning, roughly, informers and members who ran into unnecessary trouble with the law, either by provoking policemen or by committing crimes. After January 1969, the party membership was closed, and the membership grew smaller.[5] The party seems to have been able to eliminate some undisciplined members, but as events proved, it had less success in eliminating police informers because they could, after all, appear disciplined when it suited their purpose.

ALFRED CAIN, JR.:

Maybe a week or two after we had just gotten out of that case, I went down and joined the party. You see, what happened was, we realized it is very easy for a pig to kill you. Like situations we were in, when they arrested us and pulled guns out. And pigs are scared—you see scared pigs shooting up the community every day—and I realized how easy it was to get killed out there on those streets by scared pigs, so I decided, my brother decided, that if it had to be that way, that we might as well go with some brothers who were ready to deal with it.

When I first became aware of the party was when they went into the legislature in Sacramento with the weapons. It was in the beginning of 1968, I believe. When I first dug it, I said, like, these are some crazy niggers. They got a whole lot of heart. In our thing among black people, a person who has a lot of heart is right on. Because we have so many black people who have just submitted to this thing and they will not acknowledge that they have an oppressor. They do not see that you have to deal with him realistically. I realized the power of weapons. They are very useful in terms of doing what you have to do if you're being aggressed upon. You have to have them in order to defend yourself. Even before the war, when we were jitterbugging, to the extent that I was involved, you had to have your knife or your zip gun or something. You had to have something to keep the people off of you at that time. At that time it was unfortunate that you had brothers killing brothers, but because that's the way the situation was, you had to be armed to be able to defend yourself. So it's not the thing where I just became suddenly aware of this. I always realized the necessity to defend myself. We're just not submissive people; I'm not submissive, my brother's not submissive. And most of the people we relate to, they're not that way; they're not submissive.

The party first opened in Brooklyn in May of 1968. At that time we weren't really too familiar with the existence of the Black Panther Party in New York. Some people told me a couple of months after they opened it there was a Black Panther Party.

I had seen Minister of Defense Huey Newton on a short interview on a TV program, and I related to what he was saying very heavy because he explained the necessity for black people organizing movements in a political fashion and having weapons in order to defend themselves from the aggression of the pigs, and as I say, because of the fact that I had so many confrontations with the pigs, I had been aware of the fact that they were systematically committing brutality against my people, so I related very heavily to what he was saying. I just decided that because I wanted to do something to elevate the condition of black people, because of the fact that I had certain skills, that I would see if I could join the party. So I went down there and learned about the ten-point program, and I said, "Right on, I want to be part of this." What had happened was that the pigs had been running down a lot of negative publicity about the party, and right before I joined the party a couple of police had got shot up on Eastern Parkway, where the papers said they couldn't prove it was the party but they believed it was the party, and so on, and so on. So, I felt anything the pigs talked about so bad must be good for black people. I realized that anything the pig talks about as being detrimental to him is good for us. That's the conclusion I had come to.

At the time I joined, you had a lot of brothers and sisters in the party who had no political direction. In a sense the activities of the party were, more or less, to a lot of the brothers, like a throwback to the jitterbugging era, except now they were jitterbugging against the pigs. A lot of mistakes that we made could have been corrected if we were conscious enough to realize that you do not deal with the pig except when you have the advantage. I mean the brothers had a lot of heart, but they did not realize that before you actually deal with the pigs systematically you have to have the support of the people.

On Nostrand Avenue, a lot of people didn't dig the fact that the party wasn't paying any rent for the office there, had liberated the office on Nostrand Avenue, and then they came out with this thing, saying the party was supposed to be shaking down people on Nostrand Avenue, because that's the heavy business district. See, our whole philosophy has always been to do what you have to to survive as long as you don't hurt the black people. That was always foremost in our minds, and to my knowledge there was nothing about shaking down the businessmen in that community.

They busted three brothers out there one night in an incident I'm still not too clear on, on Nostrand Avenue. But they printed it up in the papers that the Panthers had come out in mass that particular night to intimidate businessmen out there and the police decided to run them all up and down Nostrand Avenue. Some madness.

They whipped the brothers up pretty bad, and put two of them in the hospital, and at that time we had a lot of people reacting to this; they were ready to move. Subsequent to that, some more people got busted. When we went to the courtroom, a whole bunch of off-duty pigs attacked about twelve–fourteen brothers and sisters and some of the white mother-country radicals out there. They whipped them up, and we had got strung out behind that; we didn't dig that at all. So, like I say, the situation seemed to be building up and building up, but at the same time you did not have enough consciousness in the brothers that you cannot move, you cannot react to the pig, you cannot react to harassment, you know, when he wants you to.

Then we started political education. Things I read before I came into the party, I read Malcolm's autobiography, *Wretched of the Earth*, a lot of things that dealt with social conditions of black people in this country. I'd been reading whatever I could get my hands on at that time. After I went into the party, we began to deal with Marxist-Leninist ideas, analysis. We were starting on specific references, *Foundations of Leninism,* by Stalin, *Private Property and the State,* by Frederick Engels; we read books written by

Lenin. We had various teachers, and I was teaching at one
time.

————————

The Cain brothers came to know some strong, smart men
in the party. Among them was Thomas McCreary, like
Bobby Seale a jack-of-all-trades: a seaman, dental technician, and organizer with a sarcastic intelligence. A short
man who wears an engineer's cap and a sparse beard, Mc-
Creary declines to conceal his impatience with all such
liberal paraphernalia as the legal process and writing
books. Before being interviewed, he said to Alfred Cain,
"This book is going to be about how Thomas McCreary
went off to the sea, and Al Cain went to college, and everyone lived happily ever after, right?"* He was equally impatient with my interview, which began as I asked him to
describe one of the people in the party.

THOMAS McCREARY:

I don't relate to this way of going about to try to express
what anybody's like; I never did that before. I haven't dealt
with too much of the emotional parts of the struggle. To me,
to write a book, I'd have to deal with tactics, I'd have to
deal with things that specifically have taken place. This is
what I would like to deal with.

It would be very simple to sit down and have a hell of an
exchange of views, if it was all over with, I had retired from
the struggle, you know, then I could bring you right up to
it. But, see, it is not over with. It is not going to be over for
a long time. And if you are around when it's all over, we'll
sit down and the conversation will be different, you
know. . . .

* In February 1972, Thomas McCreary was arrested in St. Louis, Missouri,
apparently in the company of men accused of shooting policemen in New
York. As of this writing, McCreary has been eliminated as a suspect in
the New York case, but is charged with assault in Missouri.

Before I was in the service, I didn't do much of anything. I was in high school, Williamsburg—for a minute. I left in my junior year—sick of it. I was doing a lot of stupid things, I was jitterbugging at the time. I wasn't much interested in school, there wasn't anything happening there. At the time I went into the service, I pushed my draft because I was tired of the people, I wanted to dig some other things. After basic, I went to jump school and to the war.

It's one of my faults, I can never take orders from people, and that's bad—to some extent that's bad, I realize that now. But that was a good thing in the service, because that was a fascist organization that I was working with. Like, I was one of the most—and this is not to be bragging—I was one of the most radical dudes in my company, and that wasn't radical. I wasn't political, but I just didn't relate to that type thing. Maybe it wasn't a racial thing, maybe because I just didn't—I still don't—dig authority. They were overtly racist, the people I came in contact with. There was some righteous people in the army, black and white, but the majority of the people were very sick people.

I remember the night we got ready to go to Vietnam. I was stationed on the infantry side, across the street was artillery, they had three brothers who refused to go to Vietnam. This was in '65. The company commander came up and put the three brothers under guard and they carried them to Vietnam, tried to court-martial them in Vietnam. I got kind of mad at the world. The brothers were saying they weren't supposed to be going over there, they shouldn't be there. You know, this was the first time my ears had heard that stuff. And when I got over there—matter of fact, on the ship going over—I started professing the same thing, after I'd thought about it, to a lot of people, and a lot of people related to it, they related to it in terms of what they'd do when they got back, not while they was there.

When I got into the movement it was like nonviolence had just about failed. I remember very clearly filing reports on Selma. I knew even then that nonviolence wasn't it, that it wasn't what's happening. I know a lot of other people didn't believe it either, but the mass media projected in terms of the people who did believe that way, they projected the masses of black people believing that way. See, after those little girls got blown up in that church, after that I said, Damn, unh-unh, that ain't it, that isn't the way. I had related to CORE, I had related to SNCC. To me the party wasn't too much transition to make.

I came into the party about two or three weeks after it organized—May or June of '68. I met Al [Cain] in 1968, at LIU [Long Island University]. We were having a meeting at LIU, when the party first organized in Brooklyn. We met kinda strange. He was in the same unit that I was in, in Vietnam—First Cavalry. We were having a meeting of people who had been in the military, this particular Sunday afternoon. We had the same patch, and we started to rap about An Khe.

We talked about some places we had hung out, the same places, some of the villages we had been through. We talked about the religions, the bars, the people. This was how we first became very close, by experiences over there. We had both seen some sad contradictions in terms of the war, you know. Like the Vietnamese we came into contact with, in the central highlands, they could give a fuck less about the war, all they want is to be left to do a little farming, and do a little fishing—you know, just take life easy. The area I went to, they had never seen an American plane. We came off the plane, and the people was so out of it, they was saying the plane had given birth, and we had been born from the plane.

Down at the seashore, there is a place called Cam Ranh Bay, one of the nicest harbors in the world. You can look down into thirty feet of water, nothing but clear water thirty feet straight down. The land is beautiful, mountains and all that. When the war is all over, everybody realizes—

even dudes that was in Vietnam at the time I was over there was talking about how Hilton would come in and put a big hotel there, put up a golf course and what not. When I came home, I wanted to go back to Vietnam as a citizen. I priced a ticket at Kennedy Airport—it costs you eight hundred dollars one way, so you know I couldn't be making that move, not for no vacation.

I still want to go back one day. I want to see the people— they are beautiful people—I never saw anybody like them before, you know, maybe because that was the only other country that I have ever spent any time in. Just the way they accept things, hardship and everything, they're a hell of a people. I was only over there to do thirteen months, but to the average Vietnamese fighting for the North, it's in- definite. He has more to fight for than I do. We talked about this. A lot of the things we didn't talk about, because it wasn't necessary to talk about, because we had both been there.

THE BROWNSVILLE OFFICE

In the fall of 1968, the forgotten Brownsville ghetto became overnight the focus of a furious political controversy—the public school strike. After the community governing board of the Ocean Hill–Brownsville school district transferred several teachers, the strike began, spreading to such viru- lent issues as threats of violence in the schools. One raw October day I was there, standing in front of JHS 271, the center of controversy, surrounded by thousands of angry community people and hundreds of blue-helmeted police- men. Alfred Cain was in the crowd; I had not seen him or his brother, who was then away, for months. In a way, I must confess, I was not altogether glad to see him; meeting the defendant from an unsuccessful criminal case always causes a pang, and the memory of a detestable trial and jail term in this case made it still worse. But my regret was enveloped by astonishment: Alfred had let his hair grow natural, and was wearing a *dashiki* and dark glasses. He was guarded in his greetings, saying nothing about the Black Panther Party. I did not learn about that connection until nearly a year later.

The school dispute was the first thing Anthony Cain saw when he returned to the community.

> I came back in October of 1968. I came back by bus to Manhattan, and I took the train to Brownsville. The junior high school—271—was close by the train stop. It was about four o'clock in the morning, and there were wall-to-wall pigs. They were standing completely around that block and across the street for almost two blocks straight down. That was about six blocks from my home. It wasn't until next day somebody related to me why there were so many pigs—there were something like three thousand pigs out there.

During that same fall, the Black Panthers opened their Sutter Avenue office in Brownsville. That office, near the corner of Sutter Avenue and Herzl Street, was the only one of the offices still open in Brooklyn in 1971. The black-and-blue lettering of the sign at 180 Sutter Avenue says bravely:

BLACK PANTHER PARTY

We Serve the People

I was reminded of one of the criticisms that one Panther made of SNCC in New York: "You could determine that SNCC was a *petit bourgeois* organization in the sense that it was located on Fifth Avenue and Eighteenth Street. No blacks live around there. The most logical thing would be to have it in Harlem, Bed-Stuy, Brownsville, South Bronx." The same accusation could never have been made about the Black Panthers.

In the block of buildings surrounding 180 Sutter Avenue,

the Black Panther Party office is the only ground-floor store-front that is not boarded up, or nailed shut with tin. Across the street is the burned façade of an abandoned dry cleaner's, and behind it—nothing: a field of broken bricks and charred boards. Black teen-agers stand around an ash-can in the middle of the lot, idly burning boards in it to keep warm. The odor of wood smoke hangs over the corner. The buildings have been burned, as have hundreds of others in surrounding blocks.

It is astonishing that any neighborhood in New York, where the housing shortage is acute, can be so blighted that it is literally being abandoned as Brownsville is. The houses, once occupied by white people, have in the past twenty years filled with poor black people. As the houses have de-teriorated, landlords have abandoned them, followed much later by their tenants. The buildings have been vandalized and burned, and urban renewal, with the purpose of re-building, has for the short run accelerated the process. In May 1971 there was a riot sparked by welfare cuts, during which there were more than one hundred fires. As Joseph François, former president of the Brownsville Community Council, said grimly, "When you looked at the neighbor-hood afterwards, you know you couldn't tell the differ-ence?"

Joe François is a short black man with a pronounced limp. With his organizational energy he has come, as he puts it, to wear many hats in community organizations, including the Brownsville Community Council, an antipoverty agency. At the time of this writing, he is in charge of the Board of Education's College Bound Program, whose object is to prepare poor children for college. His recollections are im-portant, because he is one of the few people outside the Black Panther Party who has intimate knowledge of the community work of the party in Brooklyn, as it began at the end of 1968.

JOSEPH FRANÇOIS:

I met the Black Panthers sometime in 1968. They came to the general assembly [of the Brownsville Community Council], an open meeting, where the community is called in. Their program described what they had done and what they intended to do as far as the antipoverty program was concerned. I'll never forget—I was chairing that meeting— I gave them the floor. They made a presentation, and then it was a very cold audience. The community people were completely turned off, because of the way they talked, the way they looked at that time—you know, "Black Panther" was a bad word. I said that I saw nothing wrong with their program, only with the public climate at that time. I saw that they were trying to do the same thing that we were trying to do as a poverty agency. And I kind of asked the community to support them in their endeavors. And then after the meeting was over, I told the leader from California —I don't know who it was—I said, "Look, we have a place over at the Good Shepherd Center, why don't you come over to talk with me so that we can arrange something?"

The Black Panther Party helped Good Shepherd and myself form a welfare rights group which I thought was excellent. They also were able to induce the community to have a sweep-out—or sweep-in, whatever—and the community would get out one day to sweep the blocks, sweep the streets up because of the very poor sanitation. So the rumors that occurred in the press that turned off many black people were soon dispelled—rumors that they were murderers, they were vicious, they were cruel, they come to beat up people.

Then they opened up a place. They got a storefront in Brownsville, and they started from there. At the same time, we were able to accommodate them at Good Shepherd with a breakfast program, which, at one time, was functioning fantastically well, an average of about thirty to seventy kids every morning getting breakfast. People, all kinds of people, women from the community, would volunteer. Parents would come in and cook: bacon and eggs, grits, orange juice—a regular substantial breakfast. What is not known about Brownsville, many of the kids go to school fantastically hungry, with no breakfast, and because of this free breakfast, the kids really came in—poured in, at times.

I was instrumental in giving the Panthers their "passport," which was a letter signed by me and my corporation, to get food. Since we had what we call a merchants committee affiliated with us, my signature meant that these were people that were reputable. When a merchant was approached—and of this I was a witness—the merchant was asked to donate food. You must realize that the merchants in Brownsville do not live in the community—all the money is taken out. The Panthers simply said to the merchant, "All right, if this is the way you feel, we're going to have the community deal with you, because you are taking money out of the community; the least you can do is to put money back into the community." And that was the strongest intimidation. Sutter Avenue became a clinic on Saturday from about nine to one. Volunteer doctors from the Good Shepherd and volunteer nurses came, and actually gave kids check-ups free. It was in the late part of '69. I visited them, and they worked very comfortably with the sisters; at Good Shepherd there was never, to my knowledge, any apprehension between the nuns and the Black Panthers. The nuns were white, by the way.

Alfred Cain was one of the ones that helped us get the welfare mothers together. He and his friends organized one of the welfare groups on one of the streets. He is another man who is highly intelligent. Al was just a little more reserved in the sense that he didn't show any tendencies of violence or roughness. He was a very gentle person and very intelligent.

Are you familiar with the rhetoric—"Right on," and all

this? He related not with so much rhetoric but with action
—he wouldn't say, "I'm going to organize welfare." When
you'd see him he had his clipboard getting names, and he
was actually doing it.

I think what frightened people, or frightened the Establishment primarily, since there were so many injustices, so
much police brutality—and still is, for that matter—was
that they outspokenly said, "We are here to protect you. If
you need a police force, and don't have one, we are your
police force to get justice," and this right away pitted them
against the Establishment. You see, because the Establishment would say, "Well, listen, we have a bunch of radicals
out here who want to take us on." But the only thing they
were attempting to do was promote justice. As you can see,
there was an attempt to deal with social injustice, and we
had a major institution like law enforcement kill it, in short.

In doing the party's community work, the brothers came
to know other men who were ultimately to be caught
in the bramblebush of the criminal courts. One of them,
Jerome West, was a husky, silent workingman who, though
only a teen-ager, had a family living near the Cains' home
in Brownsville. Alfred Junior remembers that he first encountered Jerome when the party was investigating a shoot-
out between blacks and Puerto Ricans.

> Jerome and some more of the young brothers out in the area,
> they didn't have much political direction, but they related to
> the Party at that time. The structure was very loose.
>
> We lived not too far from each other and we started relat-
> ing. If we had a little time or something, the brother, couple
> more brothers, we'd be together just about every day, because
> we were all working around Brownsville at that time, working
> on some other community-oriented projects at that time, plus
> we were just in the area together, we hung out.

Another of these men had lived a different life from the rest, with more conventional views, before he was in the party, and has lived a different life since, so much so that he asked me to set down his recollections under the name of "Fat Man." He was still only twenty-one years old at the time he told me his story.

FAT MAN:

I was going to Tilden [High School, in Brooklyn], and overnight I became a sort of rabble-rouser—you know, a demagogue, so to speak. At one time I was an honors student, but things happened where I got sidetracked. Like our first term, I was the only black in my class, and I didn't like that. In the beginning I really strived, putting extra hours into the homework. But as time went by, I got on the football team, and all of a sudden I lost interest altogether.

I wrote an article for the *Gadfly*, a newspaper at Tilden. The article wasn't that good, but it was good at that time. We were just having the Olympic boycotts. Tommy Smith and them raised a black power salute, I think it was '68. I took a very moderate view. I said this would not help us materially or spiritually towards our goals, and this was the view that everybody dug, and I got a little popularity about that. But we had many incidents—like in the *PTA Journal*, you'd find a little footnote saying the teachers and parents wanted to get the Board of Education to rezone so we'd stop having these people coming in from the other schools. Little slurs, you know. You might as well say they were mounted in my subconscious. Then it came to the point when we decided to organize this Afro-American Club.

The whole thing happened when Les Campbell* came down to speak. Now, the day before we had our little

* A black teacher then involved in a controversy with the New York City Board of Education.

demands, and [the principal had] agreed to let us have
speakers from the Muslims, the Panthers, and so forth. We
put him to the test the next day. Campbell came, and the
principal wouldn't let him speak. Campbell tried to stop
everything, but there was no stopping it—it was like simultaneously everybody just reacted. I made my change from
moderateness to—one day in the office, the principal called
me Lenin. We had a meeting with the principal—myself
and another fellow. We were supposed to be negotiating
in good faith, and he tells us, "Well, by four o'clock tomorrow we'll have everything written up." He said these things
would be mimeographed and passed out tomorrow. Tomorrow never came; he never did it; he had the blue suits in
the next day. So after that we never had any peace in the
classrooms.

I went out one day and I heard some threats about some
of the Italian kids coming. Canarsie blacks really had a hard
time. We had some incidents with some Italian fellows, and
I heard they were coming down there with their machine
guns, what not. It is foolish, to me, even to entertain the
idea, but at the time it [seemed] possible. So I said, "Well,
if they're going to be packing their bullets, I'll be going
down here and talk with somebody on our side might be
packing some bullets." So that's the reason I first went to
the party. Nobody was packing any, but that was the
image everybody had.

I first got associated with the party in April 1969. I was
never really in the party technically. You might say I was
a friend of the Panthers.

When I first came to the party, I had a totally different
idea about what I heard over the news. Just like anybody
else, I didn't know what the party was all about or what it
was really into. As the time went by, I got the feeling of it,
I began to understand what it was all about, what it was
trying to do, and what it meant to the people. I liked it. I
stuck around.

We had the breakfast program, trying to get our office together, trying to sell papers, trying to relate to the people in
the community—anybody who comes in the office who had
any problem, we tried to handle it the best we could. There
were certain cases in the neighborhood where the people
might not have gotten their welfare check, had no food in
the house, things of this nature. We dealt with things like
this. Good-neighbor stuff.

The breakfast program was a very good thing. We had
like a floating membership. On certain days, you'd have a
certain group come in, and two days later you'd have another one. I could have seventy kids or I could have seven
hundred kids. It was a very funny thing.

Look at the situation in Brownsville—you see kids running ragged in the streets, hanging out all hours of the night.
Kids are all we've got—they are our future. You got to
make a start somewhere. I think that's the only way you
can start, because while it is too late for grown-ups now, if
a kid grows up now with nothing, never had nothing, never
expects to have nothing, what's his life going to be? When
we first started the program, the kids couldn't eat the breakfast—not because it was bad, everything was top-level stuff,
the cooking, everything. Everything had to be the best that
we could provide, but they just couldn't digest the food,
because they were not used to it, because they never ate
breakfast. After we got things going they came and they ate
the breakfast, everything was really hip. We were just sort
of like picking ourselves off the ground. The program was
going well and we were thinking of starting another program. Then all this nonsense with Wilbert Thomas came
on the scene.

I was in the bag where achievement, so to speak, was
everything; in other words, if you went to college, you had
an education, you understand? After rapping with Cain and
listening to him from his over-all experiences in the street,
and . . . Cain was a very diverse fellow and could get into

some very intricate things, you know? Right away I developed a close friendship with him and had all kinds of confidence in him. He was a dynamite fellow.

Cain talked about being selfless. The average dude you meet on the street is out for himself, he goes for himself. That's the trouble with this whole country, everybody's for himself; they call it rugged individualism—that's a nice name for it, but it's just cutthroat thievery. This was what I mostly had come in contact with. But here I met this cat, he was rapping about wherever there's struggle there's sacrifice, and how if one could go out there and work with the benefit of others in mind, he'd get some feeling of satisfaction, some achievement. After dealing with the breakfast program, I got to understand what he was talking about. Like I wasn't getting any reward, the only rewards I was getting were spiritual, nothing material. I had no money; when I got arrested, I didn't have a penny in my pocket.

Cain, he could rap with you. Like after a day's work, we'd sit down and get a bottle of wine, and talk—not that we were winos. Being in this age group, a lot of kids turn to it—you know, drink wine. That was our little pleasure there. We'd sit down and talk about the day's work and what we hoped to do in the future and how we could move to make things better in the community. Well, I was the idea fellow. You name it, name the problem, I'd give you some sort of an idea. Like I wanted to get into housing down there. I wanted to organize a tenant council, engage in rent strikes, things like that, where we could make repairs. Cain thought it would be very hard to save the rent so that when everything was done and it was time for that money to be put in the right place, it'd be there. But the whole situation was hard, extremely hard. And even after being down there for that period of time, we were still confused, confused about solutions, how we were going to go about rectifying these things. After being in it for a while, you can really get lost in it and you just constantly fight. It could have been a lifetime thing if it hadn't been for Wilbert Thomas.

I'm working in the same community now, so I still feel to a certain degree I'm serving the people, whereas a lot of fellows don't want to work under these conditions. So I'm lucky I'm still doing my thing to some degree. And it gives me a small satisfaction to do a job that a lot of fellows have passed over. There's very terrible conditions here, very bad health conditions, so I'm still out here to a small, very small degree.

Ricardo De Leon, the last man in the group of Brooklyn Panthers caught up by the law, remains for me a mysterious man. Some of the reasons are accidental; I did not represent him in the conspiracy case, nor did he ever testify, and thus I have no statement directly from his lips. And apart from that, there are elements in De Leon's character that are inherently contradictory.

He was more than ten years older than anyone else in the Brownsville group, with a long criminal record, beginning from the time he grew up in Panama. He himself was to say that the party had rehabilitated him, turned him away from petty crime, while the prosecutor, in his characteristic style, claimed that he joined for the fell purpose of "corrupting young men."

I first encountered him as accidentally as I had the Cain brothers. At the end of 1968 I was advising an anarchist collective on the Lower East Side called "Up Against the Wall, Motherfucker," trying to settle police problems. Late one night in October, a member called to say there was a riot in progress on St. Mark's Place, the main street of the East Village, and a lot of arrests had been made. It had started after a Black Panther was beaten up by police on the block, and UAW/MF had put out one of its ferocious broadsides—peerless in its provocation to fight, as usual. The man had been beaten so badly, it said, that "people thought the sidewalk was bleeding." The riot had begun as police tried to move grumbling crowds away from the scene of the Panther's arrest.

The Panther was De Leon. When I went to see him in jail, he looked as tough as a man could, dressed in black clothes, his front teeth missing, with a sparse beard and mustache. He said he had been drinking, had got involved in a political argument on a street corner, and had refused to move when a policeman ordered him to. He said that the policeman had struck the first blow—but after that, De Leon had given as good as he got. By De Leon's lights, his resistance to the police was not only natural but an obligation. His frankness was amazing to me; up to that time, I had never encountered that opinion in such consistent form in a street man who was ready to act on it. About all I could think of to say was something lame about how I didn't think the criminal court would take the same view. De Leon pleaded guilty to assault and received a three-month sentence.

De Leon's friends in the Brooklyn chapter of the Black Panther Party are a little reticent about him, but they understood immediately the characteristics that I perceived only dimly.

FAT MAN:

We really didn't have much time for personal things; I didn't, anyway. There really aren't any stories to tell other than what we did, you know? As far as De Leon the man, I can't tell you about him. I can tell you about De Leon the worker. I worked with De Leon in the breakfast program, he was the cook, you know—very good cook. He was there every day, took care of the kids, went out to do a couple of other things, you know. At this point we were running ourselves to death.

He was a relentless worker. He worked and worked, and I admired him for that. The average person couldn't do those things under those conditions. Like the breakfast program, you get up at five or six o'clock in the morning, you finish the breakfast program at ten o'clock; you leave and go sell a hundred newspapers; you stand on your feet all hours of the day. That was our line of support, and that's how we ran our office, and if we needed change for the breakfast program, that's where that extra change was going to come from—paper selling. He just didn't stand there and hold the paper. I mean he pushed them. He didn't force them on anybody, but he made it in his own way. He did this every day. Day by day he got better and better. As far as being a worker—we had a saying: Social practice is the criterion of truth—and judging him by the things he did every day, you'd have to say he was for real and you got to respect this, because, being in the position that I was in the breakfast program, it got to the point certain people I depended on and certain people I knew I could ask to do more than their share of the work, and he was the cat I could.

De Leon is a very talented dude—and very emotional. He believes in what he believes in, and that's it. He is a down-to-earth brother and that's it—very high person, very good, very reactive. And very self-sacrificing—you might walk down the street and encounter five or six fellows, where you might think twice about keeping on going down the street. Well, that wouldn't stop De Leon— he would take those five or six people.

Thomas McCreary:

At one time we had people staying at the office at Fulton Street and [De Leon] stayed there for a while, and then we allowed him to live in here [at 1004 Montgomery Street] because people started living—you know, a communal-type thing—about four–five different apartments in Brooklyn.

We talked mainly about the struggle. You know, De Leon is a very intelligent person, he's very heavy upstairs. He had a way of grasping Marx that a lot of us didn't, at the time, and he would break things down. Plus, he was well read before, and he taught some classes.

He was the type of dude, like if the situation would go down, his heart would never fail him. He may have been upset over something, like the pigs moving on somebody, and his emotions would probably be upset, but in terms of doing anything irrational at that moment, behind anger, he was not that kind of a person. Drinking was the only problem he had, and I can't even say that was a problem. It was a problem, I guess, to some people who came in contact with De Leon, because of what he was doing. You know, people have a tendency to look upon you—you know, if you teach a class, then you ain't supposed to be doing them other things, from that stereotype thing before, you know, that teacher-pupil-type thing. They thought that if he had all that understanding he should be able to deal with his alcohol. If you drink, you know, everybody gets high, but he would get higher than everybody else, or maybe drunk. He wasn't violent, maybe just hard to relate to in terms of trying to tell him something that he shouldn't be doing.

JOSEPH FRANÇOIS:

He was the kind of guy that would go down fighting; you know, he had no fear. I think everyone should have a little fear. I never saw him fighting, but I think I must have seen him in circumstances where he would jaw to the police, and he would talk in such a way as would provoke a policeman, if the policeman was not cool and couldn't take that kind of rhetoric.

ALFRED CAIN, JR.:

De Leon was a stomp-down *Lumpen*. See, you have two types of people: you have strong people and you have weak people. You have black people that submit to the oppression and other brothers who are stomp-down *Lumpen,* who rebel—they might not have a systematic analysis, but it's just not in them to submit. And you can see this within a brother by the way he manifests himself. Also, De Leon has a very high political level. He's done a lot of study of revolutionary theory so that he has a guide to action, and also he is willing to do whatever is necessary to elevate the conditions of black people. You always have a certain element who is basically dealing in romantic concepts, like just looking for glory, but De Leon was a strong brother who wanted to do something to elevate the condition of black people.

———————

During the big conspiracy trial in 1969, De Leon showed the qualities of heart that Alfred Cain admired in him. During a recess, when court officers began to hustle Alfred roughly out of the courtroom, De Leon intervened between the guards and Cain. He had his hands down, but the way he stood defied them to hit him. I could catch only a glimpse, through the crack of a rapidly closing door, but I did see an officer swing a club at De Leon. After the encounter, both the court officers and De Leon looked as though they had taken punishment. Judges, of course, are not very interested in heart, and they took the dimmest view of this fracas.

In a sense, the contradictions in De Leon are those of the Black Panther Party itself. Dedicated to total social change, he worked hardest at the simplest kinds of reform. Wise in the ways of the streets, he had nevertheless gone beyond the caution which is native to that way of life, to a kind of stony defiance. That defiance was sometimes foolhardy and sometimes successful, depending on the circumstances; it might lead to endless petty conflicts with the police or to one big political confrontation. Black Panther Party leaders have criticized men like De Leon for their rashness, yet they proudly remember Huey Newton's stand-off with the San Francisco police; the difference is almost one of split-second judgment. In any case, the revolutionary defiance and the community reform were both thought to be necessary to get the affection and allegiance of black people.

4

REVOLUTIONARY MEN AND
REVOLUTIONARY HISTORY

The Black Panthers had three central fields of work, always in tension in the party, just as they were in the character of a man like Ricardo De Leon. We may call them the "military," or guerrilla aspect of the party; the "ideological," or teaching aims; and the "service," or community programs. (Panthers would have lumped the last two together under the rubric "political.") One aspect might be stressed more than another, depending on the community and the individual involved. By his own account, for example, Fat Man came to the party interested principally in its military aspect, and because of his own peaceable nature and the demands of the breakfast program, ended by being interested almost entirely in the service aspect.

The service work being done by the Black Panthers in Brooklyn at the end of 1968 was basic—food and clothing for children, elementary medical care, welfare and tenants' rights. The only shocking thing about the work was that it was not already being done on a neighborhood basis by some charitable organization, and that it had not been continuously in operation for ten years.

Law-enforcement officials later claimed that community work was only a cover for criminal conspiracies. This, of course, misses the party's diversity of aims; the Panthers worked hard and sincerely to overcome their inexperience in community work. But it is probably true that men as radically disaffected as the Cain brothers, Thomas Mc-Creary, and Ricardo De Leon could not have been interested in such reformist work at all except as part of a revolutionary cause. Plainly, this sort of basic social work was not the only end of the party, or it would not have differed from its welfare or civil rights counterparts. Part of the difference from older organizations was the spirit in which the work was done and the teaching that was combined with it. Fred Hampton explained it in a famous speech.

> The Breakfast for Children Program. We are running it in a socialistic manner. People came and took our program, saw it in a socialistic fashion, not even knowing it was socialism. People are gonna take that program and work it in a socialistic manner. What's the pig say? He say, "Nigger—you like communism?" "No sir, I'm scared of it." "You like socialism?" "No sir, I'm scared of it." "You like the breakfast for children program?" "Yes sir, I'd die for it." Pig said, "Nigger, that program is a socialistic program." "I don't give a fuck if it's communism. You put your hands on that program, motherfucker, and I'll blow your motherfucking brains out." And he knew it. We been educating him, not by reading matter, but through observation and participation. By letting him come in and work our program. Not theory and theory alone, but theory and practice. The two go together. We not only thought about the Marxist-Leninist theory—we put it into practice. This is what the Black Panther Party is about.[1]

Even the simplest social work was supposed to build a community base for much more radical change, and in that sense the law-enforcement officials were right, by their own lights, to fear it. The most logical response for the government officials would have been to undertake the social work themselves and forestall the Panthers, but that they were unwilling to do.

But the breakfast program, even with political education, did not encompass the party's aims. The great question was how to show the community that it was possible to move from reform to revolution, and how to keep that movement going. That drive was what had attracted most of the members to the party. Under constant discussion among Black Panther Party members and in the party's publications, it was part of the source of the Black Panther "image" of revolutionary violence among the general public, insofar as that image was not totally distorted by false charges of black racism and similar accusations. In a major article in the party newspaper, the *Black Panther*, for May 16, 1968, Huey Newton wrote chiefly about the military aspect of the revolutionary drive.

The Vanguard Party must provide leadership for the people. It must teach the correct strategic methods of prolonged resistance through literature and activities. If the activities of the party are respected by the people, the people will follow the example. This is the primary job of the party. When the people learn that it is no longer advantageous for them to resist by going into the streets in large numbers, and when they see the advantage in the activities of the guerilla warfare method, they will quickly follow this example.

But first, they must respect the party which is transmitting this message. When the Vanguard group destroys the machinery of the oppressor by dealing with him in small groups of three and four, and then escapes the might of the oppressor, the masses will be overjoyed and will adhere to this correct strategy. When the masses hear that a gestapo policeman has been executed while sipping coffee at a counter, and the revolutionary executioners fled without being traced, the masses will see the validity of this type of approach to resistance. It is not necessary to organize thirty million Black people in primary groups of two's and three's but it is important for the party to show the people how to go about revolution. During slavery, in which no vanguard party existed and forms of communication were severely restricted and insufficient, many slave revolts occurred.[2]

In the light of their own experience with the police, the army, and the courts, and their immersion in the teachings of the party, the Cain brothers reached their own strong conclusions about the tactics and strategy of revolution.

ANTHONY CAIN:

The system is beginning to collapse—getting to the point where the country makes war on its own babies—which was very evident during the time when they moved on the people at Kent State, just snuffed them. It's right to say nothing really dynamic came out as far as the movement is concerned, when they snuffed them, but that created such a contradiction that those whites had to realize after the thing came down, they had to realize they were vulnerable not only to whipping but they were going to get snuffed too.

ALFRED CAIN, JR.:

When you examine the control [the authorities] have over us, you realize that this control is basically psychological, because it is the oppressed people who are serving as their buffer zone, who are continuing to defend the regime of the people that control, and these people must be brought to the level of awareness where they realize they are being oppressed. Consider that you have as many brothers as you have in the army, not a significant number of brothers on the local pig force, but you do have a lot of brothers on the pig force who could be highly instrumental in dealing with the problems at that level once they realized how oppressed they are.

The only way this can be done is to educate people by doing things to break the psychological conditioning that

the system has over people. It's not so much courage, because black people have always had heart—for a black
man to cut up another black man takes a whole lot of heart,
because he knows that other black man ain't got nothing
to lose either—what we have to do is to show the people
that they can win. Black people are ready for revolutionary
change, it just has to be shown to people that things can be
changed. That's one reason we stress that black people
should examine the various revolutionary movements going
on today on this planet; to show how structures that were
supposed to be all-powerful were brought down by the will
of the people, that the people make history.

This does define a liberal to me, one who does say, "I
realize this has to be done, I realize that programs have to
be implemented on a political level, on an economic level,
to redistribute, to change the law, to reallocate funds, to
take money from the moon program to put it into better
housing for poor people," and at the same time says this
takes time. He realizes there's a need for change—total
change, complete change—yet says there's not enough
people involved. See, we can't sit back and say, well, with
time everything is going to move in a positive direction,
because the amount of change depends on what you do with
the time.

What you have to do is go on the offensive, because this
system cannot exist on the defensive, because it's been
programmed. They've never encountered a situation in
which they've had to make major concessions to the people,
so the whole system would then collapse.

You have to build to that point. That's what [people are]
doing right now, they're in the process of learning by doing,
developing the proper methods, showing people this can
be done, that when an act of aggression is committed you
can retaliate effectively, and eventually, at the point when
you have that necessary machinery, that you can move on
the offensive. And once you're on the offensive, then you've

accomplished what you have to accomplish, because you've broken that psychological hold as far as the mass of people who are oppressed are concerned, and the system cannot fail to respond to that.

You can't specify exactly the direction the struggle's going to take, in terms of stage to stage, because you have different people in different levels of consciousness.

Black people are moving at a very different rate of acceleration than the society as a whole. The reason for this is because stark reality in this country has always been the fact that this is a fascist state, and more of us realize that these pigs will commit total genocide against black people.

ANTHONY:

If you take the mass majority of white people, and program them to the fact that black people are really out there trying to do them a bad disservice, out there to rip them off, and to reverse order, they [white people] won't really care any more. And this is what's being done now—they're being conditioned to accept the genocide of black people. We can't pick up a paper any day of the week and not see they done shot some black man or sister, they print up some act of violence that some black has perpetrated against some white, and this is all part of the conditioning they're getting to more or less prepare them for genocide.

ALFRED:

This is what Spiro Milhouse is saying in so many words, and Mitchell—and that broad who winds him up, Martha —this is what they're saying, and these people are endorsed spokesmen; Martha doesn't just get on the phone [by herself] and run this down. What they're trying to do is program people to think, "Well, that's cute, what she's saying." But see, that's dropping seeds, that's putting a seed in a person's mind. Now, [it is not] for us to say they will not come into Bushwick where we are right now, or Bedford-Stuyvesant, Brownsville, Harlem, and conduct commando raids, and then write a movie about it. We're saying that this is the nature of the people who control the society, that they will do anything to perpetuate their rule and then attempt to justify it through their control of the mass media, and this is what they're doing right now.

The Cain brothers' discussion and Huey Newton's article are in many ways consistent. Their essence is that revolutionary acts, whether violent or otherwise, even if they are isolated or individual, are justified when they are done in connection with a program of radical teaching and service to the community. They can be done to break down psychological barriers to revolt, and to show that revolutionary actions can succeed. As Alfred himself had repeatedly said, this did not justify rumbling with the police at every opportunity; action was supposed to pay off, at least with limited success.

During our discussion about problems of tactics and strategy, the brothers' position raised in my mind a perennial question: how to avoid bringing down the successful repression and the bloodbath that they envisioned, precisely by the military acts, however successful, that they advocated. That question they had answered, in part, by saying that they believed the social system was on the verge of collapse, that in fact it could not withstand further pressures and contradictions. They recognized that there were risks involved in actions against the state, but we found that we differed almost completely in our estimate of them. We found that the calculation of the risks involved in taking action against the state, although it is the most serious of political issues, must differ for people who have lived different lives. As Alfred said, his estimate and mine of the risks involved, and what was to be gained or lost, could never be the same.

ALFRED:

From a subjective point of view, I do not want to have to deal with the organized fascism you had in Germany, during the 1930s, until the German fascists were ripped off. But the point still remains for us, we *always* existed in this situation. If power could be given to or could be taken by the people without having to deal with elimination of all the so-called democratic-bourgeois channels that you have to deal with your grievances, this would be right on. But the reality of the situation is that this cannot be done.

You, Paul Chevigny, might have a different conception of what this thing is than I do. We've grown up and our realities are so different. The sense of urgency we have, everything we have is different. You could say not *all* the police lie, but most of them do. To me, objectively, there's no difference because to me they're part of the powers of occupation. They would not just lie, they would do anything they feel necessary; so that's why to deal with the pigs, you can't qualify them. Then, just extending that, you cannot qualify the pig judges that you had in court, you can't qualify the politicians and say, well, he's a grade-A politician, relatively speaking, he's not as bad as so-and-so—because they're all doing the same job on a black person. That's why I say there's a different sense of urgency, because I know that you know there are things that are wrong, but at the same time *you* don't feel that you have no choice but to do whatever you have to do. But there are things that you could do to intensify the struggle. There's no limits to what you can do; the only limits are the limits you place upon yourself, saying, I'm going to move at this particular point, that particular point.

The Black Panthers struggled constantly with the apparent conflicts among their ideological, service, and military aims. The image that caught everyone's imagination was the military one, and all the leaders warned against wildcat military projects. Bobby Seale complained about members who "related only to the gun," and in 1968, the *Black Panther* published advice on the problem.

1. The purely military viewpoint is highly developed among quite a few members.

a. Some party members regard military affairs and politics as opposed to each other and refuse to recognize that military affairs are only one means of accomplishing political tasks.

b. They don't understand that the Black Panther Party is an armed body for carrying out the political tasks of revolution. We should not confine ourselves merely to fighting. But we must also shoulder such important tasks as doing propaganda among the people, organizing the people, arming the people, and helping them to establish revolutionary political power for Black people. Without those objectives fighting loses its meaning and the Black Panther Party loses the reason for its existence.[3]

The question of the legitimate use of military means was bound to be a perennial one, because the party plainly did not disapprove outright of guerrilla violence, always and in every case; the rule was that it was supposed to be integrated into a program. But that was a hard distinction to adhere to, especially when so many members were attracted by the military image. Fat Man remembered the problem with hangers-on.

You'd have people who would come into the office saying we can do such and such a thing, or I can get you such and such a thing, get it for you the easy way. Well, we were out there trying to set an example, and that's not the way we had to go about it. Everybody is doing something illegal out on the block. We call them illegitimate capitalists. Like we

always had people making these type of offers and we always
rejected them. Just like we had people who came in and
said, "Well, I'm ready to go out here and off a pig." No good.
This is not to sound contradictory, but, you know, that
wasn't it, that wasn't our way. So it got to the point, whenever you hear this nonsense—and that's what it was, nonsense—you just walk off. You wouldn't say yes or no, you
say [*shrug*].

Revolutionary groups for centuries have grappled with
the conflict between military and political work. In most
countries, any sort of "legal" military work is impossible. In
Russia before the Revolution, for example, left political
parties such as the Socialists and the Social Revolutionaries
tended to divide into a legal wing doing political work, including parliamentary elections, above ground, and a tiny
terrorist or combat wing. But the Panthers apparently never
took that route, because they believed that arming the
people was an element of political education. Although the
writings of Cleaver and Newton foresaw the entire party
being driven underground, they expected that to happen
as a result of the repression of its activities. The Black
Panther Party's activities as a whole were open and legal,
and under those conditions no public use of guns can
be made except in an act of defiance like Huey Newton's
San Francisco stand-off. When a shoot-out actually occurred, Panthers tended to take a double-edged attitude,
on the one hand maintaining their innocence and blaming
the authorities for precipitating the action, and on the other
hand praising the members for defying illegitimate authority. There really is very little choice when your aims are
revolutionary yet your activities are public.

At every stage of history, fund raising has been a central
problem for professional radicals. Some funds may come
from publications or from rich sympathizers, and smaller
amounts from poor sympathizers; but as an organization

becomes more intransigent, ever smaller amounts of money are available from such sources. It is not automatic to turn to theft under conditions of radical intransigency and official repression, but it has from time to time seemed a logical solution to money problems. There is a clandestine tradition of social banditry among revolutionary groups, sometimes denied, often disappearing, but occasionally recurring. Fund raising thus becomes, in some cases, a military as well as a political problem.

In Russia between the Revolutions of 1905 and 1917, radical holdups were common. For a Socialist, willing to undertake revolution in order to transfer the ownership of property to the people, stealing the property of great capitalists in order to keep that revolution going sometimes seemed a logical action. Socialists who sympathized with such robberies called them "expropriations." The Russian tradition of terrorist violence made taking those actions easier, especially after the disorder and fighting of 1905.

The Maximalists, renegade left-wing members of the Social Revolutionary Party, staged sensational armed robberies in Moscow and St. Petersburg in 1906 and 1907.[4] In robbing two banks and a customs truck, they took more than a million rubles. It seems that the Bolsheviks cooperated with the Maximalists, at least to the extent of supplying bombs, in return for part of the booty.[5] They went on to turn the use of robbery-expropriation into a much more systematic source of funds. Expropriations actually made the Bolsheviks financially strong, in relation to their Socialist rivals. In 1906, Lenin wrote these words:

> The armed struggle pursues two different goals . . . in the first place the goal of the killing of individual persons, higher officials and subalterns in police and army; second, the confiscation of funds both from the government and from private persons. The funds seized go in part to the Party, in part for the arming and preparations of the uprising, in part for the support of the persons who conduct the struggle. The funds

which have been seized in the great expropriations—more than 200,000 rubles in the Caucasian, 875,000 rubles in the Moscow expropriation—have gone in the first place to the revolutionary parties. Lesser expropriations have served above all, sometimes even exclusively, for the maintenance of the expropriators.[6]

Other Socialists did not fail to point out the enormous problems raised by such a policy. The Mensheviks protested that the robberies compromised the Socialist movement in the eyes of the public, and tended to justify government repression against the legal as well as the illegal activities of Socialist groups, at a time when there was no immediate prospect of revolution. It was said that banditry tended to bring gangster elements into revolutionary groups, and distort their work. Rosa Luxemburg wrote: "How could this community arise between the drama of the proletarian revolution and the guerrilla struggle of the *Lumpenproletariat* against private property, a community so hurtful to the revolution?"[7] In the light of later history, it is significant that the Russian secret police used *agents provocateurs* to build such guerrilla activities in the effort to discredit the radicals; it was this which instead finally discredited those activities among the radicals themselves.

The Bolshevik expropriations were centered in Transcaucasia, much of it mountainous and isolated, traditional bandit and guerrilla country for generations. The most famous of the robberies was staged in Tiflis in 1907, when a gang led by the bandit-revolutionary Kamo, disguised as an army officer, took more than a quarter of a million rubles from a mail coach.[8] There were probably hundreds of smaller robberies in Transcaucasia.

This peasant-bandit base for the Bolshevik expropriators is perhaps the most significant thing about them. Eric Hobsbawm, in his study of bandits, tells us that they flourish in rural societies, where communication is poor and law enforcement is weak.

The point about social bandits is that they are peasant out-laws whom the lord and state regard as criminals, but who remain within peasant society, and are considered by their people as heroes, as champions, avengers, fighters for justice, perhaps even leaders of liberation, and in any case as men to be admired, helped, and supported. This relation between the ordinary peasant and the rebel, outlaw and robber is what makes social banditry interesting and significant. It also distinguishes it from two other kinds of rural crime: from the professional "underworld" or of mere freebooters ("common robbers"), and from communities for whom raiding is part of the normal way of life, such as for instance the Bedouin. . . . In a broader sense "modernization," that is to say the combination of economic development, efficient communications, and public administration, deprives any kind of banditry, including the social, of the conditions under which it flourishes.[9]

There are examples of expropriations in modern cities, such as the Maximalist holdups in Moscow and St. Petersburg, but they are few (and in at least one of those cases, the robbers were caught by the police).[10] Successful social-bandit work, even up to the present time, seems to require an old-fashioned bandit base of operations, or something resembling it. Anarchist bandits, making raids against Spanish banks up until the 1960s, used the mountains of the south of France as their base of operations.

It is an interesting sidelight that Ricardo De Leon called himself "Sandino," after the leader of a small guerrilla army in Nicaragua who stood off the United States Marines and the Nicaraguan government for five years, beginning in 1927. The American forces themselves contributed to the blending of the ideas of guerrilla warfare and banditry, in Sandino's case, by constantly referring to him as a "bandit." Early in his career, his men did take money and supplies from local storekeepers, to get started, but he later went on to full-scale expropriations of mining operations.

He fought a small-scale war that was intended to wrest power from the government. One historian tells us:

> Shortly after the fight at Bromaderos, the Marine Corps officially classified Sandino as a "guerrilla." But the promotion was only temporary, and Sandino soon reverted to the grade of "bandit." When questioned about Sandino's status as a "bandit" by the Senate Foreign Relations Committee, General Lejeune conceded that Sandino and his followers were "called bandits for the lack of some other word." In Nicaragua General Feland explained to Carleton Beals that military men "use the word 'bandit' in a technical sense, meaning the member of a band." Beals wondered how the Marines would classify John Philip Sousa.[11]

It is not surprising for a Latin American to suppose that revolution includes social banditry, when the North Americans suppose that social banditry includes revolution.

The expropriative acts of banditry best known to contemporary radicals are attributed to the Tupamaros of Uruguay. They have been careful to make the social purpose behind their acts clear in every case. A Cuban writer, Carlos Nuñez, credits them with robbing a major finance company in February 1970 and turning its account books, showing high-level corruption, over to the press.[12] They took a quarter of a million dollars from a resort casino, and are said to have returned that part of the money which made up employees' salaries. Nuñez quotes the police chief of Montevideo as saying, after two bank robberies in 1969, that he could not prove the Tupamaros had committed them, but "the perfect organization, the good manners of the assailants, and the human touch" pointed that way. Now, that is a good bandit reputation! The Tupamaros are considered the classic case of "urban guerrillas," although in fact they too seem to have something like an old-fashioned bandit base. The police and the army in Uruguay are weak, and much of the country is poorly developed. Many people, in the city as well as the country, admire the

Tupamaros and would not betray them. Finally, the Tupamaros have friends in authority, either through genuine sympathy or through bribery. Those few things are perhaps the minimum essential to the success of such an operation.

As this is written, it seems that there are an increasing number of cases of political banditry in the United States. The best-authenticated recent case, perhaps, is that of Fred Fernandez,* a former member of the Revolutionary Action Movement, who was convicted in 1971 of a bank robbery, apparently in order to obtain funds for an escape to Algeria to avoid trial in a conspiracy case.[13] In New York, Richard Moore (Dharuba), of the New York Panther Twenty-one, has pleaded guilty to a robbery.[14]

The Black Panther Party never approved of social banditry as a policy for the party, either in part or in whole. There is nothing in the writings of the leaders which resembles Lenin's strong words, and in fact there is plenty to the contrary. But the problem was there—in the need for funds, in the anticapitalist ideology of the party, and sometimes in the background of the street people recruited for the party. They were just the *Lumpenproletariat* about whom older Socialists had once expressed such concern, and the Panthers were proud to be able to recruit them.

There were some holdups by party members on the West Coast, the best known of which occurred in San Francisco in November 1968, when a newspaper delivery truck, clearly marked THE BLACK PANTHER, stopped for gas. One of the passengers calmly stuck up the gas station, and later shot it out with the police.[15] Bobby Seale and others at first suspected that it was the work of an *agent provocateur*. While there seems to be no hard evidence of that, Seale's instinct was good, for such criminal violence was indeed just the sort of idea that would attract the attention of secret political police. The case involving the Brooklyn Black Panthers, which is the chief subject of this book, was to

---

* Mr. Fernandez's conviction was reversed in February 1972, and the "authentication," which I initially accepted, is gone.

drive that point home. Seale's comment on the San Francisco stickup put the party policy in a nutshell.

> If you get involved in that stuff then the older people in the community misunderstand the Party. You also mislead the young lumpen proletarian cat, who probably has got the guts enough to commit a robbery, but who we want in the Party so we can politically educate him that robbery isn't the way to go about solving the social problems that put him in the situation in the first place.[16]

The Black Panther Party's attitude toward robbery by nonmembers was quite different. From time to time there were stories in the *Black Panther* approving expropriations by individual black men. A typical account, from Berkeley, begins:

> On Sunday, January 29, two brothers walked into the Telegraph Avenue Co-op Supermarket to expropriate money that rightfully belongs to the people. The events that followed left one of them dead and is a clear example of a vicious profit motive system which places more value on preserving capital (money) than preserving human life.[17]

The two views are not necessarily inconsistent. Party members could applaud piecemeal expropriation by bandits as a blow struck by the people, without at all approving banditry as a policy for the Black Panthers. In the end, however, because the party condemned expropriation as a policy while expressing admiration for individual bandits, there were bound to be all shades of opinion about it. In the Brooklyn chapter, those views extended from Fat Man's on the one hand to Thomas McCreary's at the other extreme.

FAT MAN:

In the office we had a rule: You do not talk about anything that can be detrimental to the party in the office, in front of the office, or even within a block of the office. That was a rule, a very heavy rule—we related to that. We were trying to enforce conscious discipline, so when you disobeyed the rules, you knew you'd have some little extra tasks. The party at that point could not risk that type of publicity, and that wasn't our program. Matter of fact, it was once stated that if you go out and commit a robbery and you get away with it, I'll take the money and kick your ass out of the party anyhow. It was more or less a motto: If you go out there and steal, you're not stealing for the party, you're stealing for yourself. Like I say, many people join the party for different reasons. Some people relate to military things, some are just gangsters and hoodlums. We tried to weed these people out, but you don't really even have to weed them out because once they see what's happening, they drop out themselves; nobody's going to relate to these very small things that you're putting so much work into, in order to build. They might want to relate to going out there and starting a revolution tomorrow. It don't work that way, you know.

ALFRED CAIN, JR.:

You have to take a lot of things into consideration—we could start from the fact that this system has been created by the European, having come out of the caves of Europe and systematically ripping off the rest of the world, taking the resources of the whole planet, and, through the use of force, forcing the rest of the world to pay homage to him in order to get those things they need in order to survive. We feel as though it's been the labor of black people, and other poor people, Chinese people, Spanish people, who have created this monster that society has become, it's been our labor. European people have acted in the manner of gangsters by taking us off in the first place, saying that all the world's resources belong to them and therefore we have to come to them to pay rent, or to pay for communications if we have to use the telephone, we have to come to them to buy food, and if we do not have their form of exchange, that we will have to starve to death or we will have to contend with the elements. Nature provided these resources for everyone, not for the select few, not for the capitalist pigs that manipulate this society, but nature provided this for all of mankind. We black people never did get our forty acres and two mules, and if we did have them, we wouldn't have to use the methods that we do today to survive.

In the Tombs, we came in contact with a lot of brothers who were incarcerated because they had ripped off capitalists at one point or another, but the thing was that they had not really ripped them off effectively. They had been dealing with small situations. And that's one of the things we have to overcome, because black people have been programmed to think petty, they have been programmed to think in terms of individuals, in terms of getting enough for them to be able to go out there and get a car and some clothes. See, what we're saying is we have to get organized to rip off all these capitalists, rip off the banks that are out there. I'm not going to make myself a suspect in the next bank robbery that goes down, but we feel that any action that poor people have to take in order to get that capital to use in a positive manner to create conditions in the community to elevate the people is right on, if they have to go and rip off twenty banks, or if they have to go and take off Fort Knox, whatever they have to do in this direction, as long as it is significant and as long as it educates the people. You do not take off the corner candy store or the poolroom. You do not take off the ice cream vendors. You do not take off a welfare hotel, because you only have a certain number of comrades at this point who are qualified to execute against the pig; now if you put these comrades in a situation where they are risking their lives, the actions they are involved in have to be significant; they have to really be dealing damaging blows to the Establishment, and to go rip off a welfare hotel for sixteen hundred dollars, and risk three brothers' lives for doing some bullshit like that, is madness.

THOMAS MCCREARY:

I think rip-offs are very important, you know. Because if you are going to fight a war, you understand, you need resources and matériel to do it with. And if the Man or the enemy has the resources, it is your duty to take it from him, you understand. There is nothing criminal about that, once you decide and say, I'm going to be a revolutionary. You establish your own rules, your own morals. If dudes go out and take banks off, you understand, want to rob some loan company, or some apartment buildings, in terms of land-lords, this type of people, I say this is a good thing, not a bad thing. And not sometimes—any time you get a chance to do it, if you do it not for selfish gains. If the brothers want to take the hotel off, let's say they feel they'll get forty thousand dollars out of it—but that depends on the necessity; if the situation called for twelve hundred dollars, it would have been necessary. But I really don't believe that the brothers planned this thing out to go there to do no shit like that. I always say if they are going to do something, if that hotel is going to be done, it should be for one million two hundred thousand dollars.

Take the Tupamaros down in Uruguay. They pulled the most expensive robbery committed in the annals of the world recently. They even called the Interpol on it. This is the way of breaking the capitalist, because he relates to that monetary system. That's the only thing that keeps him in power—the dollar. I think the party relates to the fact that if you want to rip off the capitalist, the capitalist should be taken off, you understand, but I don't think the party relates to the fact that you take off the capitalist for a couple of hundred dollars, a couple of thousand dollars; that is irrelevant. But if you take the capitalist off to further your struggle in terms of how you're going to deal with the Man, you understand, then that's good. If you need some arms, and you want to take off the Man to go buy yourself some arms, then that's good.

I think that all the Black Panther Party leaders would have disagreed with the last paragraph. After the wildcat actions on the West Coast and the arrests of twenty-one Panthers for conspiracy in New York, it is likely that the party leaders were extremely leery of further charges of violence and were ready to repudiate anyone who acted against their policies. But the party ideology of violent socialist revolution, and the policies of appealing to the *Lumpenproletariat* and applauding expropriations, raised the question over and over again.

Many law-enforcement officials and conservative politicians would have been pleased to be able to pin the "bandit" label, pure and simple, on the Black Panther Party. Their campaign to do that is memorialized in the report of the House Committee on Internal Security concerning the Black Panthers.[18] The committee took evidence about supposed Panther crimes, some of it from the most untrustworthy of witnesses,[19] but in the end the majority wrote a relatively objective report, as they put it, to avoid making "martyrs" of the Panthers at a time (1971) when the party was split by dissension. A minority of four members of the committe of nine appended a bitter dissenting opinion, which begins:

> The present report does not give the reader a clear understanding of the Black Panther Party as a subversive criminal group, using the façade of politics and Marxist-Leninist ideology as a cover for crimes of violence and extortion.[20]

This is a most significant point of view, and it is easy to see why some congressmen and others supported it so ardently. It eliminates the Panthers, and indeed much of the revolutionary movement, as a significant political force. If the Panthers were only criminals, then all their demands for change, all their accusations against the state became meaningless prattle. Many people were willing to pay a considerable price to make that point of view prevail, and among them doubtless were many law-enforcement officials. Some were even willing to go so far as to supply the plans and the tools of violence themselves.

5

A NEWCOMER

By the beginning of 1969, the Brownsville office was established, social programs were in operation, political education was under way, and military problems were under constant discussion, but it is plain that the Brooklyn chapter of the Black Panther Party was still quite loosely organized. Interested black people were coming in off the street, and a youth like Fat Man, who found the membership rolls of the Party closed in 1969 when he came into it, could nevertheless assume much responsibility. In February, Wilbert Thomas, a slight, nattily dressed black man in his twenties, began to come around to the Black Panther offices in Brooklyn regularly. He spoke to Alfred Cain about political education, and began to collect Black Panther literature.

At that time, infiltration of the Black Panther Party in New York was in full swing. Shaun Dubonnet, a former member of the party in Brooklyn with a long history of mental illness, had told the police yarns about the Brooklyn Panthers, some of which he later admitted were fabrications. Partly as a result of his testimony, indictments had been handed down, and wiretap orders were issued by the courts for the Panther telephones. At least six black undercover agents of the New York City police had infiltrated the Manhattan Panther group, and in April, in a resounding crackdown, twenty-one members and friends were arrested and charged with attempted arson and conspiracy to bomb police stations, public buildings, and department stores.

Wilbert Thomas joined the police force in January 1969, and was immediately put to work attending all sorts of gatherings of black people in Brooklyn. It is a minor irony of history that one of his first acts was to attend and dutifully take notes on a speech by Conrad Lynn, a noted black lawyer, who was later appointed to defend Jerome West against Thomas's accusations. After he began to attend Black Panther meetings in February, his reports to the department's political surveillance group, the Bureau of Special Services (BOSS)* apparently included nothing but Panther matters. He received no formal police training, or virtually none, a practice which is customary in BOSS, in order more perfectly to preserve the cover and anonymity of the undercover agent. He was assigned the code name "René," under which he called in to his office and wrote his reports. On the other hand, he used his real name and admitted to his true past life in the groups he infiltrated, a practice which was inconsistent with previous bureau practice.

From Marion, South Carolina, Thomas's family had moved to Brooklyn, where they lived on Macon Street within a few blocks of the Cains. Thomas attended Franklin K. Lane High School, where his record was unremarkable. Unlike so many others, he was awarded his diploma in 1963. He joined the air force, where he was trained as a jet-engine mechanic. After his separation from the air force, he worked for a couple of years as a supervisor in a firm of container distributors in Brooklyn. But even there, as events proved, he showed special ambitions to move up.

The Carolinas, Brooklyn high schools, and military service—in its bare outlines, Thomas's life could have been that of any of the Black Panthers who have told their stories in previous chapters.

---

* Now called the Security and Investigation Section (SIS).

FAT MAN:

The thing is, he was born in the South. He comes from South Carolina—we come from the same state. I'm from Sumter; I left the South when I was about eight years old.

I only talked with Wilbert Thomas at any length, I think it was twice. Once was one morning when we had our old breakfast program in Bedford-Stuyvesant—we both got there early—and another time was at the other breakfast program for about five minutes—he stayed to clean up. And while he was cleaning up, he was washing dishes, and that time we just talked about broads. That was his only conversation piece—women. Which happens to be the only conversation piece of the average dude running around here in the street. See, like, the average brother always talks about women, how many broads he got here, how many babies he done made. He played the part of the average cat on the street. It was always women. This was a thing he used to throw everybody off. He was always telling us about his exploits with women; this man was dynamite with women. Whatever he got, he got it from a woman. He even said he could get guns from some broad he was messing with. Whenever you see him coming, he just came from a broad's house. He flirts with the women, all right. I'd see him rapping with the sisters, kissing them, stuff like that. But this is natural—a man and a woman, you know.

And the [other] time, I don't know how we got on it, but he said, "I can get forty-fives if you want to buy one." I think he said it would be something like sixty dollars: "If you buy six, you get a lower rate." At the time, I had to dismiss it because he didn't show me anything, number one, and number two, he never showed me any of his own personal pieces. I just said. "What the heck, where are you going to get the money?" It had to be during the summer, July or August. It seemed like nobody had no technical equipment, but this was the thing, this was a part of the image. Then the party at the time did have a rule that no Panther unless authorized could carry any pieces, so we didn't really have any need for it. Nobody was authorized. We didn't want nobody getting busted unnecessarily. If you didn't have a piece you couldn't go out there and get busted. That was sorta like contradictory in a way, too, given what we supposedly were advocating. But Wilbert Thomas at one point told me he could get .45s.

I suppose that should have made me suspicious. But you always have a lot of loose and groundless talk when you're dealing with a situation like this. Let's go out here and do this, let's go out here and do that, these things you're just talking off the top of your head. Tomorrow it's forgotten. Ninety-nine point nine percent of the things that were said were never done, because there was never time. We always had the basics to consider. Besides, he always played on our sympathies. Like the stories about his brother getting shot, about being beat up by the pigs, like, these things didn't happen, his brother being shot up, all like that. See, the party had a thing about attendance; his thing was very shaky. He was almost tossed out. He'd come up with these things, and this would give him an excuse. That's where he was basically at.

He acted like the average dude, but it was apparent that he wasn't no ordinary fellow. He didn't rap about it, but it came out that this fellow had a small amount of education and that he was different—he wasn't a street nigger, so to speak. But, everybody's different in some way. So many people in the party; you had some college people, you had people from different backgrounds. When I heard that he was what he was, I couldn't believe it. He just wasn't the personality, he looked like the quiet . . . he looked like a very, you know, bright guy.

———————

Wilbert Thomas didn't come around the party as often as the members thought he should have, and he was not very noticeable when he was there, at first. Alfred Cain can hardly talk about him except as a problem in security, a lesson in politics.

ALFRED CAIN, JR.:

The most important thing we should have done was a little more research on his background, where he went to school, where he worked, who are the people who he related to, what kind of experience did he have when he was in the army; we could have done a whole lot more research on his background to get some idea why it is that a brother feels, or *knows*, it is necessary to begin moving in a revolutionary fashion. You have a certain number of people who still aspire to be *petit bourgeois*. You can determine this if you research thoroughly a person's background. There's a natural tendency . . . say, if a person's in high school, tells somebody, "I'd like to be on the police force," or even the kind of TV programs a person watches, all this indicates the class background or his aspirations. If he watches "Mod Squad," or "I Spy," or "The Lone Ranger," then he has a Tonto complex. Whereas the majority of stomp-down *Lumpen*, they don't even relate to TV, because they realize the white fantasy world is not open to them.

———————

This approach to security came back with force after I began to do the little digging I was able to do into Thomas's background. My assistant, Seu-Wen Wei, spoke to the foreman at Thomas's old job from the period after he had left the air force. The foreman told us that Thomas had been seen talking to the people at an office for police recruitment near the plant. When Thomas left the job, he told the foreman he was going to a drafting job at $175 a week; the foreman knew that was too high for a starting salary, and assumed Thomas had become a policeman. More conclusively, Thomas came around to see his acquaintances at the plant, chiefly black workingmen, and boasted that he had become a police undercover agent. That boasting made for a ridiculously sloppy undercover agent, but more than that, the story of that boasting is very sad from the point of view of the Black Panthers. Alfred Cain is right: if the party had investigated Thomas even superficially, they could have found out that he was a policeman. But, as Fat Man says, there was no time or personnel to spare for investigating such people.

The confirmation given by the foreman to Alfred Cain's words on the need for "investigation" is striking. In simpler terms, the Panthers needed to know more about one another as people. In a way, it is extraordinary that such personal knowledge should have to be cast in the form of "research." The way they knew one another in the Black Panther Party created a problem in recognizing an informer like Wilbert Thomas. Fat Man described a part of it.

> We had a saying: Social practice is the criterion of truth. It didn't matter what he told me because I wasn't listening to him; just watching him. We were concerned with deeds; that was the basis of our whole thing: deeds. What else? The main talking we did was to discuss the platform and the program.

Thomas McCreary was much more contemptuous of individualism, and the discussion of individual problems in the party.

> Alfred came to me a week before they got busted and asked me what did I think about him [Wilbert Thomas]? And at that time, when we had our PE class, we read from Mao, and Mao states very clearly [that] you don't be talking about a person behind his back, and a lot of people practice that very

thoroughly. But it happened that people would say, "So-and-so, well, he's a jive motherfucker, he ain't doing this and he ain't doing that." You see, I wouldn't speak on that. Because Al and other people who knew me in the party at that time knew that I was very vociferous in meetings, if I had something to say about something that I felt was going wrong about somebody, and I think I made a lot of enemies for a while in terms of voicing my opinions about different people. We didn't do this in groups of twos or threes, getting out, because that's undermining unity.

The pursuit of the collective method of life assumes the consent of everyone. It is intended to exclude all the personal problems which get in the way of a general effort. Under such circumstances, it is not acceptable to say that one hasn't the time or the courage to do some piece of collective work, or that one would, say, rather write this book. In such a world, a man may be adjudged dead wrong a thousand times, but his companions assume that he will at least try to take their criticisms seriously. He is expected to share at least the endeavor with them. People involved in such a collective effort frequently know very little about one another in the personal sense—their pasts, their tastes, sometimes even their questions about ideology. The common ground is assumed, and in effect the success of the endeavor depends on good faith. The collective effort is peculiarly subject to infiltration, just because individual differences and gripes tend to be discouraged.

I do not intend this as a criticism of collective work, and yet it becomes a criticism when the collective effort becomes revolutionary. If the members simply work to supply one another's needs, and exclude the outside world, the assumption that the authorities are neutral is sometimes reasonable. But if the collective effort is action against the outside world, mutual trust cannot be assumed. Intense personal knowledge among all the participants has to be added to the common endeavor.

Of course, personal relations in a collective effort are as varied as they are anyplace else; they may be close or distant. In fact, they tend to be closest in organizations which have overtly revolutionary aims; these may break down into "affinity groups," just so that the members can come to understand one another. It is possible for a very skilled infiltrator to pass through even this screen, but it would have been hard for a man like Wilbert Thomas to do so.

If the members of the Brooklyn Black Panther Party had known more about Wilbert Thomas in a personal way, they might have been able to detect how out of place he actually was. They were not as interested in his opinions, his background, his life, as they were in his actions. So long as his actions seemed totally inadequate for their purposes, he was isolated. But if he could once make it seem as though he was really part of the actions of the party, he might succeed in gaining someone's confidence. If social practice really was the criterion of truth, a properly simulated social practice would make him acceptable.

It seems that in the Brooklyn chapter of the Panthers, among the people who have spoken in these pages, relations were strangely formal, although the bond of common effort was close. Alfred Cain's life was enclosed in ideology; the love that he felt for people was expressed in the workings of that ideology. All the experiences of his life had made it hard, hard for him to express himself except in an abstract way, a way that expressed also defiance, a determination to fight. He was perhaps not as mistrustful of the world of feelings as Thomas McCreary, but he had sunk his love for his people, his friends, his family, in ideas calculated to redeem them together with millions of others.

Wilbert Thomas, too, was cloaked in ideology. Although I cannot trace its sources as clearly as I can for members of the Black Panther Party, it will become clear from the trial, and Thomas's later words, that he adhered to an iron "antisubversive" line, one that made it impossible for him to believe that revolutionaries might have *bona fide* programs to serve the people, but that fitted precisely into the prevailing law-enforcement ideology about the Panthers. Although his life had not been so different from that of his companions in the Brooklyn chapter, something in his background had given him a fear of and contempt for the life of the street man that was the obverse of the Panthers' admiration for it. The ideology on one side looked for the spark of revolution in every black person, and that on the other rejected revolutionary talk as a mere cloak for crime. Similar experiences might have led a man in either direction. On both sides, character and ideology, suspicion of personal relations, cut both Thomas and Cain off from perceiving what was in the other's mind. In August of 1969, Cain was close to seeing the facts about Thomas, but Thomas had never understood Cain.

They did have one great characteristic in common: determination. It was determination which locked them into a course of events leading inevitably to arrest. Cain's unyielding position that there could be no real change but through revolution, and his willingness to discuss the violent means for that revolution, were bound to make him interesting to an *agent provocateur*. If he had been willing to compromise, to set himself reformist goals, he would have been of no interest to Wilbert Thomas. Thomas's will was fully as strong, but his determination led him to try to expose what he took to be the criminal nature of his companions by providing elements of their crime.

Wilbert Thomas's work was uneventful for many months. He talked to the party members, helped in the breakfast program, and sold newspapers. He received political education. On March 1, 1969, he reported to his superiors, "The BPP are studying Marxist-Leninist revolution," and indicated his grasp of its principles by defining it as "Get it any way you can." He reported making a trip with members to the East Village to buy guns, but found there were none to be had. On April 9, he was assigned to mail a package, found it sloppily wrapped, and characteristically, spent some time trying to make it tidy enough to suit him. He attended the wedding of Anthony Cain to Olaywah, another member of the party. After the service, Thomas noted, Alfred Cain read from the quotations of Chairman Mao.

On June 20, Thomas recorded a bitter line from Alfred Cain: "BPP members will have to relate to stickups because living off the few cents from the Black Panther newspaper will not make it." If Cain said it at all, it is hard to tell whether he meant it as a wry joke, but in any case it is a sad comment about the effectiveness of legal methods of fund raising for the Brooklyn chapter. On another occasion, Thomas noted a discussion with Alfred Cain about how difficult the life of the black man is, and apparently sought to gain Cain's confidence by saying that if this was living, he didn't want to see what dying was like.

The René reports reflected, without comment, the fact that there were other agents in the Brooklyn Panthers unknown to Thomas. In the middle of March, he reported that a man called Roy, or "R. C.," said that the Black Panther Party was not teaching black people what they should know, to wit, the use of guns, demolition, and guerrilla warfare. Three days later, R. C. took Thomas and a very young Panther, Frank Harris, for a ride in his car and tried to recruit them to work for the "Feds"! Thomas jumped out of the car. In July, one Sam Jones came into the Bedford-Stuyvesant office on Fulton Street. Thomas's report of his visit is inimitable.

4. At about 3:30 PM *Sam Jones*, who stated that he lives at 818 Legion Street, entered the BPP office [1808 Fulton]. Mr. Jones stated that he had .38 rifles at his apartment for sale. Mr. Jones then opened his briefcase, he had about 5 .38 revolvers inside. [*James*] *Worth* then told Mr. Jones to go outside of the BPP office, because no technical equipment was

to be brought into the office. Mr. Worth went outside of the BPP office with Mr. Jones.

5. *Mr. Worth* then returned to the office. The assigned then took the license number of Mr. Jones' car. It was a '65 or '66 blue and white dodge license number 2Z-8389.

6. About 5 minutes later about 10 police cars passed by the BPP office one right after another.

7. *Mr. Worth* then stated we are going to get that jive ass so-called Mr. Jones because he wasn't anything but a pig trying to get us busted.

It is not as odd as it may seem that Thomas did not know about these ham-handed official provocations before they occurred; it is standard espionage practice to keep agents ignorant of one another's work.

There were no René reports at all for more than a week, from June 29 to July 7, 1969. Thomas was later to offer as explanations to the Panthers that he had been ill and that his brother had been shot by Puerto Ricans, episodes remembered by Fat Man. When Thomas went back to the Black Panther office, he found he had been excluded from his already tenuous relation with the party. He nevertheless continued to go around to the offices, and in its typically loose way, the party did not physically exclude him. In his report of July 30, he claimed that Brenda Hyson, an officer, readmitted him to the party. Beginning the very next day, Thomas claimed that he began to hear remarks composing part of the conspiracy to rob and murder for which Alfred Cain, Ricardo De Leon, and Jerome West were first arrested and then laboriously tried during the following fourteen months.

PART TWO

MANHATTAN LAW

The relations between the Government and its informers are of extreme delicacy. Not to profit by timely information were a crime; but to retain in Government pay, and to reward spies and informers, who consort with conspirators as their sworn accomplices, and encourage while they betray them in their crimes, is a practice for which no plea can be offered. . . . To be unsuspected, every spy must be zealous in the cause which he pretends to have espoused; and his zeal in a criminal enterprise is a direct encouragement of crime. So odious is the character of a spy, that his ignominy is shared by his employers against whom public feeling has never failed to pronounce itself, in proportion to the infamy of the agent, and the complicity of those whom he served.

THOMAS ERSKINE MAY, 1863

6

ARREST

On the morning of August 16, 1969, at about seven o'clock, Wilbert Thomas drove a green Dodge Dart off the West Side Highway, the elevated expressway running along the Hudson River in Manhattan, and down the exit ramp at 125th Street. Ricardo De Leon was seated in the front seat next to Thomas, with Alfred Cain, Jr., behind De Leon and Jerome West behind the driver. The right-hand or eastern lane of the exit ramp was blocked by construction work, and sawhorse police barricades were drawn up parallel to the middle dividing line of the ramp (see frontispiece); the green Dart had to drive down the left lane, slowing to a stop as a small panel truck pulled across the end of the lane. Plainclothes detectives from the Safe, Loft, and Truck Squad* jumped out of the panel truck, sprang up out of the bushes on either side, and, armed with pistols and a shotgun, closed in on the car. A cab with agents from the Bureau of Special Services pulled up behind the Dart. Surprise was complete, and all four men, including Wilbert Thomas, were arrested without incident.

Alfred Cain, Ricardo De Leon, and Jerome West were arraigned that same evening in criminal court on an affidavit of one of the arresting detectives, Alfred Halikias,

---

* There is nothing irregular or unusual about an arrest and charge by officers who are not from BOSS, which ordinarily protects its agents and staff from public exposure in this way.

charging them with conspiracy to commit robbery, attempted robbery, possession of weapons, and attempted murder. The typewritten part of this short affidavit is perhaps as succinct a statement of the charges as can be made.

> Defendants, acting in concert, conspired and attempted to forcibly take a quantity of U.S. currency from the Dunston Hotel, of 142 West 131st Street, New York City. The defendants, acting in concert, were in possession of a loaded sawed-off shotgun, a loaded U.S. Carbine M-1 rifle, and other dangerous instruments. The defendants, acting in concert, attempted to shoot Det. A. Halikias, #797, by pointing a loaded sawed-off shotgun at him.

A curious charge was added on that first affidavit, in the handwriting of Detective Halikias: "Def'ts did also conspire to kill a police officer if necessary as a diversionary measure to commit said A & R [assault and robbery]." That charge was not to appear in the indictment and was never to be mentioned again until the trial, when it assumed some small importance.

The avowed purpose of bail is to ensure that a defendant will return for trial, and it is expected to vary with the finances and the background of each defendant. In this case the bail was set at $50,000 for each defendant, although their backgrounds were quite different. Obviously intended as a means of preventive detention, the bail remained the same even after the defendants were indicted and their case was transferred to State Supreme Court,* although it was obvious that the defendants were not able to post the bond.

The following day, Sunday, the newspapers reported that four Black Panthers had been arrested for the conspiracy to rob. Wilbert Thomas, it was said, had been taken to federal jail because he was wanted on federal charges. The police

---

* New York City Criminal Court can handle felony arraignments and preliminary hearings before indictment. Once the grand jury indicts, however, a felony case is transferred to State Supreme Court for trial.

said they had found on Alfred Cain a sketch of the hotel in question made on the back of a Black Panther leaflet in support of Huey Newton. Zayd-Malik Shakur, spokesman for the Black Panther Party in New York, repudiated the defendants, saying:

> The Panthers are not robbers and hoodlums. We do not go around robbing stores. We are servants of the people.

Cain, De Leon, and West were totally isolated; they had no support, financial or political.

Melvina Cain came to my office at the New York Civil Liberties Union the next day, accompanied by Mrs. West, a gray-haired, silent woman. Mrs. Cain's style had changed nearly as much as that of her sons since the last time I had seen her. She wore her hair in a natural cut, and over her shoulder was thrown a silk scarf of black, red, and green, a gift from one of her sons. She asked me to defend Alfred's case. A charge of attempted robbery and attempted murder, involving defendants whom the Black Panthers repudiated, did not present a hopeful prospect, but those were days when defense lawyers were beginning to be suspicious of any case labeled "conspiracy." Besides, I felt an obligation to and an affection for all the Cains, although I had seen very little of them for a long time, and I could as little picture Alfred Cain getting mixed up in such a case as I could picture myself defending it. The short of it was, I agreed to talk to Alfred in jail.

The next day, I went down to the Tombs, the Manhattan House of Detention for Men, and waited in the bare, tile-lined lawyers' room until the guards brought in Alfred Cain, with his familiar brass-rimmed glasses and Afro haircut. I can't say he seemed very glad to see me; he was then still hoping that the Black Panther Party would shift its ground and supply him with a lawyer.

Of course he had been in the car, he asserted, but he denied that he had been on his way to commit a robbery.

When I asked him about the sketch mentioned in the newspapers, an astonished look came over his face. There was a sketch, he said, but Wilbert Thomas had drawn it. He also said that it was Thomas's car they had all been riding in. He did not know there was a shotgun in the car, nor did he plan to commit a crime that morning. He was pretty sure, now, that Thomas was an informer, and he said he had suspected as much before he ever got into the car. He explained that he had gone out with Thomas that morning partly to try to learn enough about him to tell for sure whether he was an informer. He later said, bravely, "I found out, too," as though he had at least served the function of protecting others from Thomas.

Cain was surprised to learn that he was the one identified as having pointed a weapon at a detective. "There were so many cops there, if I had blinked an eye, I'd be dead." That sounded reasonable to me, but at that point, to establish that the charge was false without any neutral witnesses appeared almost hopeless. Thomas's having drawn the map and supplied the car seemed to me, even then, to present *prima facie* evidence of entrapment by the police, and I wanted to defend the case for that reason, but I was pretty worried about the attempted-murder charge. What would be the use of winning a conspiracy case, only to lose on the much more serious charge of attempted murder?

Within two weeks, Donald Cox, a Black Panther minister from Oakland, dropped in to explain the party's position on the case. It was clear to him, he said, that the three defendants had been entrapped, but that was no excuse for their conduct. Apart from the question of their intent, they had suspected Wilbert Thomas of being an agent, and under those conditions they should never even have consented to get into a car with him. The party, Cox said, was essentially refusing to support the three because of a breach of discipline, and what he took to be foolhardiness. I found and still find that explanation inadequate. It was plausible on its face, but it was inconsistent with other actions of the party; the Panthers defended others whose conduct was more than foolhardy, when a police informant was involved. I thought that the real reason the three were politically marooned was because they happened to be arrested late in 1969, when the party was overextended in both its budget and its credibility, and because they were from the relatively isolated Brooklyn chapter.

Cox also gave me one very odd fragment of a story. He had been at the Brownsville office a few days after the three were arrested, when a lady called in to complain about trouble with her landlord. When the members went around in a car to investigate, they discovered that they were approaching Wilbert Thomas's house and that the street was full of police. They quickly pulled out of the street, and Cox said they were all sure that it was a police trap. It might have been a coincidence, I thought, pushing the story to the back of my mind.

Cain, De Leon, and West were soon indicted on fourteen counts (set forth in Appendix B, pages 313–18). The indictment added only a little to the original complaint. It ascribed to the defendants a plan "to commit robberies so that they could obtain money to aid the Black Panther Party in accomplishing its objectives," and charged that pursuant to the plan, they had conspired to rob, and attempted to rob, the New Dunston Hotel in Harlem. They had conspired to commit murder by agreeing to "shoot to kill" anyone who made a "funny move" during the robbery (the charge of conspiracy to murder a policeman was gone). Attempted murder of a detective and its lesser-included crimes such as assault remained, and all defendants were charged with possessing the sawed-off shotgun, the rifle, a knife, and a canister of red-pepper spray. In addition, they were charged with defacing the shotgun by filing off its identifying marks.

The grand jury also indicted Fat Man on similar charges, excluding the attempted-murder charge because he had not been in the car. The essence of the case against him was that he had supposedly supplied the M-1 rifle to the others. His account of his arrest is vivid, and his recollections of what the police said about a possible assault charge are particularly significant in the light of what ultimately happened to the assault and attempted-murder charges against Alfred Cain and the others.

FAT MAN:

The day before I got busted, I was getting ready to go back to school. In June, [when] I was so disgusted, I had one credit to go, and I would have got my diploma. I got involved with the party, like with the breakfast program, and before I knew it the summer was gone. I dug the scene, and I dug the people there, but there's a saying, Revolutionaries either end up on park benches or dead. So . . . I didn't want to die, not like that. So I decided to go back, but in the beginning of September I got busted.

The first day I couldn't go down to school, because I hadn't really gotten the thing sewed together at the breakfast program so that I could leave, so I took two of the other brothers down to school and dropped them off and then I went back to finish my duties. I came home, talking to my sister that night, got up the next morning getting ready to go to school, and one of the sisters calls me up and she tells me things are behind schedule, so I said, "All right, I'll be in." I went around and got the food, and I parked the car, got out and locked the car, was walking cross the street, when the detectives approached me, said, "You [Fat Man]?" I said, "Yes." They said, "You're under arrest," and slapped the handcuffs on me. I asked them what the charge is, and they said, "Attempted robbery," and blah, blah. I couldn't even grasp it. I said, "What the hell you talking about?" I just couldn't conceive, even though Cain and them had gotten arrested like three weeks before I did. We were in such a grind, you know, from day to day, I didn't even think about it. I missed the brothers, but things have to go on, have to keep on forging ahead.

So they tell me about the charges, and me and the police were jiving. At first they were trying to be arrogant because they expected me to be arrogant. They were getting ready to charge me with assault; before I [could have] committed an assault, they were prepared to charge me. One fellow was asking the other fellow, "What about the assault charge?" He said, "We'll forget about that." At this point the only thing I was concerned with was keeping them off my head; survival was my only thought. So we go downtown, and then I see what is happening a little bit. They didn't beat me as I expected them to. I have to say they were very nice; they were scheming, but they were very nice. They were trying to get into my confidence and get me to say things. They were trying to win me over. Like I was still amazed at the whole situation; I was excited, yet I was nervous. I'd never been through this before. I wanted to find out what it was all about. When I realized they weren't going to break my head in, I just started to check out the whole situation.

So they take me down to [Assistant District Attorney] Fine. He says, "I can understand you being a member of the party. I can understand—living in that situation." After listening to a few of his words, I knew he didn't know anything about me. So I said this is all lies, and then he comes on to say, "All the rhetoric and everything: Right on; Off the pigs. It's all very exciting but now you're faced with the bitter reality of it all." That hit home. That was the only thing he said that whole day that I will remember, really, fully and truly. He says, "You can cooperate. That door is always open to you. You can go on out there to that place they call prison and rot. But that door is always open to

you." I said, "How long could I get?" and he says, "Well,
the others might get fifty years. You wouldn't get that much,
maybe twenty-five."

So I went to Rikers Island. The first month I slept because
I was so tired. You wouldn't believe it—the first month I
slept all day, even when we locked out. That's how ex-
hausted I was. At that time in the chapter we were very
susceptible to diseases because our resistance was low.

That joint had a very profound effect on me, it was like a
mind crusher. Like, I'd never been through it before, so it
was really . . . I'm kinda proud of the fact that I didn't really
break up under it. Well, to a point I was broken, you know,
I don't feel that I was strong enough, maybe it was the
maternal thing that really turned me around. My moms, she
came out every visit. She missed one visit during the whole
period I was there; it is a hassle to get out there, it involves
hours. Every visit, mail every day, things like that—charity
begins at home. Take a statement of Mao's, one of his quotations is that the revolutionary has no family, nobody.
That's where it was getting to. When I was busted, I had
time to reflect on these things, so when I came home, I decided I had to take care of business on this home front. My
whole time in the party had some heavy effects on my
family life, worried the hell out of her. At the time I almost
ignored it, but I had a whole lot of time to think about it in
the joint, how I was doing people. Besides, I didn't see why
the party should desert any of us—talking about the four
of us, you know. If they hadn't come out with that statement
when Cain and them got busted—well, they didn't have to
say nothing.

Fat Man's bail was reduced to the manageable sum of
$3,500, and he was released some two months after his ar-
rest. At first, this caused some fear that he had yielded to
the pressure and agreed to testify for the prosecution, but

he never did. In fact, the bail reduction seems instead to have reflected the flimsiness of the state's case against him. As the facts developed, he could not in any case have had very much to tell that was useful to the prosecution.

Alfred Cain was to do fifteen months in the crowded Tombs awaiting the disposition of his case, more than seven times as long as Fat Man, but he stood it a lot better. In a way, an unshakable radical is perhaps better fitted than most to stand jail, because it fits into his philosophy. It perhaps gives him just a fragment of grim satisfaction for the state to fulfill its appointed role as oppressor.

A short exchange with his father perfectly captures Alfred Cain's final, fixed conviction that he had no alternative.

ALFRED CAIN, SR. When he was in this trouble, I couldn't think right, I couldn't walk right, I couldn't do anything right. You got to think, you got to have something together. I couldn't do it when he was in there. I'd go down to talk to him and start to crying, he'd say, "Daddy, daddy, don't worry about me"—I got to worry about him, right?

ALFRED CAIN, JR. Why? What is it gonna help? It's not going to change anything. We got to do what we're doing. We don't have any choice but to do what we're doing.

A.C. SR. There's some things—well, he doesn't understand. See, I'm fifty-six years old. When you get my age—lots of things I tried to tell him, he wouldn't listen.

A.C. JR. This brother in California says, and it's true, life without freedom is, means nothing. So what I'm saying is, what is there to worry about? If you're not free, that's all you've got to worry about. Do anything you can to be free, to determine your own life.

A.C. SR. All I'm saying is, the same with all my other children after him, he's my life. What I've always tried to tell him is, don't trust nobody.

A.C. JR. All you got is black people. You got to trust black people, to the extent you can.

We are in the presence of that iron determination again, of the tragedy that befell Alfred Cain. He took a calculated risk, in riding with Wilbert Thomas, because his ideas dictated that he ought to take that risk. He understood afterward what had happened to him, and did not regret having taken the risk. To him, it was inevitable that he might encounter trouble with the law, yet he felt he could not have done otherwise.

7

THE JURY AND THE LAWYERS

While Alfred Cain, Ricardo De Leon, and Jerome West lay in jail, the first two in the Tombs, and West, being under the age of twenty-one, in the only slightly less crowded Rikers Island prison, their case slowly wound its way up to trial. All three defendants were indigent, and needed counsel. I had volunteered to defend Alfred Cain, but I did not think that one lawyer could adequately defend all the accused on a conspiracy charge. In the light of the attitude of the Black Panther Party, it did not seem likely that lawyers were going to volunteer to defend the other two as a matter of political principle, and we had to wait for more than a month until the appeals courts could appoint lawyers from their rotating list.

The luck of the draw was magnificent. Conrad Lynn was appointed for Jerome West, and De Leon drew Elliot Taikeff. The three of us came to form a perfect working team.

A small, brownskinned man with a grizzled beard and flashing eyes, Conrad Lynn has used his famous eloquence in many of the notable radical causes of the past forty years. He has defended perhaps a hundred cases charging violent crimes, often with political implications.

Elliot Taikeff had become a lawyer two years before, after getting bored with a lucrative first career in the insurance business. He had grown a Mephistophelean goatee and transformed himself into a natural trial lawyer, with a marvelous style at cross-examination; men with ten times the experience often did not do as well.

By the time Lynn and Taikeff were appointed, it was already the end of the year 1969. We made pretrial motions, with very little success. Our motions for separate trials were denied. We did learn for sure that Wilbert Thomas was a policeman, and we were given the right to inspect the sketch of the hotel. In the district attorney's office, we compared the handwriting on it with that of Thomas's application to join the Black Panthers. They looked the same, so I asked Assistant District Attorney John Fine if Thomas had drawn it. He allowed that he had. Pleased with this corroboration of our entrapment defense, Taikeff, with becoming modesty, said, "In that case, we'll offer to plead guilty to conspiracy to jaywalk." Mr. Fine emitted what in literary parlance used to be referred to as a mirthless laugh.

The most innovative of our motions from a legal point of view, although by no means the most successful, concerned police infiltration, electronic bugging, and official entrapment. We sought to limit the use of infiltration and police tape recordings of the defendants' conversations, arguing that those means of investigation were analytically no different from a search and seizure of the defendants' premises and papers; to infiltrate a political group and write reports about it, or record such reports electronically, was just as effective a damper on political activity as search and seizure. We argued that a warrant signed by a judge ought to be required, as it is for a search. The supporting affidavit said:

> The reasons are several: such intrusion without probable cause invades the privacy of persons who are presumptively, and without probable cause are likely to be innocent of wrongdoing, and in the case of political organizations, it has a chilling effect on political rights; when the intrusion is by police infiltrator, there is the added danger of entrapment

and the manufactured crime, which can often not be adequately assessed after an arrest has been made.

For somewhat similar reasons, we sought to attach a requirement of prior judicial approval (that is to say, a warrant) to the use of decoying, that is, the offer of an opportunity by the police to commit crime, which may spill over onto entrapment.

The defense will show, on information and belief, a case of entrapment. But that, we maintain, is not enough to solve the legal problem of entrapment presented in this and other cases. The defense in such cases frequently turns on delicate matters of persuasion, as to which the parties will differ. Accordingly, before commencing a decoying action such as this, a policeman should be required to show to a neutral authority evidence of the *already existing* propensity of defendants to commit the crime. Such a requirement, it is submitted, would prevent the invasion of the privacy of persons by decoying, and would reduce the likelihood of entrapment.

These were important points, and the need for them will be made clearer in the concluding chapters of this book, but at the trial level they were bound to be denied. There was no authority for them in state law, and in fact the analogous New York precedents were against us, although a few federal court decisions did seem to point our way. The weight of authority simply does not now recognize the parallel, which seemed to us clear, between search and seizure and political infiltration.

It was April of 1970 before the trial was under way. Eight months from arrest to trial—not a great delay for Manhattan—and it might even have been reasonable if the defendants had had the slightest chance of getting a bail set within their means. But everyone charged with a political crime of violence was being subjected to prohibitive bail conditions. The lawyers for the Panther Twenty-one had pursued their attempts to reduce bail to the United States Supreme Court, without success; we decided to concentrate instead on forcing the case to trial. Elliot Taikeff began *habeas corpus* proceedings to release the defendants based on the delay of the trial; as a result, we were promised a trial, and we got one. Ultimately, in fact, the case was to be heard twice, before two different juries, in trials totaling thirteen weeks.

Insofar as the time for such a thing can ever be favorable, the spring and summer of 1970 was an unusually propitious time for the defense of a Black Panther conspiracy case, at least in Manhattan. The trial of the Chicago Seven conspiracy case had been over for only a short time, and a great many people felt as I had that political "conspiracy" trials as a class were suspect. Shortly before that, Fred Hampton had been killed in Chicago under highly suspicious circumstances, which tended to cast general doubt on police testimony in Panther cases. In connection with the cases going forward in New Haven, Yale's President Kingman Brewster had expressed doubt that a black revolutionary could get a fair trial in America. This voice from within the Establishment reinforced an impression I was to get from picking the jury, that the constant criticism, from the left, of the American trial system for its political and racial bias was actually beginning to tell. Jurors, and to some extent judges, were increasingly self-conscious about the problems of racism, especially in places like New York where a jury could be rather freely chosen and the citizens were alive to the problems.

In selecting the jury, each side was allowed any number of challenges for "cause"—that is, for any proven or admitted bias which, according to the ruling of the judge, would make it impossible for the juror to be impartial—and twenty peremptory challenges, for which no reason need be given. With such ideologically committed defendants as ours, the process of agreeing on each peremptory challenge sometimes took a long time.

As in most New York felony trials, the jury in this case was selected by bringing a panel of about one hundred prospective jurors into the courtroom, choosing twelve names at random out of a wooden wheel to fill the jury box, and allowing them to be questioned collectively and individually in the presence of the others, first by the district attorney and then by the defense lawyers.* This process frequently obliges the judge to hear the juror's problem, opinion, or prejudice in a whisper at the bench, with the lawyers huddling around, to avoid prejudicing other prospective panelists.

The jury panels brought into the courtroom did not noticeably discriminate in the proportion of black people; in some panels, the proportion appeared to be greater than it was in the county population as a whole. On the other hand, almost everyone, of whatever race, tended to be from the middle class. Regardless of class, New York citizens were surprisingly conscientious about political problems. Literally dozens of prospective jurors came forward to say that they could not be impartial, nearly as many of them because of bias against the prosecution as because of bias against the Black Panthers. In both trials, the process of selecting the jury was protracted (two weeks) because of the number of jurors who freely admitted their bias. In many cases, no doubt, they were relieved to have avoided sitting in a long trial, but most of them must have been expressing real prejudices for or against the defendants. I found myself conceiving anew a respect for New Yorkers which had been getting lost in the universal complaint about the increasing grubbiness of city life. All of the defense lawyers and the defendants were making summary sociological judgments

---

* On rare occasions, jurors are put into the box and questioned one by one, out of the hearing of other prospective jurors. It is an infinitely fair and slow process.

about the character and prejudice of prospective jurors, based on what we knew about their neighborhoods and backgrounds. I discovered that we were masters of Manhattan demography: we had an enormous fund of lore about the island, and we were able to make the finest distinctions based on address, background, and occupation. And yet all our categories were not fine enough to describe the prospective jurors who came before us. They were sophisticated in ways that none of us could encompass or predict. The most astonishing types of people proved to be unshakably suspicious of the police. As the selection process went forward, I remembered why it was that I was living in New York: I could not conceive of any other people whom I would understand as well or who would understand me as well.

Theoretically, the chief purpose of the questioning of prospective jurors is to determine their bias, but some lawyers have tended over the years to shift the emphasis of the questioning toward educating the jurors about the issues in the case. In recent cases alleging crimes with a political dimension by black men, however, the emphasis by defense attorneys has shifted back to the primordial inquiry into the actual prejudice, racial or political, of the jurors. The best defense attorneys had been doing just that for years, of course, but many of us learned the techniques for the first time from Charles Garry's questions to the jurors in Huey Newton's murder trial. The defense spent hours trying to come up with questions that were revealing without being obvious. Precisely because the defense questions in our case were intended to uncover a subjective pattern of prejudice in the mind of the juror, they could not usually be effective if they were general or subjective ("Do you entertain any prejudice against black people?"). They had to be objective.

Did you move to your present neighborhood from another? What neighborhood and when?

Are there black people living in your neighborhood? In your building?

Do your children play with their children?

Do you have any black friends?

Are they business or social friends?

Do you visit them? Do they visit you?

The answers even to these simple questions could be astonishingly revealing about patterns of bias. The fact that a man lives in a mixed neighborhood but knows no black people would lead us to question him further. Sometimes a juror was so prejudiced that he would respond openly even to a subjective question about his attitudes. One man answered the question "Have you ever had any unfortunate experience with a black person in your neighborhood?" with the words "Not yet."

He was the exception. Most of the jurors, having read in the papers recently about claims of racism and other prejudice in the trial process, were concerned and on the lookout for it. They saw some of it. In choosing the jury for the first trial, the assistant district attorney at one point exercised five peremptory challenges at once, four of them against black people who seemed qualified and had revealed no obvious sympathy for the defense. There was a loud groan from the entire courtroom, including all the prospective jurors, and they began to whisper among themselves. Five more names were chosen by the clerk from his wooden wheel, all but one of white people, as it happened. One of them, who took his seat in the foreman's chair, was a partner in an investment banking firm. The defense looked him over critically. Grey suit tailored in the English manner. Hair parted in the middle. Address on the Upper East Side. Not, one would have said at first glance, a juror that the defense would instantly choose in a case like this. Mr. Fine asked him a routine question: Was there anything about this case that might prevent him from sitting impartially as foreman of the jury? Yes, there was, said the juror, and before Mr. Fine could ask him another question, or the judge warn him not to tell the other jurors his opinions, he rapped out imperiously that he thought there ought to be more black people on the jury and that one of them ought to be the foreman. The judge furiously called him up to the bench out of the hearing of the other jurors, and wanted to know what he meant. The man had been incensed by the exercise of challenges specifically against black people. The judge asked him if he understood that both sides had a right to exercise peremptory challenges for any reason or no reason, but he was unimpressed. He remained biased against the prosecution, he said, and was excused.

The lesson was obvious, and was hammered home by other jurors in less spectacular ways: any suggestion of overt racism in the proceedings was likely to backfire by prejudicing the white jurors.

Some of our questions were intended to smoke out and eliminate the hanging juror, the "law-and-order-at-all-costs" man. My favorite along these lines is the most bald and simple of all.

> Do you think it is possible that a policeman might come before this jury, swear to tell the truth, and then lie?

One woman, who had a relative on the police force, said that she did not think a policeman would lie under oath. The judge then asked her if she understood that a policeman's testimony was not entitled to more weight than that of any other witness; any witness might be lying or telling the truth, and it was for the jury to decide his credibility. She said she understood that. The judge passed her back to me, and I asked her once again:

> Do you think it is possible that a policeman might come before this jury, swear to tell the truth, and then lie?

The answer was still no, and the woman was excused.

The contrary view was perhaps just as common. A black carpenter, when he heard that policemen were going to testify, immediately asked to go up to speak to the judge. He said, out of the hearing of the other jurors, that his brother had once been arrested for disorderly conduct, and at his trial the police had said a lot of things that were not true. He was quite willing to sit on the jury, he said, but if policemen were going to testify, he was very likely not going to be able to believe them. He was excused.

The prosecution had some questions which were intended to detect bias for and against the prosecution. One of them, dubbed the "cop-killer question" by the defense, ostensibly concerned the charge of attempted murder, and the substance of it was:

> There will be evidence here that one or more of these defendants attempted to kill a New York City detective by blowing his head off with a sawed-off shotgun; knowing that, is there anything which would prevent you from sitting impartially in this case?

A more significant inquiry concerned the crime of conspiracy, and went something like this:

> If the judge charges you at the close of all the evidence that if persons intend to commit a crime, agree to commit a crime, and commit some act in pursuance of that crime, they may be found guilty of conspiracy, will you accept that charge?

This question worked quite well for the prosecution. Since the inquiry was being made while the Chicago Seven conspiracy case was still fresh in the public mind, several prospective jurors recklessly said that they did not think that merely planning a crime was itself a crime. All were struck except one, who came on in the first trial after the assistant district attorney had exercised all his peremptory challenges. The man had a beard, wrote for television, and seemed well informed. The defense was gritting its collective teeth hoping that he would not give the prosecution grounds to challenge him for cause, when he brought general gloom to our side by saying that he did not think there ought to be a crime of conspiracy. The judge then got him up to the bench and asked him if he understood that an "overt act" in pursuance of the crime was required to prove a conspiracy, and that mere "intent" was not enough. No, he had not understood that. If he were charged concerning such a crime, could he follow the charge? He thought he could. He was accepted as a juror over the vociferous objections of the district attorney.

We were not permitted to ask the jurors the details of their views about the Black Panthers, because the judges at both trials thought that it might lead to endless wrangling, and because the opinions of some prospective jurors might prejudice the minds of others. But we were able to ask the source of their opinions.

Have you heard of the Black Panther Party? [Yes or No]

Have you seen TV programs in which Black Panthers were mentioned?

Have you read about them? Where—in what newspapers, books, or magazines?

Have you ever read *Soul on Ice?* Have you ever heard of it?

We were able to ask some questions which related directly to prejudice against the Black Panthers in relation to the case on trial.

Are the Black Panthers connected in your mind with violence?

Are the Black Panthers connected in your mind with crime?

Do you think that a member of the Black Panther Party is more likely than another person to commit a crime of violence?

Do you think that if any of the defendants here was a member of the Black Panther Party, that he is more likely because of that fact to be quilty of the crimes charged here?

These questions came near the heart of our inquiry into the bias of the jurors. The judge and the prosecutor repeatedly told the prospective jurors that this was not a "political" but a plain criminal trial. Yet the mention of the Black Panther Party in the first count of the indictment by itself raised a political question in the case, and we were trying by these questions to reduce the prejudicial effect of that allegation. The first question, taken alone, proved almost nothing; anyone from a Weatherman to an FBI agent might make a connection between the Black Panthers and violence. The answers to the first two questions taken together, however, were sometimes significant. While we could not directly inquire into the prospective juror's views about when he thought violence might be justified, or even into his views about the Black Panther Party, if a juror answered that he saw a connection between the Panthers and violence, but no necessary connection between the Panthers and crime, we knew at least that he recognized the difference and could apply it to the Black Panther Party. Virtually every prospective juror realized that an affirmative answer to the fourth question constituted a bias, and no one would deliberately answer it yes unless he really wanted to be excused from the jury. But the third question brought a yes from many jurors who then answered no to the last question, after they saw where it was leading. Some, under further questioning, admitted they were biased; others steadfastly maintained that they were impartial and could decide this case on its merits.

After much inquiry, the defense lawyers concluded that we should not automatically challenge peremptorily any juror who answered yes to the third question. Other factors might weigh in the balance for a Manhattan juror, and chief among them was the police. We found that attitudes toward the Black Panthers were less important than attitudes toward the *relation* between the Black Panthers and the police. That was an equation in which political attitudes might cancel out. Several people expressed this by coming up to the bench, out of the hearing of the other prospective jurors, and telling the judge that they did not agree with the aims of the Black Panthers but thought there was a police vendetta against them.

The defense tried to reveal these attitudes about police-Panther relations through questions about the defense of entrapment.

> If the judge charges you at the close of all the evidence that it is a defense to a charge of crime if a defendant has been entrapped by a police agent into committing a crime when he would not otherwise have committed it, will you be able to accept such a charge from the judge?
>
> Do you think a policeman would be more likely to entrap a Black Panther than another person?

Some prospective jurors answered the last question affirmatively, even after they had revealed some bias against Black Panthers. It was the "plague-on-both-your-houses" or "New York liberal" syndrome, and in each case we had to go back and evaluate the juror on his background before making a decision to accept or reject him. Surprisingly, not every juror who answered yes to this question was struck by the prosecution, apparently because Mr. Fine thought there was little merit to the entrapment defense in our case.

The jury finally chosen to sit in the second trial, in August 1970, was an extraordinary assemblage. Seven members were black, the prosecution having wisely abandoned its earlier policy of challenging black people. As to the character and views of the black members of the jury, I, at least, had less knowledge than I ought to have had, going into the trial. They professed for the most part to have no opinions about the Black Panthers or the police, and most questions about racism were meaningless in relation to them. I found that racism in my own case took the form that my social antennae, by which I made guesses about the unspoken views of white New Yorkers, were largely ineffective concerning black New Yorkers. Apart from their opinions, and they professed almost none, it was difficult for me to guess their views. The defendants' and Conrad Lynn's signals, however, were strong where mine were weak; Conrad guessed that these were fair-minded black people. In any case, this was, he said, the first time in his long career that he had had a majority of blacks on a jury. Three of them were women, and five were civil servants. Of those one, a sanitation man, was a juror in a million. He had left the Sanitation Department to become a New York policeman, and had voluntarily resigned after one year. This fact was in itself extraordinary. In New York, it is still tricky for a black man to become a policeman at all, and for him to have resigned after so short a time must, we thought, indicate some disaffection with police work, even though the juror protested that it was irregular hours and family problems which caused him to quit.

One of the white jurors was nearly as much out of the ordinary at the other extreme. An airline pilot originally from Birmingham, Alabama, he had attended segregated secondary schools and seemed to have no patience with the Black Panther Party. Yet he said that he thought prosecutors tended to bring conspiracy charges when they had no real case and that the police would be more likely to entrap a Black Panther than another person. After hours of inquiry, all sides concluded that he was simply an original and that his oddly assorted views encompassed the fact that he could be impartial. Two others were young Wall Street bankers who expressed distrust of the police in relation to Black Panthers. A fourth was a self-educated workingman, toward whom all defense attorneys felt a favorable bias. The forelady was a most pleasant writer of children's stories who had no pronounced opinions. Her presence made up a jury with four women—three of them black— and five whites. All in all, the defense was satisfied with the jury and the jury-selection process; these people were in every way better qualified to hear a case than the cynical three judges who had tried the first, "little" Cain case two years before.

8

THE TRIAL:

PIG ON HORSEBACK

The case was tried twice. The first trial ended in May 1970, when the jury was unable to agree on a verdict, but that trial did at least result in the dismissal by the judge of some counts of the indictment on technical grounds.* At the beginning of the second trial, in August 1970, the defense was faced with a much simplified array of charges. All the defendants were charged with conspiracy to rob the New Dunston Hotel, on Harlem's West 131st Street. Each of them was charged also with possession of the weapons supposedly intended for use in the robbery: a sawed-off shotgun, a rifle, a knife, and a canister of red-pepper spray. Alfred Cain alone was charged with the attempted murder of a detective by pointing the sawed-off shotgun at him, as well as with the "lesser-included offenses"—the constituent charges of assault and reckless endangerment which were

---

* The charge that the defendants had conspired to commit murder by saying that they would "shoot to kill" anyone who interfered with the robbery (Count II) the judge found to be an indistinguishable part of the conspiracy to commit robbery. The charge of attempted robbery (Count VII) was dismissed because, as a matter of law, the defendants had not come close enough to their alleged goal for their acts to rise to the level of an attempt. Finally, the charges of attempted murder and assault on the detective were dismissed as against De Leon and West, because the prosecution claimed that Cain had pointed the shotgun, and there was no evidence even from the prosecution witnesses that the others had acted with him.

included under attempted murder. At the second trial, the defense had a great deal of knowledge about the evidence available to the prosecution because the witnesses and their testimony covered much the same ground.

In New York State, as in most other jurisdictions, the crime of conspiracy has three elements: an intention to commit a crime (in this case a robbery), an agreement by two or more people to commit a crime, and an "overt act," some concrete act done in pursuance of the agreement. Under these rules, it was not enough for the prosecution to show that the defendants discussed robberies generally, or even possible specific robberies; the state had to prove that they made a hard and fast agreement to commit a specific robbery.

The proof of the charge of conspiracy to rob the hotel took up the largest part of the trial, and depended almost entirely on the testimony of Wilbert Thomas. He claimed that the conspiracy had incubated for a period of about two weeks, from the end of July until the middle of August 1969, when the defendants had finally been arrested. He said that Ricardo De Leon had spoken to him alone about a robbery in Harlem on two occasions, August 4 and 8. The "Big Day" in the case, however, was August 14, when Cain, De Leon, and Thomas had allegedly polished their plan while sitting in a small park near Cain's house. On the fifteenth, the weapons were supposed to have been shown off in an apartment on Montgomery Street where Thomas McCreary lived with another member of the party, Deborah Green. The "conspiracy" was technically complete when those weapons were displayed, and probably even earlier, although the defendants were not arrested until the following day when they were leaving the West Side Highway in the car driven by Wilbert Thomas.

The weapons charges appeared deceptively simple and minor compared with the conspiracy charge, but they were in fact complex, and the charge of possessing a loaded sawed-off shotgun, at least, was very serious. It is not illegal to possess a rifle or a knife unless there is proof that it is to be used unlawfully; possession of a sawed-off shotgun, on the other hand, is a crime in itself, without any proof of unlawful intent. Conviction can result in a prison term as long as seven years, while the maximum penalty for a conspiracy to commit robbery is four years.

Attempted murder was the simplest charge of all, and the most serious. It was claimed that Alfred Cain had pointed the sawed-off shotgun at Detective Alfred Halikias from the window of the green Dodge Dart as it slowed to a stop, and had meant to kill him. Cain was prevented, it was said, only by quick police work.

The defendants denied most of the claims of the prosecution. They admitted that there had been a rifle on the floor of the Dodge, although they did not think it remarkable. They said that the sawed-off shotgun had been hidden in a bag, also on the floor, and that they saw it for the first time after the arrest. Alfred Cain, of course, denied that he had pointed the shotgun at anyone. The implication was that the gun was planted and the attempted-murder charge was a fabrication. The defendants admitted that there had been discussions about robberies with Wilbert Thomas, but they said that no specific plan had been formed, and what elements of planning there were had been promoted by Thomas. These claims presented to the jury a complex and risky defense; we were claiming on the one hand that there was no finished "conspiracy" in the sense of a specific plan, and on the other hand, that the inchoate elements of the plan were the result of entrapment by Thomas. The jury would have to decide how much of Thomas's story was true, whether his actions constituted provocation to commit the crimes charged, and whether or not the defendants knowingly possessed the sawed-off shotgun.

The testimony in the second trial began on a hot August morning before the Honorable James J. Leff, a quiet, stocky man with a healthy skepticism about lawyers, witnesses, and public officials. Seated at the bench in the large paneled courtroom with a heroic painting of Municipal Virtue in flowing robes behind him, the defendants and their lawyers arrayed in front of him at a table on his right hand, with an armed court officer seated behind each defendant, the assistant district attorney in front of him on his left hand, and the twelve sworn jurors in the box to his far left, he began quietly to take notes of the witnesses' testimony for his later charge to the jury.

As the case was presented to the jury, the complex evidence on the conspiracy charge was saved for the end. The prosecutor took up first the arrest on August 16, and the charges against Cain of attempted murder and its lesser-included crimes.

ATTEMPTED MURDER

Detectives of the Safe, Loft, and Truck Squad were assembled at their office on the morning of August 16, 1969, under their commanding officer, Captain Thomas Kissane, and went to the Bureau of Special Services, the political police, for briefing. They were told to make an arrest of the occupants of the green Dodge Dart driven by Wilbert Thomas; they heard that Thomas was an undercover agent and that the other occupants were Black Panthers who had planned a robbery. According to Captain Kissane, the detectives had information that the occupants were ready to engage in a fire fight or, as he put it, "to go for broke."

The detectives then went to the exit ramp from the West Side Highway at 125th Street, which is depicted in the frontispiece. One detective was assigned to each of the three men. All the men except the commander, Captain Kissane, were wearing bulletproof vests. Kissane was concealed behind a retaining wall on the west or driver's side of the exit ramp. Two other detectives were hidden in a panel truck driven by a BOSS officer, which pulled across the road so as to block the exit as the Dodge came to a stop.

The arrests of De Leon and West were uneventful. Kissane ran up to West with his revolver drawn, simply said, "Freeze," and arrested him. He testified that West was wearing surgical gloves and had a loaded M-1 carbine standing between his knees, apparently visible from the road. Another detective, also armed with a revolver, jumped out of the panel truck, followed closely by his partner, ran around the side of the truck, and jerked open the right front door of the Dodge, saying to De Leon, "Don't move." He testified that he pulled De Leon out of the car, searched him, and found in his pockets a hunting knife and a small canister of red-pepper spray such as is sold commercially to ward off an assailant. De Leon had no gun and no gloves.

The testimony of Detective Halikias, who was assigned to the right rear seat of the car, where Alfred Cain was seated, was the heart of the attempted-murder case. Halikias had been concealed behind an iron fence at the foot of a stairway on the east side of the exit ramp, opposite Captain Kissane (see frontispiece).

> After I left my concealed position, I was running towards the car. It was the first time I saw the defendant seated in that right rear position raise what I recognized as a sawed-off shotgun. And as I was running towards the car, the defendant—in which case it was the defendant Cain—had the shotgun in his hand and he brought it up and he was bringing it about in an arc to point in my direction. . . .

> (*Witness identifies Alfred Cain, Jr.*)

> The first time I saw the gun, it was in a raised position, and as I was running towards the car the gun was continuing in an arc to come around to point in my direction. When I arrived at the car, and when all motion was ceased, I had

my shotgun placed up against the defendant Cain's neck and his shotgun was pointed directly at me.

Halikias testified that he then took the sawed-off shotgun from Cain (also wearing gloves), removed him from the car, walked him over to a wall, and searched him. He said he found shotgun shells and the sketch of the hotel in his pockets. That was the prosecution's case for attempted murder, as it was presented to the jury.* If every word of this story were accepted, it is doubtful that the facts would constitute attempted murder, but in any case, cross-examination cast enormous doubt over the whole matter.

The detective's description of the exit ramp created one of the rare situations when it became possible to show, by examination of the layout of the terrain and physical obstructions alone, that the story did not make sense. As the detective described the exit ramp, there were sawhorse barriers running up the dividing line in the middle of the road, which closed off the lane directly in front of him (the east lane) to traffic. The Dodge had to pull into the lane farthest away from him (the west lane). The police had moved one of the barriers out of line, making an opening for the detective to run through, exactly where the Dodge was expected to stop. As the detective testified, however, the car rolled somewhat past that point.

> The vehicle did not stop, as I had thought it would have stopped, but continued on another six or eight feet or thereabouts. Then, in effect, I had to run after the car. . . .

As the cross-examination showed, the timing of the detective's run across the dirt, across the east lane of the road, through the break, and up from behind the car window

---

* Halikias had testified at a pretrial hearing that after the arrest and after warnings of his right to remain silent, Cain had said, "If I had half a chance, I would have blown your head off." This statement, which Cain denies, was excluded on the grounds that, at a joint trial, it would be excessively prejudicial to the codefendants.

simply could not be made to jibe with Cain's supposed swinging of the shotgun. Moreover, as the detective described the scene, he would have had to cross Cain's line of fire.

[PAUL CHEVIGNY]. There came a time, did there not, when you put the end of your shotgun in the window, in the back rear, in the rear right window of the car; is that right?

A. Yes, sir. . . .

Q. And you placed it against the neck of the defendant Cain, did you?

A. It eventually came to rest on the defendant Cain's neck, yes, sir.

Q. Was that while you were coming from behind the car toward the rear window? Is it as you approached the rear that you put it against his neck?

A. No, sir.

Q. When did you put it against his neck?

A. I think after I had passed the window and I was now facing toward the rear of the car, the muzzle of my shotgun came to rest on the defendant Cain's neck.

Q. There came a time when you ran past the window; is that right?

A. Yes, sir.

Q. And you then placed the muzzle of your shotgun against Cain's neck; is that right?

A. Yes, sir.

Q. There came a time when you said "Freeze"?

A. Yes, sir. . . .

Q. You didn't say "Freeze" until after you had passed the window and you were facing backwards toward the rear of the car at an angle; is that right?

A. I believe that's correct.

If Cain had had a shotgun pointed "directly" at him, the detective would, of course, have had to run across Cain's line of fire in order to stand where he did, at an angle facing toward the back of the car.

Testimony and records from other policemen did not

strengthen the detective's story. One of the detectives who had jumped out of the panel truck had run around to cover Halikias from behind with his revolver. He testified that he had seen something that looked like a gun move in the window in front of Halikias, but he made it clear that by the time he had jumped out of the truck, run around its front, turned, and faced the side of the car, Halikias was standing still. Halikias had already reached the car, and the sequence of events he described had to be over by the time the other detective saw him. That officer's testimony did not inspire confidence in the story of attempted murder. It was still further damaged by the fact, established in cross-examination, that at the time Halikias submitted his arrest report, he had made no complaint about attempted murder.

Another witness was Ron Hollander, a reporter for the *New York Post,* who had written a major story in the December 26, 1969, issue of his paper rounding up all the pending cases in New York involving Black Panthers, including our case. Hollander testified under subpoena that Detective Halikias had told him that the sawed-off shotgun was pointed in such a way that a shot "would have missed him, going over his right shoulder," and if the defendant had moved the gun any more, the detective "would have had to let one go." This story, of course, flatly contradicted Halikias's account at the trial that the gun was pointed "directly at him." Both versions are quite vivid, and do not differ in the sort of detail about which one commonly varies in telling a story. The contradiction suggested, as the defendants had claimed all along, that neither version was true.

The problem for the defense was to explain, to our own satisfaction and the jury's, what the police motive might be to fabricate such a story.

As the cross-examination went on, the attitudes of the police toward defendants such as these became clearer.

Black Panthers were said by the police to be "cop killers"; Huey Newton had been convicted of manslaughter of a policeman in Oakland, and several Panthers in New York had been accused of shooting at policemen. At the time of the arrest, some of the officers were keyed up to anticipate violence. If they did not find it, they did find, at least to their own satisfaction, that it had been planned.

Elliot Taikeff succeeded in bringing part of the motives behind the attempted-murder charge to light by an ingenious cross-examination about the discarded charge contained in the handwritten addition to the short affidavit filed in criminal court by Detective Halikias on the day of the arrest, alleging that the defendants had conspired "to kill a police officer if necessary as a *diversionary measure* to commit said A & R [assault and robbery]." Halikias described the origin of this accusation.

> I received it from two different sources. One was from prior to the arrest—I was told by Captain Kissane that these defendants intended to shoot the armed guards up at the hotel. Then, after the arrest and still in the 22nd Precinct, . . . I had a conversation with Patrolman [Wilbert] Thomas, when he described the situation where these defendants were going to go to Brooklyn and rob a bank. One of them would get on a roof top at a location, shoot a cop, and then go to Location No. B and rob a bank when all available police force was at Point A.

Both of these explanations proved to be very unwisely chosen. The story about the "Brooklyn bank" was simply a different matter altogether; in fact, it was hard to see how a "Brooklyn bank" could have had any connection with our Manhattan case at all.

[ELLIOT TAIKEFF]. Now, did this alleged conduct with respect to the bank in Brooklyn have any connection whatsoever with the premises 142 West 131st Street in Manhattan, other than the claim that it involved the same defendants?

A. The only other connection that I thought then and still do think now is that the defendants in this case would have and they did discuss taking the life of a police officer or some other private detective to accomplish their plot, yes, sir. . . .

Q. But other than the fact that it may have involved the same defendants, there is no connection as far as you can tell between this alleged conspiracy to kill and rob in the vicinity of a bank in Brooklyn and the conspiracy to rob the hotel in Manhattan, is there? . . .

A. My answer would have to be the same. The only connection that I can associate with this is that they did intend to kill someone to accomplish their deeds.

Q. But that's not my question, sir . . . I'm asking you whether there is any direct connection between the so-called plot involving the Brooklyn bank and the so-called plot to rob the hotel in Manhattan, except for the claim that it involves the same defendants? That's all I'm asking. . . .

A. Then I would have to answer no to that.

Q. No connection whatsoever?

A. I would have to answer no.

As for the supposed shooting of armed guards, the "diversionary" element was lacking.

Q. You are saying that as far as your understanding of this case is concerned, that on August 16, 1969, the owner of the hotel —whoever it was who was supposed to be held up—was accompanied by armed guards; is that correct?

A. Yes, sir, this is my understanding.

Q. And that these armed guards were policemen?

A. This is also my understanding, yes, sir. . . .

Q. So I gather that it's your testimony that Wilbert Thomas told you that as a diversionary tactic in the commission of an armed robbery at 142 West 131st Street, the defendants in this case were going to shoot the armed guards at 142 West 131st Street?

A. I can only best respond to that, sir, by saying that this was my reasonable cause and belief at the time I prepared this affidavit. . . .

Q. Could you tell us how it came that you used the expression diversionary measure when you said in your affidavit that the defendants intended to kill a police officer as a diversionary measure?

A. I can only honestly say at this time, hearing my instructions from Captain Kissane that they intended to kill the armed protectors of this money. Then subsequent to the arrest, speaking with Patrolman Thomas regarding the shooting of a police officer as a diversionary measure, I may have joined the two thoughts together. At that time it was my honest belief that this was what they intended to do.

In short, all the stories the police had heard about the defendants, from Wilbert Thomas and others, were lumped into one vague and insupportable charge, because they combined in the minds of the police to prove that the defendants presented a threat to them. The police felt they were justified in placing the heaviest possible charges against the defendants because they were getting rid of men who were potentially dangerous. The testimony calls to mind the words of Fat Man, who said that at the time of his arrest, one officer asked another what was to be done about the "assault charge" when no assault had been committed, and the second said to forget it. In other words, an assault charge (attempted murder is the extreme form of assault) was available if the police considered the defendant enough of a "bad guy" to warrant it. Luckily for him, Fat Man was not considered enough of a bad guy, but the other defendants were. From Wilbert Thomas's stories the officers thought that the arresting detectives had risked death that morning, just as they had feared they might, and that if the defendants were not jailed, other policemen might have to risk their lives with these defendants again.

Whatever individual detectives or patrolmen may have thought, some of the circumstances of the arrest suggested that persons at a higher level did not seriously expect violence. Only four men directly surrounded the car, and of them only one (Halikias) had a shotgun. The commander was not even wearing a bulletproof vest. If the defendants had been ready to do serious violence, this would have been an enormously risky way to arrest them; a detective really might have been killed. Under the law of conspiracy, if all the allegations of the prosecution had been true, the three could have been arrested and charged with conspiracy with much less risk at an earlier point—the night before, say, after the weapons had been displayed, and while they were asleep. It was the over-all improbability that the defendants would be arrested under conditions so dangerous to everyone which ultimately suggested to me that they had not been heavily armed, and that someone among the police knew it.

The most dismaying thing about the attempted-murder charge was not the flimsiness of the evidence against Alfred Cain so much as the fact that the charge had originally been made against *all three* defendants. Taking the police testimony at its face value, and without any cross-examination, if you assumed Alfred Cain had pointed a gun at a detective (and didn't get killed doing it), there was no reason to charge Ricardo De Leon and Jerome West with "acting in concert" to commit the crime. Attempted murder requires an intent to kill, and those two could not possibly have intended to shoot a detective, because they never expected to see a detective. For the district attorney to have charged attempted murder against West and De Leon seemed to me inexcusable. At the close of all the evidence in the first trial, the judge had dismissed the charge against them, but left it standing for Alfred Cain, Jr.* At the close

---

* In that trial, the jury failed to announce a verdict as to any charge, including those of attempted murder and assault. Two jurors later stunned the defense attorneys by telling us that the jury had actually agreed to acquit Cain on those charges, but had wrangled so much over the others that they deadlocked. At the second trial, I made a motion to dismiss on grounds of double jeopardy, which was denied because the jury had not announced the verdict.

of all the evidence in the second trial, Judge Leff threw out every count against Cain relating to assault and attempted murder except the last, reckless endangerment (Count VI), a general charge requiring no specific intent to kill or injure, but instead only a vague "reckless disregard for human life." The second jury acquitted Cain even of that charge. I could not help wondering how the three judges who sat in the Cain brothers' misdemeanor trial in 1968 would have decided that count and its lesser-included offenses; if we had been in their hands, our persuasive defense might have meant nothing.

In the perspective of police work, we were still back in the world of the Cain brothers' misdemeanor case in Chapter 2, a world in which the police make use of false charges and arrests to eliminate those who constitute a threat to them. The attempted murder never happened, but the charge at least existed in a universe of police charges with relatively simple motives. In Wilbert Thomas's stories about them, these Panthers had suggested killing a policeman, and that justified the most serious charges against them. But the testimony about the conspiracy and weapons counts took place in a world of police work with deeper motives, harder to calculate. We were not yet quite ready to understand those motives.

CONSPIRACY AND WEAPONS

A preliminary witness for the conspiracy charge was a fat man with a pronounced Middle European accent, the landlord of the New Dunston Hotel at 142 West 131st Street in Harlem, the supposed target of the conspiracy. The landlord was there for the simple purpose of establishing that there was something to rob: that he had brought some sixteen hundred dollars in cash to the building on August 16, 1969. But his testimony became an unintentional sketch

of the ills of ghetto housing. The "hotel" was in fact a rooming house, largely occupied by welfare recipients. The
landlord was accustomed to bring a large sum of cash on the
first and sixteenth of the month, to be able to perform the
service of cashing the welfare checks, and to take out his
rent. At the first trial, we knew almost nothing about the
character of the "hotel," but shortly before the second
trial, it became by coincidence the object of a public protest in Harlem. People in surrounding houses and parish-
ioners of the church next door demanded that the building
be closed because it was a center for drug addiction and
crime. They picketed, and held a rally at which local
politicians pledged to shut the place down. The City
Buildings Department did find plenty of reasons to clear
the house; it had once been an apartment house that had
simply been broken up into single rooms, and the ventila-
tion and toilet facilities were inadequate to handle all the
roomers. In an unusual procedure, the Buildings Department issued an order to vacate the house, and by the time
the landlord came to testify at the second trial, it was empty.

The details of the controversy in Harlem over the building could not have been known to the defendants at the
time of their arrest, and were not admissible at the trial.
The jury and everyone else, however, heard from the landlord that the New Dunston Hotel was a welfare rooming
house which had been closed by the city; the implication
that he was a "slumlord" was strong. This suggested a possible political motive for the defendants to have robbed
the place, although the defense was able to show that the
landlord had not been in the building during most of the
day on August 16, so that any violence would have had to
be directed against the superintendent and other black
people present in the landlord's office during the day.

Patrolman Wilbert Thomas's testimony consumed some
six days of trial time, much of it in cross-examination.
Dapper and unsmiling, he gave his testimony without notes,

but in words which were nearly unvarying for the many occasions he was called upon to repeat his story. His direct testimony related statements and actions of members of the Brooklyn Black Panthers on some nine occasions between July 31 and August 16, 1969. Although the pattern underlying Thomas's words was not to emerge until the cross-examination, there were some hints of provocation in the direct testimony, as well as phrases repeated until their recurrence stretched the limits of credulity.

The testimony about the first days, July 31 and August 1, painted a world filled with the desire for the ownership of guns and for crime.

July 31, 1969

At . . . Black Panther Party headquarters, the defendant Cain stated that if the word comes down from Brenda Hyson or the Black Panther Central Committee giving them the authority to pull robberies, then it would be a pleasure.

The defendant Cain stated that he was looking for a .45 or something of that calibre firearm, and that if he got this gun the only words he would know is "stick them up," and all of these trust companies and armored cars had better watch out. . . . The defendant Cain asked me did I have a gun. I said yes. The defendant stated if you don't have one, you better get one, otherwise you'll miss out on all of the excitement.

Mr. De Leon stated he was looking for a gun and that if he got a gun he would pull quite a few robberies and kill a couple of pigs while he's at it.

August 1, 1969

. . . [A]t . . . Black Panther Party headquarters . . . [d]efendant Cain asked me could I get guns for members of the Black Panther Party organization. I said maybe I could get guns, but not money. The defendant Cain said that if I could get guns for the Black Panther Party organization, that the Black Panther Party would have the money ready for the guns.

The narrative skipped the next two days to a Black Panther Party meeting at Deborah Green's apartment which "involved getting guns for members of the . . . organization." According to Thomas, Brenda Hyson from the West Coast, who chaired the meeting, was opposed to the members "being able to carry guns," but the members "argued strongly" in favor of it and Brenda Hyson was overruled. After the meeting, Ricardo De Leon invited Thomas to the roof of Deborah Green's house, and Thomas recounted the conversation.

> The defendant De Leon stated that he [and] Al Cain, went on plans to pull a robbery, sixteenth of August, 1969, to liberate three thousand dollars or more. The defendant De Leon stated that he could get a shotgun but he would have to have the barrel of the gun sawed off.
>
> I told the defendant that I had a piece, also. The defendant De Leon leaned over the edge of the roof, said, "Wow, this would be a nice place to shoot a pig." The defendant Ricardo De Leon stated we would talk about this more when we got the technical equipment that we needed.

The major part of Thomas's narrative picked up again on August 8, when he was again at Deborah Green's apartment. De Leon was in the kitchen cooking the People's Dinner (the communal party meal). He asked to borrow Thomas's gun, Thomas said he did not have it with him, and De Leon went on to tell him again about the plan "to liberate three thousand dollars or more" on August 16, 1969, supposedly using exactly the same phrase to describe the plan that Thomas had attributed to De Leon on August 4. De Leon said that the robbery was to be "on the lower side of Harlem" and informed Thomas "that Alfred Cain had purchased a sawed-off shotgun."

At this point, Thomas recounted the first of several visits to a man who was supposed to be an illegal gun seller, Hensley Johnson, who lived at 90 Legion Street, within a

few blocks of the Black Panther office. Thomas said he
went there with De Leon and Leroy Floudd, another member of the Party. De Leon rejected Johnson's offer to sell
.22s because they were "too small a caliber firearm," and
Johnson said that "he would have some guns coming in
later that evening, and that we could come back and check
around."

On August 11, Thomas said, there was a Black Panther
meeting at which one Al Carrol, from the national office
in California, said that members of the party were "going
out secretly" in "groups of threes."

> Mr. Carrol said that if a member of the Black Panther Party
> organization was caught liberating something then the Black
> Panther Party would disown him. But if the member liberated
> something and got away then the Black Panther Party or-
> ganization would reap in the profits.

On August 13, Thomas said he paid a second visit to
Johnson. He claimed that Johnson admitted having sold a
shotgun to one of Thomas's "friends," and described the
friend "with bushy hair, 'the bumpy-faced guy.'" Thomas
recognized this as Alfred Cain (even though, according to
his own account, Johnson could never have seen him with
Cain) and then walked around to Cain's house at 1833 Park
Place. Alfred Cain denied having a shotgun and stated
that he had a derringer. The supposed plot for August 16
was not mentioned; instead, they had a more general discussion.

> The defendant Cain and I discussed various robberies and
> . . . defendant Cain said he would like to pull large robberies
> instead of small robberies where we would pull maybe six a
> week. The defendant said he would like to pull one large
> robbery a month or one robbery every six months. The de-
> fendant said we could pull robberies, reap the profits and
> serve the party.

The defendant stated—Cain stated that we needed some

brothers that we could trust, someone that wouldn't cop out
when the going got tough.

I asked the defendant Cain could he get in touch with the
defendant De Leon. He said sure. He would call me later that
afternoon and let me know.

According to Thomas, August 14, 1969, was the "Big
Day" when the three men, Cain, De Leon, and Thomas,
were finally to meet and confer. It opened auspiciously

[a]t Hopkinson Avenue, Good Shepherd Center, at the breakfast program. . . . The defendant De Leon asked why was I
looking for him. . . . I asked the defendant was the plan still
on. He said right on.

But first, De Leon said, "he had to take care of some
business." He and Thomas walked around to a local welfare center and applied for emergency relief on the ground
that they had just been released from jail. They both received checks for twelve dollars, De Leon cashed his, and
they went on to Alfred Cain's house. All three sat in a little
park near Cain's house.

The defendant Cain asked me what did I have in mind to
liberate. I said I wanted to relate to them; that I would, you
know, listen to them. . . . The defendant Cain said that the
bank on Pitkin and Saratoga Avenue had quite a number of
businessmen making night deposits between five-fifteen and
five-thirty on Friday afternoons. . . . The defendant Cain
stated that some of the businessmen had pig cops with them,
so they must have quite a bit of money. The defendant Cain
stated that there are all kinds of pigs all over the area out
there.

The defendant De Leon stated the remedy to get the pigs
away from the area is to get up on the rooftop away from the
bank and shoot a pig. This way all the pigs would go to one
area and the other brothers, the defendant Cain and myself
could do the actual taking and getting away.

The defendant Cain asked me did I know anyone that
worked in big department stores so that we could get some

inside information and pull a good job. The defendant Cain
stated that he wanted to get ten or twenty thousand dollars
when we pulled the job. I said yes, maybe I did know some
people that worked in big department stores like Mays.

The defendant Cain talked about the robbery that had
taken place at Abraham & Straus and the men got away with
$300,000 or more. The defendant Cain talked about three
young brothers that robbed a bank and got away with $58,000,
and no one ever knew or heard of them since. . . .

. . . Ricardo De Leon said that he knew of a place where
we could get ten or eleven thousand dollars. The defendant
De Leon said it would be easy, because the guy, the landlord
only had two bodyguards with him. . . .

[DISTRICT ATTORNEY]. Now, you prior testified once De Leon
    mentioned something about $3,000; now ten or eleven thou-
    sand dollars. Were those De Leon's own words?
MR. CHEVIGNY. I object.
A. Yes.
Q. At this time he inflated the figure to ten or eleven thousand?
A. Yes.
MR. CHEVIGNY. I object, your Honor, to whether he inflated a
    figure.
THE COURT. Ask the witness a question without leading him.
Q. Go ahead. What happened, officer?
A. The defendant Ricardo De Leon said that we would get
    some handcuffs to detain the men when we did the actual
    robbing. The defendant then said, "No, we can't get any
    handcuffs at this late date." I suggested tying the victims
    with rawhide. The defendant De Leon said, "No, that takes
    too long. We might as well go ahead and kill them." I said,
    "Wow, that's rather drastic, isn't it?" The defendant Cain
    said, "We could get some ether and spray it in their faces
    and put them out." . . . The defendant Cain, the defendant
    De Leon, and myself talked about getting a car to pull this
    robbery. The defendant De Leon couldn't drive a car. The
    defendant Cain stated that he didn't have a driver's license.
    They wanted to steal a car the night before the robbery, the
    night of the 15th of August, 1969. . . . It was agreed upon

that I was to get the car. So I agreed; I said, "Yes, I'll get the car." The defendant De Leon said, "Well, we will go to the place and look the area over. We will get a general idea of what we are in for." The defendant Cain stated that he had business to take care of at this time.

Q. Did he tell you what was the business?

A. No, he didn't. . . . He was pretty shaky at the time.

Q. What do you mean by that?

A. Well, Cain is a very sneaky person, individual; no one really knew what was on his mind. . . . The defendant Cain knew that I had taken drafting and he said, "You taken drafting." And I said, "Right on." The defendant De Leon said we would go up to the area and I would draw a map, a diagram, of the layout and show it to the defendant Cain the next day or later that night. I agreed to draw the diagram. I said, "Sure, I will draw a diagram." Then I suggested to him, to the defendant De Leon, I said, "Why don't we go up and look the area over?"

The defendant De Leon and I took the subway up to Harlem. [When] it had gotten a little dark, the defendant and I walked to the Dunston Hotel, 142 West 131st Street. . . . The defendant pointed out the office. It was the door on the right-hand side as you walked into the building. The defendant and I walked up to the third floor and looked the joint over. De Leon pointed to a fire-escape in the back, a possible escape route in case we were apprehended, in case we were hemmed up in the building. . . . We started walking out of the building.

De Leon said that on August 16th, 1969, when the robbery was to take place, we would have one man in the car behind the wheel. We would have one man outside as a lookout. We would have two men in the building, one to the left, one to the right, to do the actual taking. De Leon said if there was any resistance or if there were any funny moves by the super and his armed guards, we would shoot to kill. . . .

I had asked the defendant De Leon would Leroy Floudd be the fourth man. . . . Mr. De Leon said Leroy Floudd is too shaky; Jerome West would be the fourth man. . . . De

Leon said that the defendant Cain, myself, De Leon and West would stay overnight at Deborah Green's apartment. The defendant De Leon said the defendant Jerome West purchased a sawed-off shotgun. The defendant De Leon said he would get a gun from Al Cain. The defendant De Leon and I walked back across the street, towards the Dunston Hotel. There we talked with a female named Vickie, that stated she lived in the Dunston Hotel, Apartment 2-A-1.

De Leon and Vickie and some other unknown male Negro drank wine at this time. De Leon and I then departed and went to the State office building at 125th Street and Seventh Avenue. There was some type of debating between Black Panther Party members and various people from the community, different organizations. At this time I left the defendant De Leon in Harlem.

The following day, August 15, the machinery of BOSS was in full gear. Wilbert Thomas had been given a tape recorder to attach to his telephone, and that morning he recorded a telephone conversation from De Leon, of which the transcript used at the trial appears in Appendix A (pages 309–12). The tape of the call was identified by Joeharry Williams, a detective with the Special Services Division, who reassuringly told us, among other things, that at the time of the trial (September 1970) he was spending ninety percent of his time on electronic police work, but in August of 1969 he had only been spending about fifty percent of his time that way. BOSS also supplied the car which Thomas had agreed to get, a green Dodge Dart.

Thomas went around to Deborah Green's apartment early in the evening and found De Leon cooking again. Thomas McCreary and Miss Green were looking at her .22 rifle, for which she had recently acquired a permit. Thomas claimed that De Leon pointed it out the window and used exactly the same words he had used when he had looked over the edge of the roof on August 4: "Wow, this would be a nice place to shoot a pig."

They took the People's Dinner around to the Black Panther office, where Patrolman Thomas ran into Fat Man and told him that "Ricardo De Leon, Alfred Cain, myself, and one other brother would be in on a plan to steal ten or twenty thousand dollars" (although, even in Thomas's account, De Leon had never mentioned such a large figure). After Fat Man left, Thomas said that De Leon tried to get him to join in the holdup of a store on the corner, right then and there, but he refused. Thomas mentioned that they walked around by Hensley Johnson's place again "to see if [they] could buy guns," but he failed to mention the result of the visit.

The two of them went looking for Alfred Cain. They did not find him at home, but Thomas left his .38 pistol with Alfred's sister Jessica so that he would not have to carry it around in public. When they finally returned, to find Alfred at home, De Leon took the pistol from Jessica and withheld it from Thomas, who claimed that he had to scuffle with De Leon to get it back. De Leon hit him in the mouth, he said, and Thomas "wrestled him to the floor" (something no one else has apparently ever been able to do to De Leon).

Alfred Cain, Ricardo De Leon, and Wilbert Thomas picked up Jerome West, at Cain's insistence, and went back to Deborah Green's apartment. She and Thomas McCreary were at home and, according to Thomas, looked on while the conspiracy came to a head. De Leon gave surgical gloves to West, Cain, and Thomas; he gave a knife to Cain and kept one for himself. West pulled a sawed-off shotgun out of a folding couch, loaded it, showed it around, and put it away. Cain asked Thomas to draw a diagram of the layout of the New Dunston Hotel, explaining the placement of corridors and exits.

Outside the apartment, in the Dodge, Thomas said they went over the plans. "The defendant Cain said that if anybody made any funny moves, we'd shoot to kill, kill anybody that interfered with us."

Patrolman Thomas and De Leon dropped off Cain and West, and drove out to see Fat Man. De Leon got an M-1 carbine from him, and they then drove back to Deborah Green's, where they slept until 4:45 on the morning of the sixteenth. Thomas went on:

> I woke first. I asked [De Leon] did he want me to call Cain and did he have the number. . . . I called Cain, asked him was he ready, was the deal still on.
>
> Cain said yes, pick him up about 5:00 or 5:30 that morning. . . . I told the defendant De Leon that I was going to get the car; would he be ready when I got back. He said yes. I went, picked up the car, came back. The defendant De Leon was standing on the opposite side of the street of Deborah Green's apartment with the guns in his hand. . . . The defendant De Leon was getting in the car. At this time I saw a small bulge in his pocket. . . . It appeared to be the canister of spray.

Thomas picked up Alfred Cain and Jerome West, and they began their journey. In the car, driving through Brooklyn and Manhattan, Thomas said that they discussed the placement of the men at the robbery. Thomas was supposed to stay at the wheel of the car, and De Leon tried to take his gun because he had none himself, but Thomas would not let him have it. He said that Cain once more said "if anyone made any funny moves, we'd shoot to kill," and De Leon later repeated it (which made at least four repetitions by two people). West just nodded and said, "Right on."

Finally, at the end of the exit ramp from the West Side Highway at 125th Street, they came slowly to a stop . . .

And the rest we already know.

The thrust of the defense was to show, under the conspiracy laws, that there was no finished "plot" to commit a robbery on August 16, 1969, and that such elements as existed were precipitated by the actions of Wilbert Thomas. Thomas's story looked fairly plausible on its face; lawyers who heard his direct testimony for the first time were inclined to flee the courtroom, their faces averted from the disaster awaiting the defense. Nevertheless, it was not impossible to break Thomas's story down by cross-examination. Long evenings comparing his direct testimony with his voluminous earlier statements in the René reports, before the grand jury, and at the first trial made it possible for the defense to piece together some of the facts. Yet the lines of inquiry we could see at the start of our work were narrowly restricted by the legal limitations on the process of cross-examination.

Under existing rules, the defense was entitled to obtain the prior statements and reports of any prosecution witness for the purpose of searching for inconsistencies or new evidence. Throughout the proceedings we renewed our motion to obtain reports prepared by police officials other than just Wilbert Thomas, particularly his superiors and any other infiltrators, to show what instructions he was given, what criticism he received, and what contradictory evidence there was. As Conrad Lynn pointed out on one occasion when the motion was renewed and denied, the defense of entrapment was especially difficult to prove without access to "what the Police Department has on the directions for infiltrating the Black Panthers."

By the second trial, the defense had an enormous volume of material for cross-examination, but all that material was restricted within the narrow compass of what Thomas himself thought relevant, and it was not until near the close of his testimony, after a brilliant sally by Conrad Lynn, that Thomas opened up enough so that we could get outside the strict confines of the contradictions among his various accounts of the conspiracy.

At the outset of the cross-examination, then, we were on

the trail of distortion and exaggeration in Wilbert Thomas's various accounts. In his story of the very first words in the conspiracy, those of July 31, 1969, we were able to uncover the seeds of all the weaknesses in his testimony.

According to Thomas's direct testimony, Alfred Cain had said that "if the word comes down from the Black Panther Central Committee giving them the authority to pull robberies, then it would be a pleasure." But Thomas had told the grand jury, at the time the defendants were indicted back in 1969, that Cain had said:

> It would be a pleasure to rob, steal and loot and do anything else that would be profitable for the Black Panther Party organization.

His René report for July 31 was even more revealing.

> Ricardo De Leon, Babu (Sam Skeets), Henry McIntosh and Alfred Cain stated that if the word comes down or if they get the opportunity to have stickups in order to get some money, it would be a pleasure.

Thomas claimed that the sentence meant "the persons present were Babu, Henry McIntosh, Ricardo De Leon. Now, Alfred Cain stated if the word comes down, it would be a pleasure to pull stickups." But the explanation makes the sentence incomprehensible. It plainly states that four people said exactly the same thing, and if there is any element of truth in the paragraph at all, it implies that the four people *assented* to the proposition. The theatrical phrase "it would be a pleasure," as Conrad Lynn was later to say to the jury, sounded like the style of Wilbert Thomas.

This suggested that Patrolman Thomas exaggerated ("rob, steal, loot and do anything else profitable"), twisted the facts to fit the individual case, imputed his own words to others, and was concealing his agitation for criminal action.

There were other examples, both major and minor. Thomas quoted Alfred Cain as saying, at the time they talked alone together about robberies on August 13, that "he would like to pull large robberies instead of small robberies where we would pull maybe six a week." In other testimony, Thomas had quoted Cain as using the phrases "four or five robberies a week" and "a couple of robberies a week" in this connection, and it was clear that Thomas was supplying his own idea of what "small robberies" might have meant.

We had one indisputable record of a conversation, the tape recording of the telephone conversation with De Leon on August 15.* Thomas had summarized that conversation for the grand jury.

> Ricardo stated, "Well, I called to let you know we are to spend the night at Deborah Green's apartment, and that things are going for tomorrow to pull the robbery."
>
> He said, "I'll discuss this later with you. Meet me at 4:00 o'clock at Deborah Green's apartment."

It is useless to try to enumerate the ways in which this account distorts the telephone conversation. A glance at the transcript in Appendix A, however, will show at least that Thomas was ignoring his own role in the conversation, and that the plan to stay overnight at Deborah Green's was entirely missing.

Because Thomas's account of the defendant's words was so unreliable, we proposed to the jury to deal with the concrete circumstances revealed by the testimony and the reports. We looked, for example, at the testimony we had concerning guns. Thomas himself said that up to the evening of August 15, none of the defendants either showed off or admitted to possessing a weapon that was useful for the robbery. Despite all the talk of guns, there seemed to have been few of them actually in hand among the Black Panthers. But Thomas said he had a gun on July 31, August

---

* There were an additional few seconds on the tape, recording a conversation between De Leon and Thomas's wife, in which De Leon said he was looking for Thomas, and that he would meet him at Deborah Green's.

4, August 8, and repeatedly thereafter. That unique property naturally cast him in a peculiarly "militant" role, and it was hard to believe he did not behave in accordance with it. Moreover, he was the only link among the supposed conspirators up until August 14. He claimed to have discussed the job with De Leon on August 4 and 8, and then with Alfred Cain on August 13, but not with both together. At the end of his talk with Cain on August 13, Thomas had asked him to call De Leon. On the morning of the fourteenth, he came looking for De Leon and asked, "When were we going to get together and find out something about the deal?" (René report). De Leon replied that he had other business to take care of, which turned out to be the trip to the welfare office.

It appeared that Thomas was the binding force among the supposed conspirators. The crucial question remained of his provocation or agitation for violent action in the Black Panther Party. A natural place to look for provocation by Thomas was in the René reports for the days about which he did *not* testify. In the René report for August 2 (which was not even mentioned in the direct testimony), the following appeared:

> While selling newspapers, the assigned was hit under the eye by accident while entering a building.
>
> When the assigned returned to the BPP office at about 6:30 P.M., the assigned's eye was slightly swollen. The assigned informed *Roscoe* [the officer of the day] that the assigned was selling newspapers on Second Avenue and 8th Street and a pig on horseback from the A Squad tried to run the assigned down with a horse, and the assigned fell over a small chain fence and hurt his eye.

Roscoe's reaction was anger. Thomas smugly quoted him as saying:

> If a pig tried to vamp on a BP member, the Panthers are going to get together and try to annihilate the pig.

I closed my examination about this passage with the rhetorical question, "Mr. Thomas, will you now tell the jury that you did not entrap these defendants?"

Passages such as this showed the methods of provocation that Thomas used, but it remained for us to show how these methods as well as others were applied on August 14, the "Big Day" when Cain, De Leon, and Thomas finally sat down together. The first notable fact which he had left out of his direct testimony appeared in paragraph 12 of his René report for that day.

> At about 3:25, the assigned went to buy some donuts, Mr. De Leon asked the assigned to buy Mr. De Leon a pint of wine, Mr. De Leon drank about 6 pints of wine during the day.

Thomas's report showed that he also paid for some wine later in the day, and that De Leon was still drinking when they were up in Harlem together.

After the two of them got together with Alfred Cain, the three sat around in the little park, still drinking wine. Thomas virtuously said he did not drink any of it but left it all to the defendants. The three paragraphs in his René report for August 14 which described Thomas's part in the discussion were amazing.

> 23. Mr. Cain and Mr. De Leon stated that we will have to have a getaway car, the assigned stated that he would supply the car for the job, because the assigned knew how to hot-wire a car.

> 24. The assigned suggested looking at the place so that they would know what they were in for. Mr. Cain said he couldn't go along this afternoon because he had some business to take care of.

> 25. The assigned suggested that he and Mr. De Leon could go and look at the place and the assigned could draw a diagram and then show Mr. Cain the diagram.

These passages contradict much of Thomas's direct testimony. There is in this version no suggestion by the defendants that Thomas should get the car, by De Leon that they go to Harlem, or by Cain that Thomas draw a diagram, as there was on direct examination (see page 156); here it all comes from Thomas. He tried to mitigate the effect of these paragraphs in some cases by saying that his "suggestion" came only after urging by the defendants, but he could not destroy the impression that he had acted provocatively, and had concealed his provocations. In the interests of clarity, the defense moved for the admission into evidence of all the René reports, running all the way back to February.*

Another suggestion of provocation by Thomas was his flippant description of Alfred Cain as "shaky," when Cain supposedly ducked the trip to Harlem on the evening of August 14. Thomas's use of the word is hard to explain except by his contempt for the defendants and his sense of superiority to them in everything—even, perhaps, in the planning of crimes. He tried to say that the word "shaky" implied to him the ideas "sneaky" or "slick," but it wouldn't do; he had already quoted De Leon saying that Leroy Floudd was not to be included in the plan because he was "too shaky," and, as the defense pointed out in cross-examining Thomas, that certainly was not intended to mean that Floudd was "too slick" to be included in the robbery. The term plainly meant "unreliable" or "fearful," and by using it Thomas implied that he thought Alfred Cain unreliable as far as the robbery went.

The use of the phrase "business to take care of" by De Leon and Cain was a similar sort of telltale that Thomas was the one who was pushing the idea of robbery. De Leon was quoted as using it when Thomas asked him on the morning of August 14 about the supposed plan; Cain was supposed

* These were hearsay, but since the prosecutor did not object (in fact, he was astonished at our foolhardiness), the reports could be admitted.

to have used it later in the day when he was "shaky"; and
De Leon used it again on the morning of the fifteenth, in the
transcribed telephone conversation, when Thomas pressed
him to sit down and talk. Throughout the telephone conversation, it seemed, Thomas was urging that they get to
work, while De Leon continued to talk of other things.

Our inquiries concerning provocation and inducement
were intertwined with questions about the nature of the
plot, in the effort to find out how specific it really was. By
his own testimony, Thomas did not know the precise loca-
tion of the project until he went there (at his suggestion)
with De Leon on the night of August 14.

In the light of this fact, Thomas's earlier conversations
with the defendants take on a rather different cast. On
August 13, he went to see Alfred Cain alone, and according
to him, Cain exhibited no knowledge about the Harlem
job either specifically or in general. Instead, he denied
having a shotgun, and said he was looking for men he could
trust; various robberies were supposedly discussed. Extraordinary performance for a co-conspirator! Cain described in detail some great robberies of the past again on
the fourteenth, according to Thomas, saying he wanted to
get ten to twenty thousand. From the words of Alfred Cain
quoted earlier in this book, the reader can imagine that he
did not express any aversion to expropriation on the grand
scale, but it did look as though he was not part of a plot.

De Leon was supposed to have mentioned a specific job
on two previous occasions (in practically identical words),
and to have brought it up again at the meeting in the little
park. One curious thing about the job was that Thomas
quoted De Leon as having said on one occasion that they
could get three thousand dollars, and at the park meeting,
that they could get ten to eleven thousand. De Leon's
lawyer, Elliot Taikeff, was convinced that he must have
been talking in a general way about different projects, and
he commenced to bring that out in his cross-examination.

Thomas's explanation for the change in the figures was that De Leon had enlarged the sum to try to "sweeten the deal" for the others. Thomas, however, forgot he had testified at the first trial that De Leon had said at the park meeting that they could get "three thousand dollars or more" (rather than ten or eleven thousand). When confronted with that, Thomas claimed that De Leon first said three thousand and then raised the figure, leading to this exchange:

Q. What did you say to Mr. De Leon about this inflationary trend that was apparent at that point?

A. What would I say to the man? He said $3000 or more. "More" could have meant 10 or $11,000. I didn't know what the job —how much money the job consisted of. He said $3000. Then he said 10 or $11,000. Maybe he tried to make it sound sweeter to the defendant Cain and myself. I do not know.

Q. Didn't you say to him, "Are you talking about two jobs?" Or "Is this one job you're talking about?" Did you say that to him?

A. No, I didn't. Did I?

It did look rather strongly as though De Leon had discussed more than one subject until Thomas insisted on pinning him down.

That was not quite all on the issue of amounts of money; there was more in Patrolman Thomas's René reports, as hard to interpret (though not as rewarding after translation) as the Rosetta stone. Thomas could not have believed, by any interpretation of the facts, that the defendants expected to obtain ten to twenty thousand dollars by their supposed Harlem robbery; yet in his report for August 15, the day after the meeting, he wrote this paragraph:

Outside of Black Panther Party headquarters the assigned asked [Fat Man] where would Mr. De Leon be. [Fat Man] said he would show the assigned. The assigned and [Fat Man] started walking towards 90 Legion Street. The assigned told [Fat Man] that the assigned, Mr. De Leon, Alfred Cain and one other brother were in on a plan to get ten to twenty thousand dollars up around the lower side of Harlem. [Fat Man] said to the assigned not to tell him any more, because if they get caught, he didn't want the finger pointing at him.

This automatically prompts one question, which was put by Elliot Taikeff:

So I gather by that time you had inflated the figure from ten to eleven thousand dollars to make it look good to [Fat Man], hadn't you?

It further prompts gloomy reflections upon the fact that Fat Man was indicted for a conspiracy to rob. Thomas had attempted to interest him in a plot, he had refused, *his refusal was recorded in a police report,* and yet he was indicted for the very conspiracy (enormously inflated) that he had asked not to be told about.

This portion of the cross-examination left me with the conviction that Thomas had tried to make something concrete out of what was largely talk on the "Big Day," August 14. The parties to the supposed plan were not ready without him. They had no specific plan, nor the intention to carry one out, and they were too broke to get the weapons or the automobile to commit a Harlem robbery.

Harder problems were presented by the testimony that the tools of crime, including a sawed-off shotgun and gloves, were distributed the night of August 15, and by the irreducible fact that all the defendants were in the car on the morning of the sixteenth.

A long cross-examination about the surgical gloves showed that there were not enough pairs to go around; De Leon had had none at the time of his arrest, and Thomas varied his reports in such a way that he could have added a pair. Cain and West supposedly were wearing theirs at the time of the arrest, although it turned out on Thomas's cross-examination that they had arrived in Harlem hours before the landlord was expected, and it seemed unlikely that they would have worn the gloves continuously while they waited for him. Of course, the defendants steadfastly maintained that the gloves had been concealed by Thomas, along with the shotgun.

No one was contesting that an M-1 carbine and a knife were in the car. Possession of them was not a crime without unlawful intent, and it was no great surprise for Black Panthers to have such weapons. The real problem was that sawed-off shotgun, and we had to canvass every mention of weapons before we could begin to understand where it might really have come from.

The starting point was that Wilbert Thomas always had a weapon, even when the others did not. As early as August 1, Thomas had said that he could get "guns, but not money" for the Black Panther Party. This was a curious statement, in view of the fact that he did not say that anyone had asked about money but only about guns; indeed, the connection between guns and money was to be part of the key to the problem.

It is hard to tell how much is true in Thomas's account of his visits to the man he called an illegal gun seller, Hensley Johnson, but it does point at least to the conclusion that neither Cain nor De Leon had bought a gun from Johnson as late as the day before the robbery was supposed to happen. According to Thomas, he first went there on August 8 with De Leon and Leroy Floudd. They had no luck; he and Floudd went back on August 11 and were told to return August 14. Thomas claimed he dropped by there on August 13, to ask Johnson if he had sold a shotgun to "any of my friends," and Johnson said he had sold one to "the bumpy-faced guy," meaning Alfred. This of course is ridiculous, because Hensley Johnson had never seen Cain and Thomas together (supposing Johnson was fool-hardy enough to tell anyone else about such an incriminating sale). Thomas remembered returning there, as Johnson had told him to, on August 14, and again on August 15 with De Leon, supposedly without success.

The circumstances of the visits to Johnson suggested, on the other hand, that Thomas must have been ready to pay for guns. He was reticent about what happened in the latter two trips (August 14 and 15), failing even to record one of them in his reports; he tended to attribute similar words to the gun seller on every occasion. Thomas claimed that he and De Leon went there on the fourteenth right after De Leon had cashed his welfare check for twelve dollars, an assertion which led to this line of questions:

[PAUL CHEVIGNY]. Did you have any discussion with Mr. De Leon before going to Hensley Johnson's concerning where the money was going to come from to buy a gun?
A. No, I didn't.
Q. Now, sir, did there ever come a time when Hensley Johnson quoted a price to you for guns?
A. Yes....
Q. And what price did he quote you and for what gun?
A. About forty dollars for a .35 Smith and Wesson—.38 Smith and Wesson.

Similarly, De Leon and West went to Hensley Johnson's on the fifteenth after the transcribed telephone conversation in which De Leon said he needed money and Thomas said he had "a few bucks" (see Appendix A). Thomas maintained that he was not authorized to spend those bucks for anything but "beverages" and similar things, but it was hard to see what use it was for De Leon, who was broke, to go see a gun seller with Thomas unless Thomas was willing to contribute.

Hensley Johnson himself turned the gun problem into an even deeper mystery. A heavy, laconic black man, he took the stand for the prosecution in both trials. He contradicted Thomas on nearly every point. He said he had seen Thomas only once, not five times, and at the first trial he said that Thomas had asked him "what happened with the guns that are supposed to come . . . here." He did say that he had seen

Cain once, and that Cain had asked him about "some funny name, a shotgun or something," but he denied ever selling a gun to anyone, and in fact he claimed that he had merely heard at second hand about another man with guns.

The prosecution argued that Johnson was frightened, that he was afraid to tell the police he had in fact sold a gun, and afraid of the Panthers if he testified against them. The problem with that argument is that either or both of those fears would have been excellent reasons for Johnson to say nothing at all to the police. But he did not quite say nothing; he appeared to have some knowledge about guns, and of the defendants. The whole prosecution approach to Johnson was puzzling. If he really was an illegal gun seller, from a police point of view he had to be one of the most dangerous men in Brooklyn, because he was a source of supply very close to the Black Panther office. It was hard to see why the police would have let him alone out there on Legion Street unless he was willing to give them something extraordinarily valuable in return, such as solid testimony against the defendants. The testimony he gave certainly did not fill the bill. It was possible that he was telling the truth in his testimony that he never did sell guns, or more likely, that he had some evidence to give against the police, which protected him from reprisal on account of the equivocal testimony he did give. All the circumstances, Wilbert Thomas's earlier apparent willingness to obtain or supply guns, the implication that he was willing to buy guns if he or the defendants located any, the improbability of his story about Hensley Johnson having described a "bumpy-faced" purchaser, Thomas's reticence about other visits, and the truncated story from Johnson, combined with Johnson's improbable insulation from legal trouble, led us to the thought that the shotgun came from Thomas, and that he might have bought it from Johnson. We were to have stronger support for the argument that Thomas was the source of the gun later, from the defense witnesses,

but the cross-examination of Thomas and the strange dupli-
citous testimony of Johnson at least suggested it.

Thomas's positive statement that he saw Jerome West
pull the shotgun out of a couch at Deborah Green's on the
night of August 15 could not, of course, very easily be
attacked by cross-examination. That also had to wait for
defense witnesses. Thomas did testify on direct examination
that De Leon told him Jerome West had purchased a shotgun, but he had no such story in his reports, suggesting
that he might have introduced West and the shotgun into
the narrative in order to lock the youth firmly into the
conspiracy. Thomas had also attributed a shotgun to Cain
and De Leon in earlier reports, which raised the possibility
that he was looking for the best man to assign the gun to.

To my way of thinking, we had by this point in the cross-
examination pretty well established that there would have
been no finished plan without Thomas, and we had suggested an origin for the shotgun. It remained to give the
jury (and ourselves) some insight into Thomas's character
which might enable them and us to understand how these
things could have happened. That understanding came to
us as a result of new lines of inquiry opened by Elliot
Taikeff and Conrad Lynn.

Conrad Lynn cross-examined last, and by the time of
his examination Wilbert Thomas had loosened up to the
point where his testimony was positively reckless. His contempt for the black people with whom he had to deal began
to show through in Lynn's examination.

Q. Now, you knew a woman at 142 West 131st Street named
   Vickie?
A. I didn't know her until August 14, 1969. She seemed to like
   me. . . . I must have smelled better than the company she
   was running with.
Q. Since you smell so much better, she would like to see you; is
   that correct?

A. Yes.

Q. And you went to see Vickie quite often, didn't you?

A. I never seen her again.

Q. That was—that affair came to a sudden stop, didn't it, just now?

A. She was not my type.

Part of Lynn's technique was to ask Thomas about crimes or plots of the Black Panthers other than the plan of August 16, 1969, as a general test of his credibility.

Q. . . . Did you take them as a part of a plan or did you consider them just rhetoric or, in other words, loud talk. How did you regard that?

A. No rhetoric. When the man spoke, he was dead serious. . . . Wow, if you could just be out there with them and listen to some of the things they talk about, I imagine it would turn your hair greyer than it is now. . . .

Q. . . . [W]hat was the first deadly serious plan you knew the Panthers had formulated?

A. Well, I've heard talk at breakfast programs about killing policemen.

Q. All right, where were these policemen to be killed?

A. I imagine any place they could kill them.

Q. . . . [A]nd who said we are going to kill policemen? Can you specify who that was?

A. I was at the Antioch Baptist Church on Greene Avenue and there was—well, I can't tell you their names, but they seemed to be Panthers at this time. One . . . fat woman and a man that she said was her husband, they were working at this breakfast program, they were coming to Panther meetings left and right and their thing started working up about killing policemen again. . . .

Q. Do you know the month that plan was being announced? . . .

A. I think it was around the month of June.

Q. . . . [A]nd do you now know who these people were who announced these plans?

A. I don't remember their names—I—

Q. Did you make a written report to your superior about that?

A. An oral report.

Q. Not a written report? You are certain that's not in your type-written reports?

A. I don't believe it is. It could be there, but—

Q. That was a deadly serious plan, was it?

A. Sure, if you discuss with someone about killing policemen, isn't that a plan? You talk about getting the material to kill them. . . .

Q. That paper that you examined just now, was that part of a paper that you kept your information on?

A. No. . . .

Q. Now, when did you write the notes on that paper?

A. Last week, maybe.

Q. And yet those notes were concerning an event in June, 1969?

A. Yes.

Q. And you wrote it down last week to remind you of June, 1969?

A. Well, an event that had happened about the stickups that the defendant Cain was talking about we would have to relate to.

Q. But you looked at that paper in order to remind yourself of the Antioch Baptist plan to kill cops, didn't you?

A. Yes, because that's where the defendant Cain told me about the stickups.

Q. And yet you did not make a written report about that in these reports you sent to your superiors?

A. I don't know. Let's read back through the month of June. . . .

Q. Now, on this handwritten note, People's Exhibit 32, it doesn't make any reference to any Antioch Baptist plan to kill cops, does it?

A. I didn't say that it was on that piece—

Q. This doesn't say anything about that, does it?

A. No, it doesn't.

During Thomas's redirect examination, the prosecutor John Fine tried to rehabilitate him on the issue of the "serious plots" by asking him just to list the categories of crimes he had reported. The answer was "Extortion, bombings, robbery, thefts, and murder." Elliot Taikeff later took up the matter again.

Q. Sir, will you show me, if you can, where in your typewritten reports you reported a murder (*handing reports to witness*)?
                    (*Inspecting reports*)

MR. FINE. I suggest you look at Report 9, . . . 12, 16, 17, 20, 23, 24, et cetera.

MR. TAIKEFF. Okay. Report 9?

MR. FINE. Yes, Page 2. An attempt to kill the Mayor.

MR. TAIKEFF. When you testified that you detected possible crimes of murder, were you referring, amongst other things, to an attempted murder on the Mayor of the City of New York?

A. It's possible that that was included, yes.

Q. All right. Will you take a look at your Report No. 9, dated February 27, 1969, Page 2, and tell me if that's one of the so-called murders that you're talking about.

MR. FINE (*to the witness*). You will see it on Page 2, after it says "burn Canarsie school to the ground."

MR. TAIKEFF. Your Honor, may the district attorney be instructed that he's not to prompt the witness? . . . Have you found it, sir?

A. Yes.

Q. Is that one of the murder incidents you're talking about?

A. Yes. The man said he was going to kill the Mayor. Can't you read? Didn't you see it?

MR. TAIKEFF. With the Court's permission, I'll read a portion of Report No. 9 to the jury.

    (*Reading*) "At 4:00 P.M. the assigned was informed by a Black Panther Party officer by the name of Cain that the assigned was to accompany Mr. Cain to a meeting of the Young Troopers held at 318 Livonia Avenue. The assigned attended the meeting but was stationed at the door as a guard. There were no loudspeakers in the building so the assigned could not hear what was being said. After the Young Troopers meeting was over, the assigned, Cain and a Negro male by the name of David who stated that he was a captain and in charge of the Black Panther Party in Canarsie. Along with two other Negro males . . . and a female Negro teacher at Canarsie High School, who stated that Canarsie High School is mostly black, with about 400 white students. The female Negro stated that the Negro students in Canarsie wanted an African Culture class and they got that. They wanted a section of the school library contributed to Malcolm X but there was a debate by the white teachers and they objected. The school had a fair with games and prizes. The Negro students stole the show by winning all of the prizes with a display of African Culture, so the teachers decided that something must be done with Canarsie High School, the same that was done with Franklin K. Lane, but the students said not one kid will leave the school. On the day that Malcolm X was assassinated was supposed to be a black holiday, all of the black students were to walk out of the school, but some white students were located outside and were supposed to start a fight with the Negro students. The Negro students stayed inside and had their demonstration inside the school.

"David stated that the teachers were making some of the Negro students absent with cutting cards, even if they were in class, but the students said no good, so the teachers and white students would catch the black students in the hallways of the school and would call them boy or Nigger, so they would get angry and take a swing at one of them. This way the teachers would have an excuse to transfer some of the black students out of Canarsie High School. David stated they just ignored the teachers until a Negro female had an epileptic fit, and a cop hit her in the head with a chair. David stated that he and five hundred black people will go to city hall, Friday, February 28, 1969, to see the mayor.

"They will have a petition with twenty-five demands for the black students in Canarsie. If the demands are not met by Monday, March 3rd at 9 A.M., they will try their best to burn Canarsie to the ground.

"David also stated if the police try to apprehend him or any of the black students at City Hall, the mayor will be the first to go."

[ELLIOT TAIKEFF]. Now, is that the murder incidents or one of
the murder incidents that you are talking about?

A. Yes. The man said he will kill the mayor—

Q. That's all. The question was answered yes.

The cross-examination might have ended here, with the
two last mighty examples to show the jury that Wilbert
Thomas could not or would not distinguish between the
real and the fancied, but instead it took a surprising turn,
veering away from the defendants' supposed conspiracy to
hints of a police conspiracy against the Brooklyn Black
Panthers continuing after the defendants had been
arrested. Very late in his direct examination, Thomas had
explained his inability to recall some things by saying that
after the arrest, "I had to move my family and myself out
of my house to a motel, because members of the Black
Panther Party organization were trying to get at me at
this time. They were trying to kill me."

I sat up, remembering the story I had heard from Donald Cox about the Panthers having been lured into a trap
at Thomas's house by an apparently false complaint about
a landlord. I had forgotten the story as irrelevant, and here
it was.

Thomas, however, had his own facts confused. The "attempt on his life" was not his reason for moving. He had
moved his family to a motel the day of the arrest, probably
to save them any embarrassing or dangerous questions
about his whereabouts, because he was supposed to have
been arrested with the others. The "attempt" occurred
about a week later. To Elliot Taikeff, Thomas tried to explain that people had been gunning for him the entire time.

A. But there were different people visiting my house within
that time. I was informed by my neighbor that some mili-
tant-looking guys were coming around my house looking for
me, and later—

Q. Military uniform?

A. Subversive-looking persons.

Q. Subversive types came around. I see. They were in subversive uniform?

MR. FINE. Your Honor, this amuses Mr. Taikeff.

MR. TAIKEFF. It certainly does amuse me. Unfortunately it happens to be in the middle of a criminal trial.

That lame story could not account for the fact that Patrolman Thomas was back in his apartment on one particular day, one week later, heavily guarded, when a group of Panthers just happened to show up.

Q. Now, tell us about that incident that occurred at your home after you moved to the motel?

A. A group of Panthers came to my house and tried to get me.

Q. What were their names?

A. There was Donald Cox and others.

Q. The second fellow's name was Others?

A. William Larry Smith.

Q. Who else?

A. A bunch of persons. . . . I got out of the vicinity and went back to my apartment house. I had to get reinforcements to get me out of the house. They wasn't about to just come and say hello or how are you doing. . . .

Q. Now, when Mr. Smith and the others arrived at your apartment house, were there any policemen there?

A. Yes.

Q. How many?

A. Three.

Q. Were they in plain clothes or uniform?

A. Plain clothes.

Q. And how long had they been there?

A. Well, one policeman stayed there all night. Three others came very early that morning.

Q. And what was their function, if you know?

A. They were to protect me.

Q. Now, this incident you're relating to us now occurred approximately a week after the arrest. Is that correct?

A. Yes.

Q. Now do you know anything about a woman going to the Black Panther Party headquarters, at or about the time of this incident, and saying that she was having trouble with her landlord at an address which was your address?

A. No, I don't.

The implication was very strong that a trap had been laid, using Thomas as bait to try to lure the Panthers into a shoot-out, on a day that the police had chosen. We were to hammer that home during the defense when we called Norman Ebanks, who had been officer of the day in the Panther office on the day shortly after the arrest when a woman called in, ostensibly for help with her landlord. Some members, as Donald Cox recalled, had driven around to the address and had come right up against the police. He believed that the police had wanted them to start something, and after Thomas's story I thought he was right.

This episode finally ended the cross-examination. It suggested that there was a broad police plan for all the Panthers in Brooklyn, of which Wilbert Thomas's story of conspiracy was only a small part, and buttressed our claim that if we could have got at other police records, we might have learned much more about the real purposes behind Thomas's actions. For the first time, I began to feel a little sympathy for Thomas, because it seemed to me he was being used. In part, he took literally the violent talk he heard, and his belief no doubt justified him in his own mind when he tried to pull the scattered parts together and piece them out through distortions into the appearance of a working conspiracy. His convictions about the extreme, serious violence of his compatriots meant that he must have been very much afraid when he was used as bait that morning. By his own lights, he showed courage.

The defense began with the testimony of Norman Ebanks, to clear up at the outset the story of the threat to Thomas's life. In the following days, the defense called a number of witnesses, both to refute specific points in Thomas's story and to present concrete examples of his acts of provocation.

Deborah Green and Thomas McCreary were supposed to have been closest to the conspiracy, and according to Wilbert Thomas, the shotgun, the gloves, and the knife had been revealed in Miss Green's apartment on Montgomery Street. No longer members of the Black Panther Party, but still in touch with the defendants, they were to be our most important witnesses.

Thomas McCreary was an insouciant witness, confident as always of his ability to deal with lawyers or anyone else. He said that he had in fact been at Deborah Green's apartment on August 15, 1969, and he had seen De Leon handling her .22 rifle, but he had not heard a robbery discussed and he did not see Jerome West pull a shotgun out of a folding couch. In fact, he did not see a sawed-off shotgun at all on the fifteenth nor at any other time.

Deborah Green is a handsome, soft-spoken young woman who then worked as a technician in a hospital laboratory. Calmly, she testified that she lived with Thomas McCreary in the apartment on Montgomery Street, and that De Leon was staying there as well in August of 1969. She said she had seen neither a shotgun nor rubber gloves on the fifteenth or at any other time. On that day, she had seen De Leon handling her rifle, pointing it at the window and saying, "Bang, bang—dead pig." She afforded us a small bit of insight into Wilbert Thomas's character when she said that he reacted to this by saying, "Sometimes I get tired of it all. I feel like killing everyone." She later saw Thomas "crouched on the floor beside Alfred drawing something," and describing it to him in words to the effect of "This is the way out" or "You get out this way."

Her ownership of the licensed .22 rifle prompted a discussion with the district attorney about Black Panther weapons policy, and specifically about political meetings in her apartment. She had got the rifle permit on August 8, four days after the meeting of August 4 at her house chaired by Brenda Hyson, the new defense captain sent from the West Coast. It did appear that there had been some controversy about weapons, but it was not quite as simple as Wilbert Thomas thought when he reported that the members had overruled Brenda Hyson and would carry weapons. Miss Green pointed out that members did not have the power to overrule the defense captain. The argument had been about packing a weapon in the street, as compared with keeping it in the house, and about financing weapons. Brenda Hyson had said that the party would not pay for weapons and did not think the members were ready for them. But Huey Newton had long ago said that members ought to keep a weapon in the house for self-defense, and Miss Green took that to mean she could get a rifle if she paid for it herself and kept it at home. That .22 rifle was the end result of an ideological conflict between the representatives of the West Coast leadership and the Brooklyn chapter.

The Cain family had important bits of evidence to fill in. Jessica Cain, Alfred's shy young sister, testified in a near whisper that Wilbert Thomas had come to the house on August 15 with Ricardo De Leon, looking for Alfred. Thomas had given her his pistol to put under her mattress, but when they all returned, De Leon first asked for the gun and she gave it to him. Alfred was in the living room reading, and De Leon and Thomas argued loudly about the gun. Alfred, who, she said, "doesn't like too much loud arguing," told them to take it outside. De Leon finally gave the gun back to Thomas, and there was no physical fight of the sort that Thomas described. Since the fight was also not in his René reports, it seemed very likely that it had not happened as he described it.

Melvina Cain took the witness stand, the picture of the militant mother. She had her red, black, and green scarf on, and as she turned to take the oath, she made the fist of solidarity to the defendants, in such a way that it was not visible to the jury. She testified that her son Alfred Cain, Jr., came in very late the night before he was arrested. She woke up, and he asked her to wake him at eight in the morning. Sometime shortly after four the telephone rang, and it was Wilbert Thomas. She said Alfred had asked not to be awakened until eight, but Thomas said there was "trouble in the party" in Harlem and he wanted Alfred to go along.

On the issue of Wilbert Thomas's provocations in the use of weapons, Thomas McCreary had more testimony to give. He said that about two and a half weeks before the defendants were arrested, Thomas told him outside the Good Shepherd Center that "he knew this lady that he could get thirty-eights from." He said the gun would cost between forty and fifty dollars, and McCreary said he was interested, but he did not have the money at the time. He heard no more about it. Two or three days before the defendants were arrested, McCreary found Thomas outside the Sutter Avenue office, talking about a sawed-off shotgun for which he had a "connection." McCreary said Thomas described it as a "twelve-gauge, pump-action gun, sawed off at both ends," which also neatly defines the gun introduced into evidence. He said he had begun to think Thomas was "jiving," because he had not produced any weapons, and the subject was dropped.

On August 15, when Thomas came to Deborah Green's house on Montgomery Street, he was carrying a .38 revolver. He took it out and passed it around for the others to look at. This was apparently the same weapon which was left under the mattress at Alfred Cain's house.

Leroy Floudd, with whom Thomas said he had made two trips to the supposed gun seller at 90 Legion Street, took the stand. He was a soft-spoken young black man from East New York, then working as a truck driver, and formerly a custodian at a college. He too was no longer a member of the Panthers. He testified that sometime in the summer of 1969, Thomas asked him to walk to 90 Legion Street with him.

> And while we were walking he was telling me that—a story about his father had lost his thirty-eight or someone had stole it. I can't remember, but then his father had lost his thirty-eight and he was going to buy another one for his father, and so, we walked on down Legion Street and when we got to Legion Street he spoke to this fellow. And after he spoke to him, he asked me . . . was I coming back that night and did I have the money to buy a sawed-off shotgun. I told him I didn't have the money and he offered to give me the money, if I would come back, and I said okay.

Floudd said, however, that he did not return with Thomas because the situation "rang a bell in his head"—it renewed suspicions he harbored from observing the incident about the "pig on horseback."

> When [Thomas] had came in the office and didn't want to sell Black Panther Party newspapers and didn't want to work in the community, he told me that he was knocked over a chain by a mounted policeman and he cut his eyes and some girl took him in and washed him up.

The youngest witness in the case was Frank Harris, seventeen at the time of the trial, who had been a Panther-in-training for a few months in 1968 and 1969. He testified that he had had a .25-caliber pistol while he was in the party, and sometime in April of 1969, Wilbert Thomas had offered to get him ammunition for it. He was a cool, credible witness with no apparent motive to lie—yet another in the parade of able, intelligent youths attracted to the Black Panthers at the end of the sixties.

The testimony from McCreary, Floudd, and Harris tended to show that Wilbert Thomas was agitating constantly about weapons and in particular about a sawed-off shotgun. The testimony of Floudd and McCreary certainly implied that Thomas had tried to interest each of them in the same gun which ultimately turned up in the car on August 16.

Mr. Fine's cross-examination of the defense witnesses took the general form of an attack on their credibility, to show that they had a motive to lie and would not be likely to come to court and tell the truth about weapons. McCreary fielded these questions very well. He was asked about his story concerning Wilbert Thomas's description of a sawed-off shotgun a few days before the arrest.

Q. [Wasn't it the] kind of description that might come after you having seen the gun on the 16th day of August, 1969, in the apartment on Montgomery Street?
A. If you want to repeat yourself, that's your business; but I just stated I didn't see West pull any shotgun from any mattress.
Q. . . . [A]re you familiar with the terms aiding and abetting?
A. Of course. . . .
Q. Accomplice before the fact?
A. Yes.
Q. Conspirator?
A. Right.
Q. Well, now, if you were involved in any way with that sawed-off shotgun in the apartment, you might be guilty of a crime, it's possible?
A. That's correct. Right.
Q. Are you going to come in here and tell this jury you are guilty of a crime?
A. If I would have been involved, I would [not] have come in here, period.

This was an important point; if Thomas McCreary was as deeply involved as the prosecution said he was, he very likely would not have run the risk of testifying at all. McCreary's contempt for the state was so great, however, that

he fenced with the prosecutor, and inevitably, he sometimes said some rash things.

Q. As a matter of fact, didn't you say to De Leon words to this
   effect: that you would have liked to have gone in on the job
   but they didn't give you enough time to prepare?
A. No.
Q. You would have been able to use Deborah Green's gun.
A. A registered piece to go in on a job? That would have been
   pretty bright of me.

Throughout his examination, McCreary exhibited great
confidence in handling the weapons in evidence, such as the
carbine, and in discussing others. It was plain, as he said,
that his ease came from his experiences in the Vietnam war
and in the Black Panther Party.

Mr. Fine used the same technique with Deborah Green.
One of his principal aims was to show that she had supplied
the surgical gloves, because she worked in a hospital. Hours
of testimony from rebuttal witnesses were later taken up in
showing that she had access to such gloves (although they
were not used in her laboratory), but in the end it all
proved very little, because the gloves were a commercial
product, available if desired from a number of sources.
After the first trial, when the prosecution had found out
that it was possible for her to have obtained such gloves,
detectives had gone to her laboratory and searched her
work area vainly, looking for similar gloves. If she had had
any such connection with the conspiracy, however, it was
likely that she would have kept quiet and avoided testifying.

The prosecution technique of attempting to show a motive to lie worked even less well with Leroy Floudd and
Frank Harris. They had no strong motive to come in and
invent a story. Harris, in particular, was a quick, well-
spoken teen-ager who had never been in any kind of legal

trouble and had a post office job at the time of the trial. He certainly did not need to come in and admit possession of a gun simply in order to accuse Wilbert Thomas of offering to supply ammunition for it.

The main part of Mr. Fine's examination of all the defense witnesses concerned their own and the Black Panther Party's supposed advocacy of and reliance on violent crime and subversion. He started right in with Thomas McCreary.

Q. Now, Mr. McCreary, you told us that you work serving the community and the black people.

A. That's correct.

Q. How long have you been doing that?

A. Since I came back from Viet Nam.

Q. Are you self-employed?

A. No. That's ninety per cent of the time I work in the black community. Ten per cent of the time I work as a dental technician, a merchant seaman.

Q. You do what you please ninety per cent of the time?

A. Ninety per cent of the time I work trying to alleviate some of the wretchedness of the black community.

Q. Who pays you for this work?

A. My pay is not of monetary value, where in the system you receive a salary for your job. My reward is like seeing conditions, those conditions, alleviated for the black people.

Q. And the satisfaction sustains you. Is that correct?

A. Right on.

Q. How do you go about buying your food, buying your clothes?

A. You see, I relate to a group of people who does the same thing. We live out of like a collective, and it's very economical when you live that way.

Q. Do they work, too?

A. Some of them do. . . .

Q. Now there's nothing about you physically that prevents you from working, is there?

A. No. Of course not.

Q. I see. And where do you obtain your money?

A. From the people I relate to.

Q. Friends give you money?

A. Of course.
Q. You don't relate to stickups to get money, do you, because you're not working?
A. No. . . .

Mr. Fine also questioned McCreary about explosives, which were totally irrelevant to the case; he even used articles from the Black Panther newspaper which were not in evidence. We defense attorneys objected less than we might legally have done, because we were sure that the jury would see and resent the political thrust of the questions, and that the witnesses could handle them. Thomas McCreary could.

Q. And, indeed, bombs were discussed in the Brooklyn Black Panther Party branch, weren't they?
A. No.
Q. The defendant Cain gave lectures on how to make bombs?
A. No, that was not his function at all.
Q. And guerrilla warfare.
A. No. That he wasn't qualified to do and guerrilla warfare is against the law to be taught.
Q. And you wouldn't violate the law, would you?
A. Oh, no, but we don't believe—agree with the laws even, we are trying to find ways to get around them and have them changed.
Q. And you have a list—how to get around them?
A. Yes. You use loopholes yourself in law.

The technique became even more heavy-handed in the questioning of Deborah Green.

Q. Now, it's true, isn't it, to the minutest detail that the Black Panther Party through publications and through lectures not only encouraged crimes, maybe in the name of revolution or otherwise, but encouraged robberies but also [told] how to avoid prosecution for these crimes?
A. No, that's not true.
Q. That isn't a fact?
A. No, it's not true. . . . You can be expelled for things like that.

It extended even to the classic "subversion" question.

Q. Now, the time that you were in California, did you become
aware that money was coming into the Black Panther Party
from the People's Republic of Communist China?

MR. TAIKEFF. For God's sake, everybody go home and look
under the bed for a subversive now. What kind of nonsense
is this? The district attorney knows better than to pull a stunt
like that.

THE COURT. Objection on the ground of irrelevancy is sustained.

In questioning Frank Harris, Mr. Fine combined his
"criminal violence" technique with an attempt to show that
the Panthers had tried to corrupt a mere boy of sixteen
years.

Q. But what I want to ask you, Mr. Harris, please, isn't it a fact
that People's 46 [an article in the newspaper not in evidence]
and similar things like that, as a young man who had
dropped out of school, created an impression on your mind?

A. No. . . .

Q. Now did you feel that while you were a member of the Black
Panther Party you came into contact with a number of criminals that may have influenced your thinking?

A. I came in contact with fellow human beings sharing in a
cause, but not to my recollection I've ever run across any
criminals.

Q. Would it seem to you that persons other than young impres-
sionable men would be attracted to a philosophy of robberies, as expressed in that People's 46, or possession of
weapons and stealing things, Mr. Harris?

A. I disagree. I disagree on the grounds that you say "impres-
sionable young men." But then you have to realize that
nobody is forcing anybody to do anything. They do it on
their own volition.

Q. Nobody could force you into doing anything.

A. No.

A deeper question was raised by the implications of this
cross-examination: If the authorities thought Harris an im-

pressionable youth while he was associated with the Black Panthers, why could they not think of anything more constructive to do about his condition than to send an agent like Wilbert Thomas to offer to get him ammunition for his gun? In general, the entire line of inquiry about Black Panther policies of violence backfired completely for all the witnesses. It made hypocrisy out of protestations that the trial was not "political," and it cast doubt over the firm issues that the prosecution had to present in the case.

Only one of the defendants, Jerome West, was to testify. He was twenty years old at the time of the trial, and had left school when he was sixteen in order to support a child.

He testified that his friend Alfred Cain came to see him on the evening of August 15, a Friday.

> He came around St. John's Place [West's home block]. . . . I was on the stoop with my son. He said, "Power." I told him, "Power." I walked him down [to] the corner, you know. . . . He started telling me that he suspected Wilbert Thomas of being a pig. . . . He told me that Wilbert Thomas had plans for this robbery, and that he would need my assistance to determine whether Wilbert was a pig or not. . . . I told him, "Right on." And at this time . . . the brother left. . . .

At about midnight, Jerome West, Alfred Cain, Ricardo De Leon, and Wilbert Thomas all walked over to Deborah Green's apartment. They stayed there about a half-hour, a period during which West said he did not see a sawed-off shotgun, gloves, or knives. He and Cain talked about "getting some smoke," (marijuana) because August 17, the following Sunday, was West's birthday and he said he wanted it for a party. Later, on the way back to St. John's Place, Cain told West that they were going up to Harlem the next day, and he wanted West to go along. West agreed, and went back to his girlfriend's house. He did not sleep, but watched television until about five in the morning, when Cain called with the message "Wilbert said he was leaving early, to meet him at Debbie's house."

I walked down Montgomery and I . . . seen De Leon coming towards Debbie's house and he said, "Power," and I said, "Power," and he told me Wilbert Thomas is in the car and I seen Wilbert Thomas behind the seat in the car. . . . Said, "Power," and then I opened the back door and I saw a carbine and bag on the floor. . . . The bag was on the left-hand rear and the carbine was on the right rear on the floor, kind of pushed under the seat. . . . I asked him [Thomas] what was happening with this and he said he's going up to Harlem to sell them. . . . I got in the car, and he drove up a little bit and brother Cain was sitting on a park bench and he came over to the car and got in. He said, "Power," and we took off. . . .

Entering the west side drive highway, Wilbert Thomas had passed back this piece of paper. I guess it was meant for me, but brother Cain took it. He looked at it and passed it to me and as I was looking at it, he said it's a good place to hit.

Q. Who said that?

A. Wilbert Thomas.

We came off the ramp, like, Wilbert Thomas slowed up the car and then he stopped it. As he was slowing up, I looked to the side window, rear window, I seen them—Captain Kissane. . . . He was running with a gun in his hand and another officer behind him with a shotgun and I turned around and I looked at Cain, and turned my head back and the gun was at my head and he told me to freeze and get out of the car.

He threw me up against the car and searched me and put my hand behind my back and handcuffed me. It was, like, walking to the car—it sounded like I heard him taking—it could have been taking it out or ripping the bag off fast, that's when I saw the shotgun.

In his cross-examination of Jerome West, Mr. Fine ran up against a ghetto wall. He asked West about one apparently odd circumstance in his direct testimony.

Q. Now, Mr. West, why did you stay up all night the 15th through the 16th, if you weren't going to hold up the place early in the morning the next day?

A. It was hot that night.

Q. Hot that night?
A. Don't have no air condition where I live at.
Q. You just stayed up and watched TV.
A. Right.
Q. It's just as hot watching TV.
A. It's always going to be hot in the ghetto.

Mr. Fine impeached West's credibility by questioning him about his previous conflicts with the law. West testified that he was innocent of the one crime of which he had been convicted. Mr. Fine also questioned him about a disciplinary proceeding in which the correction authorities had found him guilty of using abusive language to a guard during the year he was in jail awaiting trial at Riker's Island.

Q. Did you ever threaten to kill him when you got out—any man at the Adolescent Remand Shelter?
A. Now, if you are talking like that, you understand you get killed in that place. You don't threaten nobody in jail. You get killed. That is what it is all about. You have never been in jail.
Q. Were you found guilty of any charges as a result of using that particular language, threatening to kill someone?
A. Well, there was no Judge there, you understand? Just a Deputy. You go up there and tell him what happened and the man says, "You are guilty." If they wanted to bring it to the street, why didn't they bring it to the street?

All this finally provoked a line of irony intended and unintended from the prosecutor: "My, you are a terrible victim of circumstance, aren't you?"

Although the prosecution did not seriously damage West as a witness, his story had raised nearly as many questions as it answered. It made the point, which Cain had maintained to me from the start, that he and West, at least, were suspicious of Wilbert Thomas and were trying to find out whether he was on the level; buying the "smoke" was to be a dividend. It also tended to establish, as Mrs. Cain's testimony had done, that they had left earlier than they originally expected to. But it left unanswered what exactly they must have thought when they got into the car so early in the morning and found at least a carbine on the floor, or when Thomas produced the diagram which he had earlier shown Cain at Deborah Green's apartment.

Finally, Mr. Fine called to the stand one member of BOSS, a policewoman who had been riding with other policemen in a taxicab tailing the green Dodge. Her story had a curious side-effect. The taxi in which she was riding had been waiting on Canal Street in Manhattan on the morning of August 16; it was plainly coordinated with Wilbert Thomas's green Dodge. When Thomas had been asked what he had told his superiors the day before the arrest about his route to Harlem, he had made the conversation look casual.

> My boss asked me . . . "which way are you coming to Harlem?" I said, "I imagine the west side." He said, "Well, where will you be exiting?" I said, "125th Street ramp."

It was plain that the route required the most careful planning and briefing, and was fixed as to times and streets. Apparently, the time had actually been moved up a few hours by Thomas's superiors after his last talk with the defendants, perhaps because they felt it was too dangerous to make an arrest on the public streets as late as eight in the morning. Thomas's account partook of a general pattern, throughout the case, of concealing the elaborate police planning that had to have gone into the case.

SUMMATIONS

In his summation, Elliot Taikeff finally reached out and made the ultimate accusation against Wilbert Thomas.

> I think that the most important part and the most interesting part of Wilbert Thomas' testimony, both direct and cross, was

the last five per cent, because I tell you, in all candor, that I made a mistake in evaluating Wilbert Thomas. I thought that he was just a plain ordinary liar, that he was making up these stories maliciously.

I don't think that he did not lie. I think he did lie on the stand, and I think you know when he lied. You could tell from the expression on his face that he lied. You are the original lie detectors. That's your job.

But we learned something; and my enlightenment started halfway through Mr. Lynn's cross-examination and continued into the next morning—and it was a miraculous progress that Mr. Chevigny, Mr. Lynn, and I all came to the same conclusion simultaneously without consulting with each other.

Wilbert Thomas is partly mad. He's a madman. There's no doubt in my mind about it, because he believes the most incredible things.

I do not think now that it was necessary to go that far. Thomas was locked into an ideology much more rigid than that of any of the defendants. All of his behavior indicated that he hated and feared black street people as well as radicals. The defendants were both, and that made him willing to use any means at hand to lock them up. That was enough; insanity was too much.

No exposition of Thomas's motives would alone suffice to explain to the jury what did actually happen on the morning of August 16, 1969. Such an explanation the defense was not technically obligated to give—all we had to do was raise a reasonable doubt about the prosecution's version— but we decided that some explanation would make our case more believable. Elliot Taikeff's account comes closest to being a coherent one.

So there was a pistol under Thomas' leg and the rifle in the back and there was in the shopping bag a sawed-off shotgun and in that shopping bag there were two pairs of gloves and maybe or maybe not Wilbert Thomas had another pair; I don't know, but this thing was set up in such a way by Wilbert

Thomas because he believed from these cockeyed stories and conversations that he had with these fellows that at that point they actually would be interested in doing a robbery, and he said, Well, once they show their interest, as far as I'm concerned, morally speaking they are as guilty as if they did it. Cain and De Leon were supposed to be there and everything would have come out right, because there would be one gun for everybody. There would have been one pair of gloves for everybody, for every man in the car; but as it turned out, because of some quirk, Jerome West joined the group.

Now, if there was a real robbery in progress obviously they wouldn't let him join the group, but if they were going to Harlem for a combination of reasons, to buy some marijuana, to attend to a matter at a State site which was a political issue up there at that time, there would be no objection to letting Jerome West get in the car, and so Jerome West got in the car and that's why there weren't enough gloves to go around, because the die was already cast. The stuff was in the car. The police were waiting. There was no turning back. That's why there weren't enough guns to go around. That's why the number of guns equals the number of [defendants]. Who ever heard of armed robbers going out without enough guns, and that's why there weren't enough pairs of gloves in the car and that's why Wilbert Thomas adjusted his handwritten report; that's why he included West suddenly on the evening of August 14, because West wasn't even a part of these rhetorical conversations which are no crime, but he wasn't a part of that. He knew nothing about this. He was an innocent caught in this trap.

This account left some questions unanswered—chiefly about the presence of the diagram and the earliness of the hour. Some questions would have to await reflection after the trial.

In his summation, Mr. Fine hammered away at the most difficult point in the defense: we claimed, on the one hand, that there was no finished plot, and on the other, that the defendants were entrapped. We had said we meant to apply the entrapment defense only to those parts of the plan which existed, but it certainly was a complicated notion to put across. Apart from that, the prosecutor branded the defendants "hoodlums," calling their social programs a "disguise."

> You had talk—breakfast programs, the medical clinic, the ten point programs: Liberalism—that is what Cain thinks about them. "That is just what we tell them, to get a little cooperation from the people; because if the people see what we are really up to—" It is a guise. It is a disguise—

And again:

> Any woman that has known the terror of the ghetto knows the hoodlum at sight. It isn't hair length. It is a sixth sense. They can recognize the hoodlum. That sixth sense and sixteen police locks on the door get them through the night in Harlem. And they know that young hoodlums are the worst— West, the baby—because they have no mercy.

He closed with a quotation which at the time seemed to me an especial affront.

> And you know, in these days I often think of a line I copied from Robert Ruark's work, "Uhuru" in Swahili, which is "freedom."—"To the wilfully lawless, Uhuru is a license to rob and steal, to kill without punishment and to flout rules of decent human behavior with reckless impunity."

In retrospect, this passage seems more interesting than offensive. It embodies an extreme political view about the Panthers. The prosecution was in essence supporting the position of those minority members of the House Committee on Internal Security who had wanted to report on the Panthers as simple criminals. To them, all the talk of revolution was but a ruse to cover criminality both petty and brutal. It was one basic aim of the prosecution to prove a case of such criminality, if it could be done, and that aim is itself a political fact of some importance.

Both Mr. Fine and I had something to say about young people in the ghetto and the influence of the Panthers or the state upon them. It is fitting that we should have raised the same issue, and reached such diametrically opposed conclusions. Mr. Fine said:

> "[In] the kitchen at the Good Shepherd Center"—Now that's where they have the Breakfast Program for these little kids, little kids that associate with forty-year old criminals, little kids that associate with people smoking marijuana.
>
> Maybe that's too emotional for you—little kids that probably don't have a chance to begin with.

And I said:

> Now, what was the job of the state under these conditions? Was it the job of this state under these conditions to go out to Brownsville and Bedford-Stuyvesant to try to better the conditions? Or was it the job of the state to send an ambitious young man, an ambitious young black man, out there and try to get these young men into jail, behind bars, so there wouldn't be any more Black Panther Party? So there wouldn't be any more protest out in Brownsville and Bedford-Stuyvesant?
>
> I ask you what was the proper job of the state? Was it to lead them on in this rotten scheme, to try to ruin their lives? Or was it to try to help them to realize their ideals?
>
> And when the state does this sort of thing, it says to the Black Panthers and it says to all the black people in America, and it says to you, ladies and gentlemen, if you want your rights too much, we're going to find some way to put you behind bars.

CHARGE TO THE JURY

In his charge, Judge Leff defined the crime of armed robbery, for the purposes of our case, to be forcibly stealing property while armed with a deadly weapon. With many illustrations, he outlined the three familiar elements of a conspiracy to commit such a robbery: the intent, the agreement, and the overt act, which took the conspiracy out of the realm of a mere "thought-crime" and brought it into the real world.

For the weapons crimes, the judge charged that possession of a sawed-off shotgun was a crime per se, regardless of the intent of the person found in possession of it.* Similarly, a defendant's possession of a defaced weapon was presumptive evidence that he had defaced it. The rifle and the knife, however, were not illegal in the absence of proof of an intent to use them for an unlawful purpose, and the judge charged, quite simply, that if the jury found the defendants not guilty of the conspiracy, they should find them not guilty of the unlawful possession of the rifle and the knife, because without the conspiracy there was no unlawful intent.

Even though Alfred Cain was supposed to have been holding it, all three defendants were charged with the possession of the shotgun under a New York statute which provides, "The presence in an automobile of any . . . firearm is presumptive evidence of its possession by all persons occupying such automobile at the time such . . . weapon is found."† It was thus possible for all to be found guilty of the shotgun charge, even if the conspiracy charge was dismissed.

Jerome West's account of the shotgun, if it was believed by the jury, would rebut the presumption, as the judge charged.

The defendants state they didn't know it was there. They have a right to explain their ignorance of the existence of the

* Although the offense is much less serious, a similar rule was applied to the canister of red-pepper spray.
† This law contains an exception for the case where the weapon is actually in the physical possession of one of the occupants of the car; then it is imputed to the one individual.

sawed-off shotgun in the car. And it is then a question of fact
for you as a jury to determine whether the jury will believe
and accept the explanation.

If the explanation is accepted, then the guilt of the defendants cannot be established under this count.

I felt that this charge did not cover the case. It was irrelevant, I thought, whether or not the defendants knew the
shotgun was in the car *if the police put it there.* I later made
a request to charge of the judge.

It seems to me there is a further contention if they knew it
was there—if it was planted by Wilbert Thomas—it would
still be a defense, and the presumption is rebutted. In other
words, planting is a defense per se, and it is not solely the fact
that the defendants didn't know it was there. . . . The fact
they didn't know it was there is not of the essence. The essence [is that] they didn't know it was there and/or it was
planted by the State.

THE COURT. I am not going to so charge.

There was no law in New York State at the time requiring
such a charge, but as events were to show, state law was
inadequate on this point.

The most difficult part of the judge's charge revolved
around entrapment. That was an affirmative defense; we
had the burden of proving to the satisfaction of the jury
that the defendants had been entrapped.

In order for the defense of entrapment to succeed as to a
particular defendant, in relation to a particular crime charged,
it is necessary for the defendant to establish by a preponder-
ance of the evidence—I will point this out to you later—two
elements:

First, that Police Officer Thomas actually induced or
actively encouraged that defendant to engage in the pro-
scribed (which means "prohibited") conduct, seeking to
obtain evidence against that defendant for the purpose of a
criminal prosecution; and, second, that the methods used to
obtain such evidence were such as to create a substantia

risk that the offense would be committed by a defendant not otherwise disposed to commit it.

If that particular defendant were disposed to commit that particular crime, even without the activity or inducement of Patrolman Thomas, the defense of entrapment must fail as to that defendant in relation to the crime.

The jury came out from time to time with requests for rereading of testimony and restatements of charges. It was plain that a squabble was going on over entrapment, because the charge on that defense was rephrased several times for the jury.

Because it is not the jury's function to consider punishment, the judge did not tell them that the crime of possessing a loaded sawed-off shotgun carried a maximum penalty of seven years, while the conspiracy carried a maximum of four years. The jury surely thought that the conspiracy charge was the most serious in the case, once attempted murder was dismissed, and in fact a newspaper reporter later quoted one of the jurors saying that the jury had "adjusted" their verdict for what they thought was the "least sentence."

The extreme seriousness of the firearms count, viewed in retrospect, raises the question why the prosecution dragged in the conspiracy case at all. To hear Thomas tell it, the police had a solid case for the firearms charge on the shotgun alone. Once that crime had been committed, there was no reason, other than a political one, to enter further into any conspiracy. The anomaly in the degree of the offenses in this case emphasizes a home truth about conspiracy cases. Prosecutors often say that conspiracy is a crime like any other and that such cases are not brought for political reasons. But once an undercover agent has detected a concrete act like possession of a sawed-off shotgun, there is no excuse for the police to continue his work against the same people, unless they want to fit the defendants into some political design. Virtually any conspiracy case, detected by undercover work, which involves an overt act that is itself a serious crime must by necessity be a political case; if it were not, the arrest would be made for the overt act (here, possession of a sawed-off shotgun) and not for the conspiracy.

VERDICT

At the end of four days of deliberation, on Saturday night, September 26, 1970, the jury filed back into the dim-lit courtroom and the defendants and lawyers stood up to hear the verdicts. All four defendants were found not guilty of the conspiracy charge and of unlawful possession of the rifle and the knife. All were found guilty of possessing a loaded sawed-off shotgun, and Alfred Cain of defacing it; Alfred Cain and Ricardo De Leon were found guilty of possessing the canister of spray—all purely possessory crimes, requiring no criminal intent. Characteristically, De Leon began to denounce the jury, and Cain sat down with his back to them and began to read the Black Panther newspaper—whether to show his contempt or because he could not express his angry feelings, I could not tell.

In accordance with the curious custom, the clerk began, immediately after the verdict, to take the pedigree—background and record—of the defendants. When he was asked his occupation, Alfred Cain at first said he had been in the Tombs for thirteen months, and when he understood that his occupation before his arrest was meant, he put his face up defiantly and replied, "Revolutionary."

SENTENCE

Modern sentencing practice decrees that the punishment should fit the man rather than the crime, and in many cases that means that defendants are given long sentences if they have long criminal records. Whatever the validity of that approach as a matter of theory, it is brutally distorted by the fact that black and poor people tend to have criminal records where white middle-class people do not.

Because Jerome West had a previous felony conviction, we expected a jail term for him, and on the sentencing day, more than a month later, Judge Leff sentenced him to an indefinite term up to three years.

In De Leon's case, we were all braced for the worst. He had a long record, and his fracas with the court officers during the first trial had not endeared him to the judges. He told Elliot Taikeff that the Black Panther Party had rehabilitated him, and I am convinced that for him that was indeed the truth. While he himself and Alfred Cain saw him as a stomp-down *Lumpen,* judges and other public officials would never be able to see his open and physical defiance of jailers and police as anything but antisocial. Judge Leff said:

> I would like to say it seems to me that society requires the administration of criminal justice to incarcerate vicious, dangerous criminals. I think that the characterization of such [persons] for trial as "political persons" is inappropriate. This defendant hasn't had any behavior in the course of his adult life to warrant his receiving any consideration from me. The public at large is benefitted by having him incarcerated.
>
> I sentence this defendant to a term of imprisonment not to exceed seven years.

That was the maximum penalty the law allowed for the crime of possessing a loaded firearm, and I learned from my reaction to De Leon's sentence that professionalism had, over the years, deadened my emotions. As a man, I knew that seven years was too much for the crime of which De Leon had been convicted, but as a lawyer, I knew that his past had made any other result unlikely. I had no words of comment. The law simply should never have provided for such an enormous maximum penalty, based on mere presence in an automobile where a weapon was found.

Joseph François had kindly written a letter to the judge praising Alfred Cain's character and work in the community. On his sentencing day, Alfred Cain and I stood up before Judge Leff and heard the sentence of five years' probation. After more than a year in jail and two big trials, Alfred Cain finally walked away from the bar and down the aisle of the courtroom. Alfred Cain, Sr., threw his arms around his son, who did not respond, but stood, still frozen in ideological anger, saying that they would have to stop going to these bourgeois courts for justice. If he was thinking of his friend De Leon while he said that, I saw the point.

9

THE AFTERMATH

THE JURY'S DELIBERATIONS

Shortly after the trial, Elliot Taikeff and I had lunch with the two young white bankers who had sat on the jury. We came away with some ill-connected thoughts about the jury as a whole. Still later, we had drinks with nine of the twelve jurors, and I listened to the babble of conversation, trying to get a consensus, as they might have done themselves. I perhaps heard most from the former policeman, because I was sitting next to him. I came away with only sparse recollections to write down. Finally, I sat down with the forelady, a white writer of children's stories, and tried to record her considered thoughts about the deliberations.

The charge of attempted murder, reduced by the judge to one of reckless endangerment, had presented the least trouble. The forelady said:

> As I recall, we were very much influenced by the fact that the charge had been so very much reduced. When we started we had been told we were going to be considering attempted murder, and we wind up with something called reckless endangerment. We began to think—I did, and I think a lot of others did—Well, if they can dilute this accusation that much, there can't be an awful lot to it.
>
> The men analyzed it factually. They played soldier and pantomimed bringing guns up to the window of a car. . . .

I must say, women jurors did not attend that in any great detail—we're not as inclined to play with guns.

There were sort of variables in Halikias's testimony. It got to be a question of his right shoulder, and then the reporter quoting an earlier opinion from Halikias. We just felt there was nothing there that we could settle on for intent or reckless endangerment.

The young Wall Streeters told us that the former policeman's views were pivotal for this charge, as for others. After the jury had initially concluded that the story did not seem to hang together, they turned naturally to the ex-policeman, to ask him what he thought about it. As he put it to me, much later, "Policemen often try to make themselves out heroes, but that story was just not believable." The defense attorneys' sense about this man, that he had his reservations about the police life and that he could be relied on to tell the truth about it, was borne out.

But right as we were about the black man, we were dead wrong about the self-educated white workingman. We learned that he himself had done some time in jail, apparently surrounded by black prisoners, and he had something bordering on hatred for them. He was one of two jurors who held out until near the very end for conviction on the conspiracy charge. The forelady described the jury's deliberations on this question.

The jury as a whole swung back and forth the first couple of days, just trying to decide if there was a conspiracy. My personal feeling is that there may have been some jurors who were never convinced that there was a conspiracy, but others did feel that what was testified to sounded like a conspiracy, as the judge defined it to us. And our terrible chore was sorting out whether it was entrapment. And that was what the whole last two days was about. We had at least two jurors who were, almost to the end, anxious to convict on every single count, and they felt that everything Wilbert Thomas did was proper police procedure.

We had the written reports in our possession and we finally combed them, day by day, and kept almost a score of Wilbert Thomas's acts that he himself reported in his reports. We took notes, and then went back and weighed his own reports of his doings, in terms of the entrapment defense. It was as though you had a fulcrum of some sort; on one side was proper police work, and on the other was exceeding the bounds. You may recall, we went back and had that entrapment defense read to us, I think it was four or five times.

Finally, one of the jurors had to take notes [on the charge], because we'd get back into the jury room and start again on those written reports and start quibbling over what was entrapment.

The basic question in our minds was one of initiative. The arguments in the deliberations would be, would the three defendants have put themselves together to work on this plan, without the consistent urging by Thomas?

She showed me a small sheaf of handwritten notes summarizing and commenting on each of Wilbert Thomas's reports after July 30, 1969, made by her in the effort to bring the jury together for a decision. Each report up through August 8 was labeled "inconclusive," as to both the conspiracy and the defense of entrapment. The reports for August 8 and August 11, in which Thomas reported that De Leon told him about a plan, did contain "proof that the plan existed."

Concerning the August 13 report, because Thomas went seeking De Leon and Cain, the forelady noted, "First clear Thomas initiative *re* plan." About the conversation in which Thomas recorded Alfred Cain as talking of bigger jobs and people he could trust, she commented, "A curious assertion, three days before the conspiracy."

For the report of August 14, the forelady noted that before Cain, De Leon, and Thomas began their conversation in the park, "Wilbert Thomas invited or encouraged conspiracy talk." After a note on the meeting in the park, she wrote:

General talk of other jobs. Wilbert Thomas suggested casing the job.

Suggested that he draw a map.

If this [plan] self-sufficient without Wilbert Thomas, this not necessary.

And after a note on the trip to the Harlem hotel:

De Leon took an active role in planning.

First mention of West.

Concerning August 15, she told me:

There was some time spent comparing Wilbert Thomas's version of the phone conversation, of which we had the transcript. I remember the discussion was about whether De Leon was taking the initiative, or Thomas was.

Concerning the night spent at Deborah Green's, she wrote in her notes:

Wilbert Thomas had to make preparations for the morning job.

Encouragement?

She commented to me at last:

One thing that did not really come up was any moral attitude on the part of the jurors in their conversations about under-cover work. We all seemed to accept that as a necessity. There was no disapproval or scorn that I recall for this police officer having been ordered to infiltrate the Black Panther Party. We felt it was an individual who was not a skilled police operative. That was what our task was—to measure his performance.

A key member of the jury was a former police officer, whose comments were of immense value to all of us, in connection with proper police procedure, in trying to understand this—to us, very complicated—entrapment defense. I can remember this former policeman saying, right off the top of his head, "Well, Thomas did not have adequate training."

He had attended the Police Academy less than a month, or something, and was pulled out for this assignment. That had quite an effect on me.

It is ironical that the ex-policeman should have made just that comment, because Thomas's lack of police background was entirely deliberate on the part of his superiors; it was part of his cover. It was supposed to make him more credible, not less. In fact, as events will show, inexperience may explain his actions in some small part, but it cannot completely account for them.

One of the young bankers told me a similar story of notes he had made in the attempt to analyze Wilbert Thomas's testimony. I was pleased, of course, that our impudence in putting Thomas's reports into evidence had paid off, but I was astonished at the extraordinarily technical approach the jury had taken. Lawyers customarily think of juries as a little more emotional than they in their approach to a case, and this analysis of the reports seemed to me positively dry. Thomas McCreary was later to say, "You mean our evidence about Wilbert and the guns didn't make any difference?"

His testimony did make a difference, I am sure, by creating an atmosphere in which it was possible to take the entrapment defense seriously. The long technical analysis came about, apparently, because of the conflict within the jury. The burden of proving entrapment was on the defense, and therefore everyone on the jury had to be persuaded of the defense if it was to succeed. The easiest way to persuade those who were against the defendants was to use evidence to which they could have no objection: the police reports. If they could be convinced from police evidence that there was too much police involvement, then it would become nearly impossible for them to refuse to accept the defense. The remarkable thing is that the experiment worked: the holdouts apparently were persuaded by the analysis of that evidence. The very technical analysis of the entrapment defense was carried out, then, not so much out of personal detachment as in the search for irrefutable logic to convince the holdouts.

Every juror Elliot Taikeff and I talked to, no matter what his views about the defendants, told us how annoyed all the jurors had been by the passage in the indictment alleging that the robbery was to be committed to aid the Black Panther Party. As the forelady explained:

> It was implicit in our thinking that that was there for a [political] purpose. We thought that we could go home, if we had to be satisfied that the evidence supported that part of the indictment.
>
> One time we went back into the courtroom. We had been told not to let our questions indicate the direction of our thinking, and we went through exotic editing of the question that had to do with reading the opening statement of the grand jury indictment—did we have to settle our minds on each and every allegation in there?—and I think Judge Leff figured out what we were on to. We felt that if the indictment [had to say] they were going to hold up this hotel to raise funds for the party, we were going to throw the whole case out.

The deliberations on the weapons charges could not have been the most interesting part of the jury's work, but they were ultimately the most important, because all the defendants were convicted on one or more of the weapons counts. The forelady recalled the law and some of the reasoning.

> It seems to me it's not unlawful to get in a car with a rifle in it. I don't think we took the knife thing seriously, and the spray—I know I had seen a spray just like it at my corner drugstore for a dollar ninety-five on a display card—none of us took that seriously.
>
> I think when we got to the shotgun charge, which we'd touch on and then we'd get away from and onto this entrapment problem, we somehow believed, or some of us did— which led us to convict on that charge—the testimony about

taking shotgun shells out of Cain's pockets. I guess we felt that even if we felt the police were fabricating some of their testimony, or exaggerating it, we just couldn't believe they would get into that much detail of made-up testimony.

I was concerned whether the origin of the gun had made any difference, because I had made a request to the judge to charge the jury that it was a defense to the crime of possession if the gun came from the police, and the judge had refused. The forelady had this to say:

> I think we did talk about the testimony about somebody having the gun in his coat, but before that, where they bought it, before it was in the car—I don't think that made any difference, because I don't recall it coming up in the deliberations. We just focused on the question in our minds. Was the shotgun in the car? We said it was.

There does not seem to have been any consensus about this. One of the black jurors told me repeatedly that she had been concerned about where the gun came from, but she thought they did not reach the issue because it seemed irrelevant. One of the two young white bankers disagreed; he said they would have considered the fact if they had believed the gun came from the police. The other, who had sat right next to him during the trial, disagreed in his turn. He later wrote down his thoughts.

> . . . in our confusion, we never considered the possibility that the defendants knew that the shotgun was in the car, but that Thomas had placed it there. If entrapment was sustained and the above was demonstrated, I now believe that they could not and should not have been found guilty of possession. The nature of Patrolman Thomas's written reports, and his refusal to testify as to the manner in which De Leon was to have carried the rifle and the shotgun to the car, created in my mind a reasonable doubt that this in fact was the actual portrayal of events. However, in my confusion as to the charge regarding the possession of concealed weapons, I ignored this doubt.

These conflicts among the jurors make it apparent, I think, that the jury was confused about defenses to the charge of possessing a weapon, and that they could not focus on the origin of the gun as an element in the case.

The man just quoted also said later, with regret, that he had "compromised" on the conviction of Cain for defacing the shotgun, when he did not in fact believe that the gun was in Cain's hands.* It is plain from his words, as well as from those of some of the other jurors, that not everyone was able to be as detached about the case as the forelady. One of the black jurors later told a news reporter that he "figured the Panthers were framed."

One of the great political questions about juries, of course, is the influence of race on their deliberations. One unexpected by-product of a racially mixed jury seems to be that it leads to good race relations among the jurors. One of the bankers remarked admiringly that the character and dynamics of the discussion was in no way different from corporation merger negotiations he had attended. And months later, one of the black jurors said teasingly to the white man from Alabama, speaking of Wilbert Thomas, "He's a good nigger, Bob, but he's a house nigger." The forelady recalled:

> Color meant nothing and I felt very privileged to be able to get acquainted with people I might not otherwise meet.
>
> The question of approaching it from the point of view of your own color was discussed and everyone promptly said "No," and the one aspect of it where the white people were aware of their color, was recalling Conrad Lynn's summation where he implored us not to try to imagine what we would do in the same situation, but to make our imaginations leap into a whole other world—the world that these defendants came from. The white jurors admitted that was very hard to do—to cast your mind into that world.

* It is actually a difficult question of law whether Cain could be convicted of defacement if the gun were in the car and its possession were imputed to him by presumption.

On the matter of the women's attitude. It is true that one of the women was afraid of the defendants. She feared what might happen, years later, that a defendant might look her up and do her harm. She was truly afraid. You know whom she was afraid of? Cain. I talked to her. I pointed out the glasses frames he was wearing, they were so large and that gold—she felt he was giving her the evil eye throughout the whole trial. And she would not discuss the case, but she'd say, "Oh, he's looking at me again." I kept nudging her to realize it was just the light off his glasses.

In connection with the recorded phone conversation, and some of the raw language—it might have been shocking to white jurors, and a black juror pointed out that this was "ghetto talk." A lot of black men with no job or any prospect of one might well just be, as this juror said, "all mouth," and it was not very meaningful, and not to be taken very seriously.

I came away from the interviews with jurors impressed, on the whole, with the intense seriousness the jury had brought to their task. There was simply no comparison between the deliberateness of their decision and the decision of the three judges in the first Cain case, so long before.

ALFRED CAIN, JR.

Later, when Alfred Cain, Jr., talked about the case, he had less to say about the facts than about the jury and the system of justice. He left it to the rest of us to try to arrive at a consistent account of the facts; even the defense summations had not quite been able to do that. In his summation, Elliot Taikeff had attributed the defendants' intent in getting into the car to make the trip to Harlem to a "combination of reasons," including "to buy some marijuana." But the combination must have involved something more than that. The weapon or weapons might have been represented as intended for sale, as Jerome West testified, but the diagram of the hotel could not be explained that way. That diagram, such a convincing artifact of entrapment, was also puzzling as an index of the defendants' motives. Despite the diagram, however, I am convinced that the defendants had no clear plan to commit the robbery with Wilbert Thomas. They were unprepared, hesitant; they were suspicious of Thomas. Most important, as I began to realize toward the close of the case: if all Thomas's stories were true, it was most improbable that the Bureau of Special Services would set up a situation where an arrest would be made of the defendants when they were armed and on the move, especially when they could as easily have been arrested in their beds, after the shotgun had been displayed to Thomas on August 15. It seemed more reasonable to assume that the shotgun was concealed, as the defendants said it was. The only explanation which seems to fit all the facts is that some or all of the defendants were trying to find out the truth about Wilbert Thomas, and see what he would do, without being totally opposed to a robbery at some future time if he proved to be what he pretended to be. Jerome West suggested as much in a phrase he used in the first trial: "I didn't think anything was going to jump off that morning." And in their telephone conversation of August 15 (see Appendix A) De Leon told Thomas, "Hey, relate to the bitch quick, because she living up there, we're going to be around there to deal with the situation," an admonition which does not seem to contemplate a robbery the very next day.

If my suggestion of the "combination of reasons" is anything approaching the correct one, the defendants were extraordinarily careless to have got in the car at all, once they saw the rifle. On this point, Alfred Cain said:

> I just didn't think the rifle was enough. Actually, I did make a mistake, because I hadn't even decided to go with him [Thomas] until the night before we left. And I said, right

on; we had been in situations before where the pigs had tried to set us up. See, we were of the opinion that the only time they would make a move like that would be to have us doing something where they would have us in a position where if they couldn't kill us, understand, they would have according to their definition enough evidence against us to put us away for a long period of time. But it had got to the point that we realized that it's necessary to begin to take procedures to put some kind of protection on yourself as you are organizing the people. It's necessary to find out exactly who are the infiltrators to expose them and put them out of the party. This is what we were working on, because at one time one of my functions had been to deal with security in Brooklyn.

His justification was to say, "I found out, too." But if he is right, he had the foolhardiness of the desperate, and he totally underestimated the police.

In the last analysis, a definitive answer to the question of the defendants' motives is not so necessary as it might otherwise have been, because the elements of provocation which went into the case were so strong that it was clear that whatever elements of a real plot there may have been were gathered together and pushed by Thomas.

Alfred Cain's comments on the trial process are a good deal more explicit.

ALFRED CAIN, JR.:

We realized that our particular situation was not an isolated incident, but it's just another part of the aggression that's committed against black people. We didn't expect to receive a fair trial, because we had been in the Tombs for about ten months when the first trial began, and we had spoken to a lot of brothers and realized the practices that the DA uses.

You know, pigs would come in, sit down, and figure out

what was the highest crime they could charge a brother for, and then what they would try to do is get the brother to take a plea to a lesser degree in order to save the state a trial. This is what happened with our case, and this is what happened in general in the Tombs.

When we went into the trial, we didn't expect to get justice. Look at the fact of the way the indictment was drawn up—being that the state had a weak case, what they were trying to do was give the jury some means to compromise by putting up fourteen charges against us—which is eventually what happened.

The tactics that John Fine used, the tactics of trying to create paranoia in the minds of the jury by saying that we were receiving aid from the People's Republic of China, and saying we were supposed to be cop killers; other statements of Wilbert Thomas to the effect that we were supposed to be subversive-looking people. We weren't surprised at these tactics, because we realize the nature of the system. The courts' function all during the time that this country has been developing has been to oppress black people. When those punks wrote the Constitution and the Declaration of Independence they were selling black people for molasses.

The pigs kept saying, this is not a political trial, this is a criminal case, and we were indicted for being members of the Black Panther Party, which in itself makes a political trial. If it was only a criminal trial, then the fact that we were members of the Black Panther Party had nothing to do with the charges at all. This was to create that paranoia in the minds of the people.

One of the things that did surprise us was that you did have people on the jury who were obviously members of the Establishment who did see contradictions. I remember some white dude that got up said that he believed the police was arresting for laws that weren't even on the books. This was a dude who had money—I think he was in investment banking. Also some dude who had worked for United Fruit down in Ecuador, he got up and said that he believed that the police were out to destroy the party, to kill and jail members of the Black Panther Party as quickly as possible. We felt that this was very strange, because we remembered that people in this country are among the most naive in the world, subjected to the most intense programming by the media.

We expected because there were the black people, the second jury would be more attuned to the tactics that are used against poor black people, Spanish people, and against poor white people by the state. At the same time, we realized that this was not truly a jury of our peers because some of these people still suffer under an illusion that they are middle class. They feel as though they have a certain degree of security within the society and therefore it's to their interest to maintain the values of this society, and if the state arrests us, being that the state is the paragon of this society, therefore we must have done something. If you're charged with fourteen counts, charged with attempted murder of pigs, charged with attempt to commit armed robberies, these people have been programmed to acknowledge the idea that we must have done something. We think that the verdict itself, which was very contradictory, bears that out. It's because of the fact that we were hooked up the way we were, with fifty thousand dollars bail.

———

I have thought a lot about these words since the time that Alfred Cain said them and I transcribed them. Considering the jury as people, it is plain that Cain has underestimated them, even though he recognized their surprising freedom from class doctrine. It is true, nevertheless, that white people and even black middle-class people do retain reflexes of race and class that they cannot control, and that these do affect their decisions. They have specialized ex-

pectations about officials, and also about defendants, which
are impossible for them to ignore.

The essence of what Cain has said, however, is that the
problem is not so much with the jury as it is with the bail
system, the way charges are drawn, the way the trial is
conducted, the laws themselves and the way they are given
to the jury. That statement is true; the jury, however well
chosen, does not have the freedom that it could to make a
fair decision.

INTERVIEW WITH WILBERT THOMAS

It goes without saying that Wilbert Thomas does not talk
about the "New Dunston Hotel" case, as he calls it; he
studiedly refrains from doing so. He did keep an appointment in January 1971 with a woman reporter from Community News Service, Norma Sue Woodstone. Mrs. Woodstone is a straight, sympathetic interviewer, and Community News Service is a venture, partly funded with Ford
Foundation money, intended to help fill the national gap
in minority news. I have tried to report everything as she
told it to me.

Mrs. Woodstone met in a Greenwhich Village restaurant
with Wilbert Thomas, perfectly groomed in a sport coat, a
pink shirt, and a wide tie. She had called him at his office,
the Bureau of Special Services; he said that the call had
been recorded and his superiors had advised him not to
come. He had come, nevertheless, he said, because he was
"curious" about her and about Community News Service.
She showed him a folder of some of the work of her office—
news releases and the like—and he said he was familiar
with the information because part of his job was to read
community newspapers, such as the *Manhattan Tribune*
and the *New York Courier*. This would have been part of
the standard "overt" intelligence work of the political po-

lice, and it is likely that it was indeed part of his job. They walked up to her office, some blocks away, Thomas looked it over, and they returned to the restaurant.

Mrs. Woodstone asked Thomas what he was going to do for BOSS, now that he had "blown his cover" by testifying in the conspiracy case. He said, in the first place, that the case was not over; there were "several more men" who had got out on bail in the conspiracy case, whom he still had to deal with. This was apparently a reference, cloaked in obscure language, to the indictment against Fat Man (not several more men), then still pending. Thomas sounded a recurrent theme of his interview—loneliness. He said dramatically that he had been "all alone on the case." It bothered him that Alfred Cain was out on the streets on probation.

Mrs. Woodstone suggested that they might write a book together about his life as an agent (presumably the obverse of this book). Thomas was interested, although he did not see how he could do it while he was working for the Police Department. He suggested some titles—each of which again emphasized his aloneness. He said that he could sell "a million dollars worth of information"—the FBI and the Internal Revenue Service had contacted him. "There is such a thing as the CIA, too, you know," he added. He talked of doubling his income if he became a lawyer. He said he thought he could have done a better job on his conspiracy case than the prosecution. He knew more about it than "the judge, the defendants, the defense, and the jury." He told Mrs. Woodstone that one had to know how to handle all of them as a lawyer, and he could do it. He would be able to be a good lawyer because he could "snow everybody else while not losing control of things."

Mrs. Woodstone went on:

We were talking about the car he supplied to the robbery. I was asking him, wasn't he the criminal? He just went sideways. He always went sideways into some little personal things. He said that he was a race driver and a speed demon.

Thomas expanded on the theme implied by this. He said, "When the situation requires you to drink well, you drink well, to smoke, you smoke well, and, well, anything else you have to do." He said that he had the very best of stereo tape decks and a big record collection. He sang along in "a nice alto voice" with some of the records playing on the jukebox in the bar. "Particularly, there was a song about loneliness where he really knew everything—he sang it and did a whole bit."

> Originally when we were having beers, some woman waitress was serving us. And then this guy—sort of faggy—came up for the food orders. Right away Thomas's whole personality seemed to change—he wasn't the tough little street kid any more. . . . They started this little conversation about their accents—the waiter had this foreign accent. They started talking, and the waiter said he was a Creole. Thomas started talking to him about his accent, and then, at that point, that was when Thomas started saying he was Dutch or of Dutch descent. Somehow he was trying to say, "We have something in common."

Wilbert Thomas, it will be remembered, is from South Carolina.

Relations with women came up repeatedly in the conversation, more frequently, indeed, than any other subject. This is in harmony with what we already know about Thomas's constant talk of women from Fat Man, who told us of Thomas's boasting, and from Fat Man's and Thomas McCreary's recollections that Thomas said he had a source of guns who was a woman.

During the conversation, Thomas remarked several times that he preferred the company of women to that of men; he said he had twelve intimate friends, and they were all women.

He opened up this fat wallet with a lot of money and credit cards and pictures and stuff like that in it, and started flipping up pictures of these girlfriends. He identified nobody by name, but mostly by what they looked like, or where they lived. Here was his black girlfriend, and here was the girl-friend who was mixed—either Mexican-Jewish-black or Mexican-Jewish-Indian. And he has another girlfriend who lives in New Jersey. He was flipping these things across the table at me.

He said—this is not a direct quote—that he thought I would enjoy his friends and they would enjoy me. . . . There was going to be this party that Friday night that I was sup-posed to come to. He was supposed to call me about that. . . .

Oh, he started putting together that we had all these nice contacts in the community that we were getting our stories from, that I would be an effective member of his department and that they had a lot of trouble recruiting women, until he got there and he had recruited a lot of woman members in the [bureau] when no one else could.

This kind of thing led naturally to some banter, which took an odd turn.

I've this little pen that says "Property of U.S. Government" on it—that's one of my favorite pens—a little ball-point pen. I had it out on top of the legal pad that he wasn't letting me write notes on, and he picked it up and saw the "U.S. Govern-ment," and said that since I had taken the pen, I had stolen it. But if he took the pen from me, it wouldn't be punishable by the law because he is the law, so he could get me on some kind of theft rap. . . . At that point, he started naming dif-ferent charges and years. We went through things like "class-something felony," and he would tell me how many years that would be. He was doing this whole little run-down to show me how well-educated he was in the law. And then later on I had this gold watch that I wear around my neck, and I think I was kidding him that I didn't need to take notes because it was a tape recorder and I was getting all of this down anyway. And he said if it was, and he went and busted it, then I could get punished for having tried to

tape-record him when he specifically forbade me to do it
in the first place. Then he kept doing this number . . . that
he could put so many charges up against me that the judge
would drop some of them but not all of them, and I'd be gotten on some little thing. . . .

He used the word that I could be "gotten to," and he suggested that he could go to my family or my job. And I said
I work for myself and he said, "This makes me re-evaluate."

He had written on her pad with her pen, apparently un-
awares, "How can I identify myself with your faults?" She
read this upside down and wrote, also upside down, "I have
none." He was startled and interested by the trick.

Mrs. Woodstone finally asked Thomas if he considered
himself a hostile person, and he replied that he had to be, in
his job.

I said that I had just had my traumatic birthday, and that
anybody who knows women as well as he is supposed to
know them should know that I was talking about I was
thirty, but he didn't and couldn't guess how old I was. And
at the same time I couldn't guess how old he was. I said that
he looked very young, somehow, but he backed off and suggested that he was older than twenty-eight. He had decided
from my phone conversation that I was a radical, and he
came because he was curious. And it wouldn't have mattered
if I was and I was laying there and waiting for him with ten
guys, because "I would have shot them." . . . He was wearing
a gun when he came.

For a few days after the meeting, a white man reading a
newspaper was stationed in the building which housed
Community News Service, apparently doing surveillance.
The fact implied that Wilbert Thomas might have conned
his superiors somewhat about the purpose and results of
his meeting. He had apparently represented in some way
that he had learned that the news service was a radical organization, which might repay investigation. In the months
following the interview, Mrs. Woodstone was occasionally
bothered by calls purporting to be from the FBI.

PART THREE

HISTORY, THE LAW, AND THE PEOPLE

An *agent provocateur* is a police agent who is introduced into any political organization with instructions to foment discontent against a government, or to fake a case in order to give his employers the right to act against the organization in question.

VICTOR KALEDIN, COLONEL,
IMPERIAL RUSSIAN MILITARY INTELLIGENCE

The secret agent, in order to justify his salary, naturally tends to invite confidences by uttering with feigned violence his grievances against the regime, and the temptation is great to build up a complete conspiracy in order to gain later the merit of having discovered it.

JEAN GALTIER-BOISSIÈRE,
Mysteries of the French Secret Police

10

STATE AND REVOLUTION:
POLITICAL PROVOCATION IN EUROPE
AND THE UNITED STATES

Wilbert Thomas was but the latest (surely not the last) figure in a long and disreputable history. Provocation to crime by the government is not rare in history, although until recent years it seems to have occurred infrequently in this country, at least in connection with crimes of violence or for purely political purposes. There is confusion about the term *agent provocateur*, because some writers have used the notion interchangeably with that of "infiltrator." Infiltration does present legal problems of its own when it is used against a political organization, by interfering with the privacy of the members, and when it is discovered or suspected, by putting a damper on political agitation. It is a widely accepted view that every infiltrator tends in addition to become a *provocateur*, but as we shall see, the accuracy of that prediction depends on the political pressures on the infiltrator. In any case, even if there is such a tendency, it is still necessary to decide whether a given informer has yielded to the temptation or not, that is, whether he is a *provocateur* or whether those he has accused would have completed the crime without his intervention.

At the outset, provocative action by the government presents a problem in politics, posed neatly by the two passages quoted as epigraph to Part Three. That problem is whether provocative action typically originates at the top, from rulers or administrators and as an instrument of policy, or as a result of overzealousness on the part of the agent, without (or rather, regardless of) explicit directions from above.

It is not unusual to find historians, by implication, entertaining both views, and in fact the two are not directly contradictory. It is possible for the authorities to lay out the plan for their agent, and it is also possible that the conspiracy reported by the agent may simply fit into an existing policy. The higher authorities may have a theory about their political enemies which they wish to prove, and the story of the agent may fit that theory.

In times of political paranoia, the authorities may even accept the ravings of a madman as gospel. It is an index of the strength of the official fear today of black militants that information from a certified madman, Shaun Dubonnet, was used against the Black Panthers. Partly as a result of his testimony, warrants were obtained from magistrates, and several Panthers were actually indicted. Dubonnet's constantly shifting stories of bomb plots and other violence were accepted as reliable, presumably because they must have appeared to the police to be inherently probable—or because the police supposed that the stories would appear probable to others.

Under such conditions of official fear and expectation of violence, it is difficult to make a choice between the two theories of the source of provocative action. The agent may act as part of a program directed from above, or he may simply recognize the need of his superiors to have their theories fulfilled. It may in fact be nearly impossible for an informer or infiltrator to maintain his position as an informer without producing some sort of plot, because his superiors are not ready to believe that there is no plot. The point here, finally, is that whichever view you take, the actions of a *provocateur* MUST ultimately be rooted in policy; even if he acts on his own, his zeal must be motivated by the conviction that he is telling his superiors what they want to hear, and that his story will be accepted for prosecution because his superiors find it believable or expedient to accept it—that is, because it harmonizes with policy.

Much of this will probably seem quite exotic both to citizens and to many policemen in the United States, who will be at a loss to imagine a policy to which provocation could be well suited. The history of old cases in other countries and recent cases here, however, gives an astonishingly uniform picture of the political reasons for provocation, and shows a repeated pattern of provocative practices. The political reasons for the increasing tide of domstic cases, including the New Dunston Hotel prosecution, are really very difficult to conceive and understand except in the light of history.

In the nature of secret political infiltration, it is impossible to know when official provocation was first used as a political tool. It has been said by an expert on the imperial Russian political police, the Okhrana, that the modern type of *provocateur* originated with that organization,[1] but it is clear that the practice was fully developed long before there was an Okhrana.

My working theory is that provocation was originally a tool of international espionage, brought over into domestic politics. Time out of mind, international incidents have been faked for the purpose of justifying aggression. For example, during the earliest period of domestic political provocation, under Napoleon Bonaparte, a Jacobin adventurer named Mehée escaped to England. In 1803, with the connivance of Napoleon's secret police, he organized a supposed Jacobin-Royalist alliance of *émigrés* against Bonaparte, and incidentally received some 192,000 francs from the British government to finance the conspiracy.[2] In this sort of scheme, the domestic and international (not to speak of personal financial) aspects are dovetailed. Napoleon's police used the existence of the conspiracy to rally support for the emperor at home, as well as to intensify hostility against England.

This sort of intrigue has never been rare in international relations. Vladimir Dedijer tells his favorite *provocateur* story, about a British agent who, posing as an Irish militant, led the Fenians in a disastrous invasion of Canada in 1870;[3] this provocation too was basically an exercise in foreign intrigue. The ethics and law of domestic politics, which are strictly codified in the Anglo-American system as rules of due process of law and have some claims even under an autocratic regime, have never been much applied in international politics. There are, of course, no effective tribunals to expose international fraud. Apart from the freedom from legal and ethical strictures, the reason for the success of such tricks perhaps lies in the nature of xenophobia: citizens are unable to predict what wild plots might emanate from foreigners, although they are better able to judge the credibility of charges against their own people. Moreover, they are not easily incensed by what is done abroad and to foreigners. It is still true up to the present time that the most brazen provocations are executed by international spies; and even in domestic police work, the boldest provocations commonly have an aspect of foreign subversion.

International provocation is generally an aspect of propaganda, and as such it is so common that a jargon has grown up around it. Paul Blackstock, who has studied the problem, tells us that documents or incidents which are made to appear to emanate from the "enemy" are called "black" propaganda, while such information emanating from its true source is called "white" propaganda.[4] The purpose of black propaganda is outright provocation. Perhaps the most famous of black-propaganda documents is the *Protocols of the Wise Men of Zion,* which purports to be the record of a Jewish plot to control the world.[5] Its provenance has been traced to the Paris office of the Russian Okhrana, and to its chief in the 1890s, Ratchkovsky, a man peculiarly notorious for his provocations, who produced it to feed the flames of reaction and anti-Semitism, especially in the pogroms of Russia.

Such black propaganda as the *Protocols of the Wise Men of Zion* brings out in high relief one of the characteristics of political provocation: while provocation may be desirable as a way of eliminating potential enemies, its impact on people friendly or neutral to the government is equally if not more important. Provocation is, in one of its chief aspects, simply propaganda—a means of manipulating opinion.

Cases of pure forgery like the *Protocols* raise the question why governments or agents who wish to "fake a case" against their political enemies—to use Colonel Kaledin's phrase as quoted in the epigraph to Part Three—would ever bother with anything so dangerous as infiltration and provocative action. Why not just manufacture the evidence and be done with it? The most obvious reason has already been mentioned: the provocation may originate with the infiltrator rather than his superiors, and thus may appear genuine even to them. Moreover, the use of provocation is commonly blended with simple surveillance, because the authorities do want to know who their real political enemies are. There is in most provocation situations an interplay between a real revolutionary impulse and a provocation to put it into action. The authorities do not, except in the rarest of cases (such as the politics of anti-Semitism in imperial Russia), want to fake a case against people who are not in some way a potential danger. Finally, there is a practical legal difficulty which does not exist in international intrigue, but which cannot be eliminated in domestic cases short of a totalitarian judicial system. That is the problem of proof; it is very hard to establish a credible story of conspiracy without actually dealing with the people involved. An individual might be framed on a simple charge—such as, say, possessing explosives—but a conspiracy is difficult to fabricate without some cooperation from everyone involved, including the defendants. Even in an autocracy, defense attorneys and judges are often independent enough to expose such fabrications.

The problems are illustrated well in a case now more than a hundred years old, and at one time very celebrated, arising out of the repression following the Revolution of 1848.

The Prussian archives, now in East Germany, contain the following memorandum from King Frederick William IV to his prime minister, Otto von Manteuffel, dated November 11, 1850:[6]

> I have just now read Kinkel's report. This has brought me to a thought, which I will not altogether classify as pure. To wit this: whether *Stieber* is not a priceless personality, to expose the web of the Liberation Conspiracy, and to give the Prussian public the long and justly yearned-for spectacle of a *discovered* and (especially) *punished* plot. So hasten with Stieber's *appointment* and let him make *his trial*. I believe the thought is rich in possibilities and I lay great stress on its *quick realization*. Remind Niebuhr in my name of the most important thing to attend to at present, the search for the English alliance through Radowitz and Bursen—Moses and Aaron. There is not a minute to lose. *Burn this paper.*
>
> Vale
> Friedrich Wilhelm

Stieber was a Prussian criminal lawyer who had already done some work as a *provocateur*.[7] He himself recounts that as a police agent he had been at the forefront of a crowd demonstrating around Frederick William, and had ingratiated himself with the king by getting close enough to tell him that he was in no danger. Frederick William's memo was apparently one of the results. It appears on its face to deal with two unrelated problems, a domestic plot and relations with England, but as events developed, the two ideas were to be connected in fact as well as in the memorandum.

In May 1851, eleven Communists in Cologne were arrested and charged with a conspiracy to overthrow the government. The charges were at first dismissed, having been based solely on the writings of the Cologne group, but they were reinstated after Stieber produced new evidence.

Stieber had gone to England, where the chief group of Communists, headed by Karl Marx, was living. Stieber's agent, Hirsch, joined the group, but was shortly excluded after the members learned of his police connections. Hirsch then produced reports of their meetings out of whole cloth. At this point, it was a case of failed infiltration and provocation.

At the trial in Cologne in 1852, Hirsch's reports were introduced, and Stieber dramatically brought in a "Minute-Book," purporting to contain the records of Communist conspiratorial meetings in England. It was such a botch that in some cases the first initials of members of the London group were wrong, and supposed dates conflicted. Stieber himself finally had to admit under cross-examination that he doubted its authenticity,[8] although he claimed to have been duped himself. Karl Marx, who was accused of being one of the international conspirators, succeeded in getting Hirsch to admit before a London magistrate that the Minute-Book was a fraud, and Hirsch fled from England.[9]

Under the trial conditions existing in Prussia, seven of the eleven defendants were nevertheless convicted of various offenses, but it was not the "yearned-for spectacle" that the king thought the Prussian public wanted, and it did not improve relations with England. The redoubtable

Marx made himself heard all over the world, notably in a blistering dispatch to the *New York Tribune*.[10]

This is, of course, a case in which the fraud was authorized, or at least encouraged, at the highest level. It involves an "international conspiracy" as part of a supposed domestic threat, and it is one of the first cases of a reactionary legal attack on a recognizable left ideology. Most of all, it illustrates the weakness of a totally faked case as contrasted with a living conspiracy (even one raised in a hothouse); the truth tends to come out. Most policemen, in all nations, have been neither so crooked nor so arrogant as Stieber, and for all the reasons discussed above, provocation has been greatly preferred to fabrication.

FRANCE

Provocation must have become more common in domestic politics as it has become more general to connect domestic subversion with foreign influences, and as it has become more accepted to use the methods of political espionage, including infiltration and surveillance, against the domestic population. Thus its modern use can be traced at least to the period in France following the Revolution, when Joseph Fouché established the first modern political police, and there was constant intrigue, both real and fancied, from abroad. Bonaparte was constantly on the alert for plots against himself. During his consulate, according to his secretary, Bonaparte authorized his private police to suborn a conspiracy to assassinate him, for the double purpose of encouraging public support and eliminating his political enemies.[11] The Arena Conspiracy, so called after a Corsican deputy who opposed Napoleon, was the result. It was the classic sort of political case called an "amalgam,"[12] involving real conspirators—although provoked by the police—and mere political opponents, tried and convicted together.

During the First Empire, Fouché is said to have had ten thousand *mouchards* (informers) in Paris alone, and a tale survives that two of them at a banquet "vied with each other in making bold remarks against the government."[13] They then separately went downstairs, and each tried to arrest the other. Whether the story is apocryphal or not, the Parisians' assumption that such provocation would be advantageous to the *mouchards* must reflect that there was talk from the authorities higher up about opposition plots. It was at this time that Mehée was at work on his machinations in England.

During the Restoration after 1815, the repression, and with it the provocation, increased. As laws became more restrictive of expression and came closer to making opinions into crimes, provocation became proportionately easier. Under Louis XVIII, the mere artistic representation of Napoleon I was a crime, and some artisans were arrested after executing busts of the emperor upon the order of undercover agents.[14]

Canler, a policeman at the time, and later a prefect of police, records in his memoirs the origins of a most important political device: staging bogus riots to influence public opinion. The night before the first elections, November 18, 1827, a riot began in St. Denis, a liberal Paris district.[15] Liberal households were supposed to have their windows lit that night, and the rioters erected barricades and threw stones at unlighted windows. Canler himself recognized one of the rioters as an ex-convict in the pay of the police, and he could not get the gendarmes to arrest the man. He wrote, "It was the political police who, on the evening of the first electoral scrutiny favorable to the Liberals, deliberately prepared and fomented disorder in the government's interest." This sort of practice approaches total fabrication, which as we know can be disastrous, but it is less dangerous if no arrests are made. Of course, none need be made in a riot, and if any are made, they can be selectively prosecuted.

Provocation by the French police reached its zenith in the Second Empire, when the political police were under the command of Lagrange. After the collapse of the empire, Communards sifted through the police records and reported to the prefect that, without police interference, nearly all the sedition cases of the previous ten years "either would not have occurred or would not have produced any trouble."[16] That was an embittered revolutionary opinion, but it is clear that there was a consistent policy of provocation. Claude, later chief of the Sûreté, reported that 140 million francs a year were spent for secret political police work.[17] Some of the money at least was used to pay "the lighters," informers who stirred up anger by radical speeches at secret-society meetings.

Lagrange used the whole arsenal of provocation, including plots against the emperor, international intrigues, and "revolutionary" riots. In 1869, a plot to kill Napoleon III was uncovered when a man named Baury was arrested and incriminating papers were found on him.[18] One of his co-conspirators, Guérin, had written reports under an assumed name to the police concerning *his own* activities, including the manufacture of bombs. The reports were used against Baury, and it was not discovered until after the Revolution of 1870 that the informer and the bomb maker were the same man.

In the "Plot of the Four Italians," a supposed revolutionary visited Mazzini in Italy to plot against the Emperor Napoleon.[19] He picked up arms and accomplices in Italy, and was arrested in Paris by Lagrange, who had arranged in the first place for him to visit Mazzini.

Finally, Lagrange continued the "riots" familiar from

the St. Denis incident. He followed his own famous dictum, "If we had a battle in Paris, the empire would be consolidated for ten years,"[20] with three days of riots in 1869, led by agents singing the *Marseillaise* and building barricades. The affair, known as the "White Shirt Riots," had been so carefully staged that Lagrange was able to sit in his office and criticize the accuracy of the reports of inspectors, saying that at such and such a place the erection of a barricade should have been reported. A bogus revolutionary act for the purpose of frightening the bourgeoisie came to be regarded in the nineteenth century as a peculiarly "French" police specialty. It was, in fact, so deeply ingrained in French political life that neither the Commune nor the Third Republic could exorcise it. Still another police prefect, Andrieux, recounts in his memoirs that he engineered the bombing of a statue of President Thiers in Lyons, blandly explaining, "It was necessary that the act be done, so that the repression would be possible."[21] Even the evidence fabricated against Captain Dreyfus can be viewed as a kind of anti-Semitic black propaganda.

GREAT BRITAIN

The British, of course, supposed that everything suspiciously wicked and deceitful originated on the Continent, and that included police work. For them, then, there was something especially shocking about the first great cases of political provocation, which broke upon British public life in 1817.

The Home Office had long infiltrated English radical groups, to such an extent, in fact, that Edward Thompson believes "a convincing history of English Jacobinism and popular Radicalism could be written solely in terms of espionage upon the movement."[22] That there was at least an element of provocation in such infiltration from the first is reflected in a Rule of Order introduced in the Jacobin London Corresponding Society in 1795:

> Persons attempting to trespass on order, under pretence of showing zeal, courage, or any other motive, are to be suspected. A noisy disposition is seldom a sign of courage, and extreme zeal is often a cloak of treachery.[23]

The police actions did not come to public notice until much later, however, after there had been disturbances among the working people, arrests had been made, and cases had been brought on for trial. There were three such cases within the space of less than four years, after the Napoleonic wars. At that time there were thousands out of work, agitation was strong, and the government hoped to be able to repress it. The reformer Cobbett sensed the mood of the Home Office in 1816.

> They sigh for a PLOT. Oh, how they sigh! They are working and slaving and fretting and stewing; they are sweating all over; they are absolutely pining and dying for a plot![24]

At Spa Fields, London, in December 1816 there were three days of large demonstrations, of which the leaders included the ultra-Jacobins Dr. James Watson and Arthur Thistlewood, and a certain John Castle.[25] After the first day of demonstrations, Castle offered a toast at dinner, paraphrasing Voltaire: "May the last of Kings be strangled with the guts of the last priest." The next day, Castle loaded arms in a cart, which was wheeled to the meeting at Spa Fields. The leaders were drunk, and there was indeed a riot. On the third day of demonstrations, Castle and Dr. Watson's son were talking of a *coup d'état*. Watson, Thistlewood, and a few others were arrested and charged with high treason; Castle turned out to be an agent of the Home Office, reporting regularly to the Home Secretary, Lord Sidmouth.

The public was to have no knowledge of Castle's work

until the time of Watson's trial, in June of the following year. In the meantime, the House of Lords reported on the riots, finding evidence of a "traitorous conspiracy," and Parliament passed severe repressive legislation, including a Seditious Meetings Act and suspension of *habeas corpus,* designed to eliminate all the radical clubs.

During the same few months at the beginning of 1817, a much more complex problem than the Spa Fields riots was under surveillance. There were revolutionary committees in several towns and cities, especially where the agitation among the hand weavers was strongest. These groups had little regular correspondence or other strong links, and they were hoping for leadership from London radicals. This was supplied by William Oliver, an agent of Lord Sidmouth.[26] He professed to represent the London committee, and at first went about with a genuine Jacobin to the provinces. After the latter was arrested in May, Oliver was for more than a month the only known link among all the towns. According to the report of another informer, he promised to the Nottingham people that 70,000 were ready in London, and "they were very ripe in Birmingham."[27] He showed off a "plan of campaign." Based on these promises, there were risings in several towns on June 8 and 9, 1817, most notably in the village of Pentridge, near Nottingham, but each of the groups was surrounded by soldiers and arrested.

Dr. Watson of Spa Fields went to trial in London that very day, and the *Leeds Mercury* broke the story of the role of Oliver on June 14, before Watson's trial was over. Some small part of Castle's provocation was brought out on his cross-examination, and the jury found Watson not guilty. At the trial of the Pentridge group, the government was more careful; Oliver did not testify, and proof of entrapment was not admissible. Five of the defendants were convicted of treason and condemned to death, and the others pleaded guilty to avoid the death penalty.

The last of the three cases is remembered as the Cato Street Conspiracy.[28] The Jacobin Arthur Thistlewood, having escaped conviction for the Spa Fields business in the public revulsion against Castle and Oliver, inevitably became involved in further agitation, which the government as unfailingly infiltrated. In February 1820, after the passage of the repressive Six Acts, Thistlewood and his companions were arrested at a house in Cato Street, distributing arms for an attempt upon the lives of the cabinet members. One of the conspirators, George Edwards, was an agent of the Home Office, and a London alderman presented depositions to Lord Sidmouth from those who had known Edwards, in an effort to force an investigation.[29] One of the deponents swore that he had heard Edwards offer pistols and propose an assassination, and there were other affidavits to the same effect. At his sentencing, Thistlewood said that Edwards had proposed the attack. Sidmouth took no action on the complaints, and the conspirators were hanged. Thompson remarks, "The arrests created the sensation which the Government required to justify the Six Acts, and also to help them through a General Election."[30] Indeed, it is plain that the provocative activities in each of the three cases were known at the highest level, and were sponsored for quite as specific political purposes as were any of the provocations on the Continent.

The work of these British infiltrators in the early years of the nineteenth century resembles that of the *agent provocateur* as we know it today. Thompson painstakingly shows that there was some interplay between live revolutionaries and infiltrators, rather than mere fakery or a mock-up of a plot. Liberal historians before him had tried to prove that the men arrested in the Pentridge rising were complete dupes, illiterate countrymen framed by the government, in the manner of some of the Continental "outrages." That view, however, is not only very patronizing to the victims, who actually were ready to fight the ruling class, but makes the events themselves all but incomprehensible. Thompson's analysis is that in the spring of 1817 there was a will to rise up, however fragmented and weak it may have been. What Oliver supplied was the links to complete a conspiracy, and the confidence that there was force enough for it to succeed. This clearly was provocation, however ferocious the revolutionaries may have been, because there is no reason to suppose that the revolutionary impulse would have been put into action without the false links and the false confidence. A similar analysis could be applied to the Cato Street Conspiracy; the participants were violent radicals, but it seems likely that they would not have tried to execute their plot without Edwards. This concept is essential in grasping the nature of political provocation in its modern form. The *provocateur* generally works with explosive materials, but they need not go off unless he sets them off; in cases where it is clear that they were set to go off in his absence and he does no more than report the facts, then the accusation of provocation is not justified.

Thompson has put his finger on a peculiarity of the persons provoked, as well. Both in the Pentridge rising and in the Cato Street Conspiracy, the victims seem to have sensed at the last that their efforts were all but hopeless. Indeed, at the time of the Pentridge rising on June 8, 1817, there was already a rumor that the plot had been betrayed, yet the men went through with it.[31] Once inspired with confidence by agents, the people caught up in these things are, in the most literal sense, "desperate"—willing to take almost suicidal risks to show their courage and defiance of the authorities.

The aftermath of the three cases provoked by agents of Sidmouth tell us a great deal about the dangers, from the government point of view, in using *provocateurs* as an instrument of politics. The exposure of Oliver's game especially left a permanent scar upon British political life; there was a public outcry and a parliamentary investigation of the "Continental Spy System."[32] The revelation contributed to the acquittal of the Spa Fields group, and made it a risky business for many years to bring any alleged conspirators to trial upon the testimony of informers. It helped to solidify the opposition to the government from two directions. On the one hand, it tended to discredit and eliminate violent plots as a political tool, and on the other, it tended to drive the moderates and liberals into a coalition with the radicals, because of their common opposition to the government's police methods. The difficulty the British authorities encountered is inherent in the fact that much of the propaganda value for the government in a political conspiracy lies in the arrest and the state trial; if the conspirators simply "disappear," by being shot at the time of arrest or in some other way, the propaganda point is largely lost. On the other hand, when there is even a pretense of a free press or a fair trial, the constant risk of exposure means that the long-run interests of the government are ill-served by provocation. The discovery of even one major provocation introduces a well-nigh permanent element of ambiguity into political life. Accusations of violent conspiracy are forever afterward open to the counteraccusation that they have been created by the government; credibility is irreparably damaged. Moreover, as in England, the exposure of provocation tends to create a generalized "antirepression" coalition against the government.

IMPERIAL RUSSIA

The Okhrana, the imperial Russian political police, is generally thought to be the paradigm of modern political infiltration and provocation. It is just a little overrated, however. Many of its practices were well established outside Russia before the Okhrana was started in 1881. Ratchkovsky, at one time head of the Paris office of the Okhrana, was in fact accused of having imported into Russian police work the "French" practice of manufactured "anarchist outrages."[33] One of his agents, Yagolkovsky, had at his direction bombed the cathedral at Liège, Belgium, and it does seem that this was then a device new to the Russian police.

The characteristic of imperial Russian secret police work was a kind of interpenetration between the police and radical groups. The police tried to control the radicals by placing their agents inside the groups; those agents not infrequently failed to tell the police all they knew, and policemen themselves were sometimes friendly to the revolutionaries. Vladimir Burtsev, who made an avocation of tracking down and exposing agents, got some of his information from a former police chief, Lopuhin. Much of the police work did not result in provocation to crime so much as in a normative influence over radical politics.

One aspect of this was the "Zubatov Idea."[34] Zubatov, head of the Moscow Okhrana after 1898, had come to share with some other officials a recognition that social agitation had to be dealt with in some way other than by repression. He wrote:

> There is hardly any doubt that economics are for the working man infinitely more important than any political principles. Satisfy the people's requirements in this respect, and they will not only not go into politics but will turn over to you all the radicals.[35]

This is hardly a sinister view of the social question. The idea of getting the labor movement out of politics is familiar to us at least from the time of Samuel Gompers and the AFL, if not earlier. The notion of controlling or co-opting radical ideas in the interest of the government may be found in Bismarck's social legislation as well as in the New Deal and the War on Poverty in the United States. The difference is that in Russia, because there was no free press nor opposition political structure, there was no legal way for such ideas to be put to work except through the police. Social policies which in the United States and Western Europe could with some difficulty be pressed by the workers themselves, or could become an open governmental policy, in Russia had to be expressed through police infiltration and control. Under the resulting system, called "police socialism," Zubatov sponsored labor unions dedicated to bread-and-butter issues, trying to lure working people away from the revolutionary ideas of the independent radicals. In 1902, a delegate to the Russian Congress of Social Democrats said gloomily, "In Moscow, revolutionary social democracy has given way before police socialism."[36] The social situation was so explosive, however, that there was no controlling the unions, and after some police unions joined a general strike in 1903, Zubatov was removed.

The policy of normative control had, however, become deeply ingrained in imperial Russian police work. Zubatov's successors, abandoning the formation of police unions, intensified their infiltration of already existing radical groups, to the point where the police had policy-making functionaries in nearly all of them. Father Gapon, leader of the workers at Bloody Sunday in 1905, received police sponsorship, and in the Bund of Jewish Workers, the terrorist Kaplinsky was a police agent.[37]

The strangest of these agent-revolutionaries was Yevno Azev, a Social Revolutionary who was in the pay of the police for nearly fifteen years.[38] Ever since his exposure by Burtsev in 1908, his career has been a subject of dispute, in the effort to find out just how much he was an *agent provocateur*. He had been directly responsible for several assassinations—of Plehve, the minister of the interior, in 1904, of the Grand Duke Sergei in 1905, and of Father

Gapon in 1906 (the latter on the grounds that he was a police agent!)—and had a hand in a number of others. The news that Azev was a police agent was so shattering to the revolutionaries that two survivors of the period, Theodore Dan and Boris Nicolaevsky, have independently concluded (the words are Dan's) that "his exposure dealt a blow to the tactic of political terror that it never recovered from."[39]

In 1903, Azev had become the chief of the Combat Organization of the Social Revolutionary Party, a tiny group dedicated to political terror and little known to the "legal" members of the party. Azev assumed that leadership partly because other members had been arrested, and he, being a police agent, of course could not be arrested. He assumed the role with the approval of Plehve, whose death he engineered a year later. He thus stood in the position of Oliver before the Pentridge rising in Britain in 1817, as the leader and connecting link, but he did not use his power in the same way.

Revolutionaries who heard of Azev's "treachery" at first assumed that all of his actions were in some way those of an *agent provocateur* for one or another element of the police. His actions, however, are practically inexplicable on that theory. There was no solid political motive for the police to instigate the assassinations for which Azev was responsible, and more important, in those cases he never betrayed to the Okhrana his own role or even the names of his closest associates. Without a betrayal, it is nearly impossible to believe that he was an *agent provocateur* in those assassinations. In fact, the socialist court of honor which tried Azev could not be convinced that he was an agent, because he acted so little like one, until the ex-policeman Lopuhin came to testify.[40]

Everyone who has studied Azev's actions, from his biographer Boris Nicolaevsky on the left to his superiors at the Okhrana on the right, has concluded that Azev was not acting as a police agent in his important cases. Vasilyev, the last head of the Okhrana, in his memoirs put his finger on a central weakness in the Okhrana's policy of control over radical organizations, arguing that he had opposed police alliances with "people who were themselves at the head of revolutionary societies," because

> the man who is directing a treasonable organisation can never unreservedly pass on to the police all he himself knows. . . . If he betrays these secrets to the authorities, the inevitable consequence will be that he will run the risk of being found out by his comrades and accomplices.[41]

Thus Azev betrayed certain secrets to the authorities, throwing to the wolves those revolutionaries whom he thought foolish or incompetent in order to maintain his standing with the police and to strengthen his own power, but he did not—partly because he could not—betray anyone in any case which might arouse suspicion of his own role either on the revolutionary or the police side.

An abiding mystery surrounds the motives of a double agent like Azev. Nicolaevsky ascribes all his duplicity to the greed for getting money from both the police and the revolutionaries, and there is evidence to support that view. Azev initially contacted the police himself, when he was a poor student in search of cash, and in later years he did consume a great deal of money. Nevertheless, it seems to me that his game is too complex and dangerous to be explained by greed alone; he did not have to undertake actual murder to maintain his standing in either camp. There is the thread of a policy in Azev's actions. He was a Jew, and there is general agreement that he had resolved to kill Plehve because the latter was responsible for the pogroms. All of the major assassinations for which Azev was responsible, in fact, occurred during times of savage repression. When a measure of reform and representative government was established after the Revolution of 1905, betrayals to the police by Azev became more frequent, and he finally dropped out of the Combat Organization until the repression was clamped down again. I venture a guess, then, that Azev was not merely greedy but—in the words of Colonel Kaledin—"a genuine revolutionary, who in his work fulfilled more the role of a double spy."[42] It seems, roughly, that Azev adhered to a policy of terror so long as there was only autocracy and repression in Russia, but when the political situation began to thaw or when other revolutionaries made plans which conflicted with his own, he betrayed them. This is a little like the phenomenon with which we are all now sadly familiar, that of men advancing their own policies by denouncing to the authorities those to the left of them.

I felt a glimmer of understanding for men like Azev after I interviewed a young man who came to me saying he had agreed to work for the FBI, hoping to be a "double agent." I thought him very nearly mad, but his macabre explanation of his own motives struck a chord. I wrote down his words as exactly as I could.

> I was very afraid of being arrested. I am terrified of the police, but I wanted to do revolutionary activities. I wanted to do "heavy" things, and have the security of not being arrested. I thought I could get away with a lot more, agitate more, without getting in trouble. I could make a speech that would radicalize other people, and if an undercover agent heard it, I would not be arrested. I could openly say that I was a violent radical.
>
> This way, I thought I could get the government to finance movement activities. I could give information about the government to the movement, and not hurt myself.

These words, I think, bring us near the heart of the secret agent: he seeks hard reality, sometimes violence, but he wants to cut himself off from it. He seeks the exhilaration of power—power over others, the power of violence—but he is not able to take responsibility for it. These words are nearly as true for the *agent provocateur* as for the real double agent like Azev. All seek the thrill of being near violence and of having control over others, but at the same time shield themselves from their criminal impulses by their allegiance to the authorities. They experience danger in safety. The difference between the double agent and the *provocateur* is that the former has some real policy which he wants to advance and for which he uses the police as a shield, while the latter has none, but is the creature of a repressive policy.

Azev was not the only Russian double agent in the years before the Revolution of 1917. Bertram Wolfe tells us that Kaplinsky betrayed other terrorists but refused to give up any member of his own organization, the Bund of Jewish Workers.[43] The conclusion is inescapable that Vasilyev was right: the policy of recruiting men near the top of revolutionary organizations as informers necessarily entailed the risk that they would use the police as a shield. Police surveillance at the time was so pervasive and the power of the police, even over life and death, so great that it was inevitable that the Okhrana should be able to put even genuine revolutionaries in a position where they had no alternative but to cooperate. It was equally inevitable that some of them should be strong-willed enough to play a double game.

The police policy of control reached its zenith with Roman Malinovsky, a confidant of Lenin and a Bolshevik deputy to the Socialist Party Congress of 1912 and later in the Duma.[44] The record shows incontestably that Malinovsky was directed by the Okhrana to take an intransigently radical position in the party and the Duma, so as to intensify the split between the Bolsheviks and Mensheviks, and with it the fragmentation on the left. According to Vasilyev:

At his [Chief of Police Belyetsky's] instigation, Malinovsky provoked a violent discussion among the members of the

Socialist Party in the Duma, and guided it so skilfully that a split took place.[45]

Fortunately for Malinovsky at the time, that was also Lenin's policy, so the police instigation was not detected until after the 1917 Revolution. Malinovsky's speeches were approved by both Lenin and Belyetsky.

This practice is not, in itself, the same thing as provocation to commit a political crime. It is not so much directed toward destroying an enemy and justifying his destruction to the public as it is toward control. As such, it is today one of the most widespread of counterintelligence practices. Our State Department and CIA have served just this function in labor unions abroad; their brand of ideology, in an ironic echo of the Zubatov Idea, has been called "State Department socialism."[46] In the same style in domestic politics is the quiet funding of certain charitable foundations by the CIA, for the purpose of multiplying the ideological effects of their work.

The control of the policies of radical organizations, although not quite the same as political provocation, presents some problems of its own, as the CIA control of foundations has helped suggest to us. In the first place, such control reduces political debate to a charade by making the opposition the creature of the government. Moreover, if the government influence is strong enough it may lead to provocation, when the authorities decide that they want to eliminate their opponents and justify the repression.

The prevalence of normative control in Russian political police work does not mean that there was no criminal provocation, when it suited the police to have it. The deep penetration into radical groups, and the power of the police agents, made some provocation unavoidable. Police agents established such basic policies and operations for the radical organizations that any arrest for those operations could be said to have resulted from provocation. Thus, for example, after Azev helped to establish a printing press in Finland for the newspaper *Revolutionary Russia*, the press was moved to Siberia and the publishers were arrested.[47] And provocation was still used directly as a tool of policy. Premier Stolypin seized upon a conspiratorial circular planted by a police agent as one pretext for dissolving the Duma in 1906, in preparation for new limitations on the franchise, designed to exclude the radicals. In considering Russian police work, however, we cannot assume that every act of violence, or speech advocating violence by a police agent, was intended as provocation to political crime. It may have been, as in Malinovsky's case, an attempt to divide or control the left, or it may have been a real revolutionary act, unknown to the police.

The policy of control, although it seems daring and subtle, did not work well in the end. It did finally discredit the government. Moreover, it even played into the hands of the revolutionaries: the terror was continued by double agents, and Malinovsky's divisive speeches strengthened the extreme left. In short, the policy of repression in Russia intensified the drive to revolution.

GERMANY AND FASCIST ITALY

By the 1920s, provocation had become so ingrained in the public image of European political police work that nearly every act of violence the authorities tried to attribute to the left could be, and often was, blamed on the police. Among the most famous and plausible of these accusations, accepted for thirty years, was the claim that the Nazis engineered the burning of the Reichstag in 1933 for the purpose of frightening the voters before an election and consolidating their power. The Nazis, with their arrogance and internal quarreling, did much to strengthen the impression. They had stacks of blank warrants for the arrest of

Communists, which they proceeded to execute immediately after the fire. Göring, having been accused by some of his cohorts of responsibility, speculated grotesquely on the witness stand about the possible guilt of other Nazis. It appeared then to be the last and worst of a long series of provocations in Europe.

Yet the whole controversy now seems to have been a political puppet show. The Nazis took advantage of the fire to repress the left, and the left took advantage of the fire to prove Nazi provocation, but the fire itself, it appears, was set by an incendiary, Marinus van der Lubbe, acting alone and without provocation.[48]

The same cannot be said about the cases of those who were tried with Van der Lubbe. In their effort to link the fire to a left conspiracy, the police arrested, among others, a Communist Reichstag deputy, Ernst Torgler, who had been seen to leave the Reichstag chamber shortly before the fire. Van der Lubbe admitted having burned a Berlin welfare office before setting fire to the Reichstag, and Torgler was linked to that fire by one Willi Hintze.[49] Hintze swore that he had heard the Communists plotting the welfare office fire, that he had seen Van der Lubbe, and that Torgler's name had been mentioned. The strangest sort of vagrant coincidence emerged at the trial: Hintze was "*schwindel*-Hintze," a police agent with a long criminal record, who had himself been urging the unemployed to attack the same welfare office and offering to supply arms. He had warned the police about the impending attack shortly before Van der Lubbe chanced to burn the place! He admitted at the trial that he had "played along with the police" in making the link to Torgler and Van der Lubbe. Through tiny links such as this to an *agent provocateur*, the criminal trial of Van der Lubbe for incendiarism was turned into an "amalgam" of the trial of a real crime and a fancied conspiracy.

During periods of totalitarian rule in Italy, Germany,

and Russia, provocation has been used as a tool of international intrigue against political refugees in other countries. Mussolini's OVRA (Opera Volontaria Repressione Antifascismo) planted explosives and weapons as evidence in the homes of distinguished *émigrés* and organized a plan, led by a grandson of Garibaldi, to draw *émigrés* into a plot to assassinate Mussolini.[50] This perfect mirror image of the Four Italians plot of 1869 planned by the French police was itself uncovered by the French police after Garibaldi's arrest.

Strange as it may seem at first glance, provocation as we know it hardly exists under a mature totalitarian regime as a tool of domestic (as distinguished from international) politics. Such a rule is characteristically so tight, so all-pervasive, that there can be no interplay between a revolutionary impulse and the authorities. A revolutionary impulse is not permitted to exist long enough for any provocation to occur.[51] To be sure, there are show trials of a political nature, but they are usually based on the carefully rehearsed confession of the defendant. Everyone—the judge, the defense attorneys, the witnesses—has a set role. If a case like the Cologne Communist trial of 1852 had been tried under a mature, modern totalitarian state, the Minute-Book would have been perfect, and there would in any case have been none to question it. Otto Kirchheimer has spoken of the vagaries of trials using the testimony of *agents provocateurs* under nontotalitarian governments.

> Police organisations all over the world may have a creative mind, with do-it-yourself kits at hand in case their enemies are not willing to oblige. But such devices have only limited usefulness where the emphasis rests on piloting a case successfully through court in which testimony may be freely examined.[52]

These words are true, as all the cases described above bear witness, but it is equally true that the use of *provocateurs* occurs, not in totally regimented societies, but in societies—even despotic or dictatorial ones—where the process of trial retains an element of true inquiry. The use of provocation is characteristic of a government attempting to maintain the status quo against a strong impulse for change. It is always repressive, and it may mark a stage on the road to fascism, but it is not the creature of totalitarianism itself. The presence of a *provocateur* implies that there is still some sort of political conflict, however unequal. The paradox is that those very governments which use *provocateurs* are also those which run the risk of their exposure. Provocation is truly an act of political desperation, and it certainly implies a drive onward toward fascism, to eliminate the paradox and the embarrassment of exposure. The next step is to want to get rid not only of the radicals but of the independent judge and jury, and avoid all those unpleasant risks.

UNITED STATES

At a time when official provocation was already old in Europe, when it had helped to discredit terrorism as a political tactic as well as to discredit the governments which made use of the provocation, and when some governments were beginning to dispense with provocation by dispensing with dissent, the practice seems still to have been new in the United States. While there were cases of "entrapment" into crime in the legal sense by government agents, they were rarely or never involved with political crimes, or indeed even crimes of violence, but rather, usually, with prohibitions upon prostitution, gambling, drugs, or some other morals crime.[53] Part of the reason for the lack of official political provocation was the loose and sometimes rudimentary government structure in some parts of the country, which left many police functions in the hands of private organizations. In the chief social conflict of the time, that between capital and labor, much of the police work was done by private detectives rather than by government police. To be sure, there were provocations and outrages manufactured by the private police, although they are extraordinarily difficult to authenticate with certainty.[54] It seems that Tom Mooney, later convicted of a bombing in San Francisco on evidence manufactured by private detectives of the utilities companies, was framed as early as 1913, when explosives were planted in a skiff he had used.[55] One commentator on the Mooney case has significant words to say about the police situation at the time.

> . . . company detectives were an inescapable necessity because in 1913 California neither had nor desired a state police force. The experience of striking workers in Europe and Pennsylvania (which had the only state constabulary in the country) had convinced the labor movement that any state law-enforcement agency in America was far more likely to be used to protect property than to protect persons; and businessmen and landowners, for their part, took pride in their local resourcefulness, which included, in extreme cases, local vigilante traditions. In short, nothing could have been more alien to the concepts of freedom espoused by labor, business and agriculture than a California state police force.[56]

While it is true that there was often cooperation between the political authorities and management in such cases (two attorneys from the Pacific Gas and Electric Company assisted the prosecutor in Mooney's 1913 case), nevertheless a provocation created with private funds and by private means, in a conflict between capital and labor, remains an essentially different political creature from a provocation originating with the state. Such private problems are really beyond the scope of this book.

The federal Justice Department, acting through the FBI and its predecessors, infiltrated the Communist Party from its inception. During the period of the Palmer raids in 1919, it was reported that some radical meetings were called by agents on convenient days, in order to collect subjects for dragnet arrests and deportations.[57] In the main, however, the work of the Justice Department for many years was directed to normative control rather than to provocation, in a sort of pale caricature of the Okhrana. FBI informers penetrated the highest levels of the party, and on at least one occasion the Justice Department apparently experienced the characteristic problem of such high-level control: the double agent. In 1920, Ferdinand Petersen, the FBI's chief agent in the party, was shown to have been reporting to the party on the bureau's activities.[58] The bureau even had its own "Malinovsky"—Agent K-97. At the secret party conventions in 1922, K-97 cast a decisive vote on the question whether the party ought to remain underground or become a "legal" political party. The bona fide members were evenly split, and K-97 voted to remain underground.[59] So close is this to Malinovsky's divisive actions, although on a much smaller scale, that even the Leninist name of the defeated faction in Russia and the United States—"The Liquidators"—is the same. In both cases, it was the faction that wished to liquidate party differences and illegal activities. Americans who are inclined to smugness over the devious and "Byzantine" policies of the Russian secret police should never forget Agent K-97.

In January 1940, at a time when a request for an increase in funds for the FBI was pending in Congress, Director J. Edgar Hoover announced the arrest of seventeen members of a Christian Front Sports Club in Brooklyn on charges of plotting to overthrow the government. Hoover alleged that their plans included blowing up bridges and power plants. At the trial four months later, the case hung on the testimony of an informer, Denis Healy.[60] A film showing military maneuvers of the Christian Fronters was introduced, but upon cross-examination it developed that Healy had obtained the ammunition used in the film from a National Guard armory. The conspiracy was supposed to be established further by tape recordings made in Healy's home, but the tapes revealed only a maudlin party under the influence of Healy's liquor. Nine defendants were acquitted outright, and the jury hung as to the other five; the charges were finally dropped. The *New Republic* commented:

> Is it only a coincidence that the FBI's attempt to convict these men in the newspapers was made when Mr. Hoover was trying to get money out of Congress? Mr. Hoover was asking, and after his publicity about the plot he obtained, a 33-percent increase in his annual appropriation, four times as much as his Bureau received a decade earlier.[61]

Here at least was the shadow of FBI policy behind the provocation; the Christian Front case is a right-wing dress rehearsal for contemporary cases.

During this period, the New York City police force was slowly developing its own political police. The New York Police Department has had a "Radical Bureau," as it was then called, since 1912, and during the period of labor unrest it apparently expanded its work to include the patrolling of strikes.[62] It was officially called the Bureau of Special Services—familiarly, BOSS (or BOSSI, for Bureau of Special Services and Investigation)—until it was changed in 1969 to the Special Services Division (SSD), and once again, a year later, to the Security and Investigation Section (SIS). Inspector Anthony Bouza, the unofficial chronicler of BOSS, tells us that it was "quiescent" during the fifties but came to life again in the sixties.[63] David Burnham of the *New York Times* reports that as long ago as 1969, the Police Department admitted spending some $660,000 a year for BOSS.[64]

Much of the intelligence work of BOSS is not done by undercover agents, but simply by keeping track of suspected radicals, clipping news stories, and attending demonstrations. The information is correlated through "desks" assigned to cover particular areas of agitation.[65] The undercover work is a different matter. In its use of undercover agents, BOSS has tried to avoid some of the more obvious problems. Bouza has this to say about the use of informants who are not policemen but turncoat radicals:

On the positive side, it furnishes data that come straight from the target, there are few risks for the agency, since the informant is not connected to the government by any official bounds, and it is relatively inexpensive and easy to control. The paid informant is generally under economic pressure to furnish information, so he may fabricate some to keep the money flowing. The conscientious informer frequently loses his enthusiasm after he evaluates the risks and experiences the boredom of the assignment. There is also the possibility that the informant is "planted" for the purpose of deliberately misleading the agency. Frequently the use of two or more informants in one group, unknown to each other to be furnishing information, serves as a verifying control. The information furnished must always be subjected to the test of verification.[66]

To avoid fabrication and the "Azev problem," BOSS relies on actual policemen as infiltrators.

The undercover man is an extremely valuable investigative tool because of the control that can be exercised over his activities. As a salaried employee and as a motivated and dedicated policeman, he can be ordered from one group to another and from one activity to another. His functions can be guided and directed at every step of the process, and his loyalty is generally far more assured than that of an informant.[67]

The use of such police infiltrators in militant black organizations at first followed an especially rigid pattern. It began, apparently, with Ray Wood in about 1964. He was inducted into the police directly as an undercover agent, using a

fictitious name and background, and without attending the
Police Academy. According to Inspector Bouza, "no police
records were available on him until after he had been surfaced," a method of total cover which had been adopted
from the procedures of foreign espionage. Wood infiltrated
CORE and other civil rights groups, gradually making himself known as a militant; he was even convicted and fined
after an attempted "citizen's arrest" of Mayor Robert Wag-
ner. He finally surfaced in 1965 to testify in the spectacu-
larly successful prosecution of three other black men for a
conspiracy to bomb the Statue of Liberty. He was promoted
to second-grade detective, decorated, and only then began
to attend the Police Academy.[68]

The Police Department was apparently so pleased with
Wood's work that it followed almost the same scenario with
Lee Howlette.[69] After taking the qualifying exam as a policeman, Howlette was interviewed by BOSS and taken
onto the force in July 1965 without regular police training.
He infiltrated the Black Brotherhood Improvement Association in Queens, and finally surfaced in 1967 to testify at
another sensational and successful prosecution, this time
for a conspiracy to kill moderate civil rights leaders, including Roy Wilkins of the NAACP. Howlette, too, had been
promoted to the rank of detective within less than two
years of coming onto the force.

The trial records in these two famous cases do not afford
much hard evidence of provocation.[70] In the Statue of Liberty case, Ray Wood drove one of the defendants, Robert
Collier, to Montreal in a rented car to obtain explosives
from Quebec Nationalists. In the second case, Howlette
bought a simple road map of Queens, and the defendants
rode in his car to look at the home of the victim. He also
made up a leaflet with words cut from a magazine, intended
to set forth the reasons for the assassination. What these
cases do establish is a set of standard procedures and ideas
for police involved in "black militant" cases. It is as though

each major element in the New Dunston Hotel case had been drawn from the previous cases: the car, the map, the trip to the scene. But of course, the difference is always one of emphasis, a matter of who *suggests* each step in the process.

By the time of the New Dunston Hotel case, and the prosecution of Black Panthers generally, the New York City Police Department, like other law-enforcement agencies, had become noticeably more slack, or more eager, in the recruitment of undercover agents. Little attempt was made, as we know, to conceal Wilbert Thomas's real background. The demand for black undercover agents was so great that a national conference of black policemen in Philadelphia in 1971 publicly opposed the growing tendency throughout the country to transfer black policemen to undercover work.[71] They are being recruited as fast as police departments can get them.

In the late sixties, the amount of police intelligence work throughout the country, especially at the local police level, expanded enormously. Between 1968 and 1971, BOSS increased its staff from 60 to 90 (a figure which does not include an unstated number of undercover agents), and the Los Angeles Police Department doubled its intelligence division in the single year 1969–70.[72] In Chicago and Philadelphia, in the words of Frank Donner, more police are engaged "on political intelligence assignments than are engaged in fighting organized crime."[73] The expansion has been heaviest in college communities and black ghettos, although it has extended across the board to right-wing organizations. An article in the *New York Times* for March 28, 1971, lists fifteen major colleges and universities with authenticated cases of the use of undercover agents,[74] but it is probably safe to say that no college campus with any pretense to diversity of opinion is free from undercover infiltration, with or without the consent of its administration.

In this growth of surveillance, there has been an increase in the use of *agents provocateurs* in political cases. In the pages that follow, I have tried to describe the contemporary cases across the country which present well-authenticated instances of provocation at the time this is written, based on the admissions of the authorities or some other reliable source.[75]

The best known of these incidents, although not the clearest in outline, revolves around Thomas Tongyai, called Tommy the Traveler or Tommy Traveler.[76] Tongyai, who held a job as a traveling salesman, acted as a "regional traveler" for SDS and later in a similar role for Newsreel, the radical film group. In 1969 and 1970, he agitated on the campus of Hobart College in Geneva, New York. The testimony of witnesses is overwhelming that he repeatedly demonstrated and offered to demonstrate bombs and that he took students out to practice with an M-1 rifle. In April 1970, he tried to recruit a secretary of the Hobart ROTC office to help destroy its files, offering her a hundred dollars.[77] Some days later, three fire bombs were thrown into the ROTC office after a meeting between Tongyai and some freshmen, and the perpetrators were arrested on information supplied by him.

Tongyai was apparently in the pay both of the local sheriff's office (his local work was supposed to concern narcotics) and of a federal agency, not at all an uncommon arrangement. Tongyai's father, who was half Siamese, seems to have worked as a CIA agent in Thailand, but it is likely that Thomas Tongyai worked for the FBI rather than the CIA. The ideological and historical link to foreign intelligence work is important, however, because Tongyai's career shows the effect of the techniques and attitudes of foreign espionage. In an article in *Esquire,* Ron Rosenbaum surmises that Tongyai may have got "almost religiously anticommunist ideas" from his father.[78] Thomas Tongyai was disappointed when students did not respond to a display of weapons and bombs, because he thought, from his right ideological point of view, that as radicals they *ought* to respond, and also because he himself was excited by weapons and by conspiracy. In his undercover work, he could both eliminate "dangerous foreign influences" and indulge a taste for violent adventure. Like Wilbert Thomas, he was attentive to women and seems to have confided more in them than in men.

A case from the University of Alabama at Tuscaloosa, revolving around the actions of a former student, Charles Grimm,[79] is similar to the Hobart College incident, except that the violence was more serious. The arrests, in fact, occurred less than a month after the arrest for arson at Hobart, during the nation-wide campus protests following the shootings at Kent State University in the spring of 1970. Like Tongyai, Grimm was paid by the local police as a narcotics informant, as well as by the FBI for political work, and before the cases in which he participated were brought to trial, he was warned by the local police to leave town. His role was revealed by George Dean, a lawyer who had represented Grimm as a client along with many other students, but repudiated him after he learned Grimm was an informer.

Grimm admitted to witnesses that he burned Dressler Hall on the Tuscaloosa campus on May 7, 1970, an event which prompted university officials to request more police assistance. On May 14, 1970, he threw three Molotov cocktails into the street in front of an apartment building occupied by students, which attracted a crowd and subsequently brought the police. The same night, he met local and state officials at a Holiday Inn, although what he said to them is not known. At least one student was beaten that night, and at a meeting on May 16, Grimm urged students to avenge that beating.

Grimm's work culminated on May 18, 1970. In the words of the lawyers' report:

On the 18th of May, 1970, Grimm threw a bicycle pedal, a softball and a brick from the east balcony of the Student Union Building at police officers gathered in front of the building. After the objects were thrown, Major John Cloud of the Alabama Highway Patrol declared an unlawful assembly in that area. Approximately 45 students were arrested that day in and around the Union Building pursuant to Cloud's orders. Grimm has admitted throwing the objects and we have interviewed two witnesses who saw him throw one or all of the various missiles.[80]

If we know less about Charles Grimm personally than we do about Tommy the Traveler, the reasons of policy for Grimm's actions seem much clearer. They were intended to cause "outrages" which would precipitate arrests and increase the police presence on the campus—it is difficult to see how any other explanation is possible.

There is at least one other plain case of police provocation in a "campus riot" during the spring of 1970. On April 29, a group of students at the University of Ohio in Columbus shut the gates of the university as a symbol of protest.[81] The state highway patrol came and opened the gates by force. The crowd grew to three thousand people, and finally the National Guard was called in to restore order. At a university disciplinary hearing for one of the students, a photograph was introduced in evidence by the prosecution showing four men closing the gate at the beginning of the incident; two of them were admitted to be undercover agents of the highway patrol. In this case as well, the policy of provoking violence so that more police will be required is clear on the face of the facts. All three of these campus cases occurred in the spring of 1970, and they cast a somewhat lurid light over the allegations of "campus violence" during that period.

Undercover agents have also supplied weapons to conspirators in recent cases. The most spectacular example emerged at the trial of the "Seattle Seven" in federal court

in Tacoma, for an alleged conspiracy to cause a riot in protest against the trial of the Chicago Seven for an earlier
conspiracy to cause a riot (we may be faced with an endless hall of mirrors in these protest–conspiracy–protest
cases). Horace Parker, an FBI undercover agent, testified
that he had infiltrated a Seattle Weatherman collective and
was directed by his superiors to make an offer to purchase
dynamite and blasting caps.[82] He also bought and delivered
five pounds of potassium chlorate, supposedly for igniting
Molotov cocktails. He provided firearms instruction, pass-
ing himself off as a former Green Beret. Parker may have
justified all this in his own mind by a rigid ideology similar
to those attributed to Tongyai and Wilbert Thomas, because his hatred for the defendants was so great that he did
not even make a decent prosecution witness. Under cross-
examination by one of the defendants acting as his own
counsel, Parker said that he would lie if necessary to destroy
the defendants.[83] As of this writing, the case has not been
finished, because it ended, shortly after Parker's testimony,
in a mistrial.

Other cases in which radicals have been given explosives
by the government present more obscure but at the same
time more suggestive situations. In Los Angeles in 1969,
Shirley Sutherland and Donald Freed were arrested for
violating a federal statute which forbids the transfer of
hand grenades without having filled out a federal registration form. United States District Judge Ferguson chose
to dismiss the indictment against them upon technical
grounds. Those grounds must have seemed the best
ones open to the court before trial, but they ultimately
proved unfortunate for the defendants, because the Supreme Court set a precedent in reversing the dismissal of
the indictment.[84] They are doubly unfortunate, because it
is obvious from the judge's remarks to the United States
attorney that what really concerned him about the case was
that the grenades had been delivered to Freed shortly be-

fore his arrest by a man named James Jarrett, a Los Angeles policeman.

Private investigators for the defendants had traced Jarrett's past,[85] and the results were astonishing. He had worked for the CIA in Indochina, Africa, and Latin America; the violent nature of the sort of experience he had had is indicated by the fact that he came to the Los Angeles police to help train a special weapons and tactics ("anti-sniper") squad. He came to know Freed and Sutherland in the Friends of the Panthers, where he posed as a disaffected Vietnam veteran. Freed claims that Jarrett talked constantly of violence, and it is easy to believe him.

Not much more than the fact of the transfer of grenades and the background of Jarrett is clear in the case as this is written, because it is still awaiting trial. The chief disputed question is whether the defendants actively sought hand grenades, or whether, as Freed claims, Jarrett had offered to get some canisters of Mace and outright framed the defendants. The question is interesting because it throws light on the government's justification for pressing the case. Here is a bit of the colloquy between the judge and the United States attorney at the time the case was first dismissed:

THE COURT. [I]t appears to me that when you take the problems of this case, you take a police officer who goes to the Navy, who gets some hand grenades for the sole purpose of delivering those hand grenades to one of the defendants so that the defendant can be arrested and charged with a federal crime. That is the whole purpose of the whole thing.

He didn't give them the hand grenades so they could blow up the City Hall, did he?

MR. KINNAIRD. Well—

THE COURT. Or maybe he did, I don't know.

MR. KINNAIRD. Well, inherent within this fact of the hand grenades, your Honor, is the question that there are not any legitimate uses for hand grenades.

THE COURT. The only reason he gave him the hand grenades

was so that Freed could be arrested and charged with a federal offense.

MR. KINNAIRD. Or in a sense, your Honor, we only gave him what he wanted—

THE COURT. The opportunity—

MR. KINNAIRD. The opportunity to—

THE COURT. You didn't give him the hand grenades to do any damage with them, I hope?

MR. KINNAIRD. We certainly did not intend to let them remain that long—

THE COURT. All right, all right.

MR. KINNAIRD. —to do any damage, or to have them fed back.

THE COURT. All right.

MR. KINNAIRD. But the man did have the propensity to want to acquire them. There is no way of knowing if a person is acquiring weapons from underground sources or from a black market, the agent was certainly in a position there of selling himself as one who was able to acquire them, not from the Office of Naval Intelligence at least, but you are dealing in a sub rosa culture that was attempting to stockpile destructive devices and we merely gave him the opportunity, under a control situation, where we could minimize the danger to society and, we believe, bring the man to justice for the criminal activities that he desired to do. And that was the only point—

THE COURT. You desired to bring him to justice for the thing that he was planning to do, not for the purpose of what he did.

MR. KINNAIRD. He did, because he did take possession of the hand grenades. We gave him the opportunity to do it.[86]

In short, the government believed that the transfer was justified if the defendants wanted those hand grenades. The underlying question, whether the supposed conspiratorial impulses of the defendants might have had no result at all if the government had not made the transfer, appeared to concern the court but not the prosecutor.

If we think about the government's attitude, and the character of the agent involved in a case like this, we can begin to understand how the government comes to be in the position of supplying instruments of violence. The agents have a taste for those instruments of violence.[87] At the same time, they tend to subscribe to rigid views that justify ridding the country of radicals at any price. Finally, the government attorneys agree that if the radicals really *want* weapons, they ought to get them from the government so they can be arrested before they get them from someone else. It is not an entrapment within the meaning of the law to give contraband to a willing recipient, in the government's view (a technical point of law discussed in the next chapter), and so there is no bar to the prosecution. Although the government attorneys may fail to recognize that the defendants' unlawful designs probably would never come to anything without the government's assistance, they cannot fail to see that supplying contraband must subject the government to public criticism. They obviously believe that the need to eliminate the defendants is greater than the danger of public criticism, which is nearly the same thing as saying that they do not care whether the defendants have been entrapped or not. The prosecution of a case which is based on the government supplying weapons or explosives, as in the *Freed* case, *must* be a matter of policy, because the government cannot be ignorant of the actions of its agent. At the time the decision is made to press the case, the government knows who delivered the goods, and decides to try to convict the defendants simply because of a belief that they are dangerous. It is a classic case where, whether he acts on orders or not, the agent takes an action which fits in with existing policy.

There is an extraordinary case of provocation against members of an extreme right-wing group in Mississippi, the White Knights of the Ku Klux Klan. The White Knights adhere to a virulent anti-Semitic ideology, and a number of bombings of Jewish homes and synagogues in 1967 and 1968 were attributed to them. After the bombing of a syna-

gogue in Meridian, a large reward for the capture of the
perpetrators was collected, chiefly through the Anti-Defa-
mation League of B'nai B'rith. The FBI believed that the
two chief bombers were Danny Joe Hawkins and Thomas
Tarrants. The FBI and the local police agreed to pay two
other members of the White Knights, the Roberts brothers,
to arrange a bombing by Hawkins and Tarrants. In the
words of Jack Nelson of the *Los Angeles Times,* who
learned the facts from the Meridian police, "The original
deal called for the brothers to share a total of $69,000 . . .
but that was if Tarrants and Danny Joe Hawkins . . . attempted the bombing."[88] According to Nelson, Meridian
police memoranda show that the police urged the Roberts
brothers, and they in turn urged Tarrants and Hawkins, to
meet a deadline for the bombing.

It seems that the intention was to lure Tarrants and
Hawkins into ambush and kill them. Anthony Dunbar says
in his article about the case:

> The FBI was aware that some jurors, especially in a Missis-
> sippi Klan case, frown on the testimony of paid informants.
> The Roberts brothers began to consider the dangers of testify-
> ing against fellow Klansmen, especially if they were acquitted
> or released for appeal after conviction. A new plan began to
> form. The FBI agents in Jackson had a great deal of profes-
> sional as well as personal animosity toward the men they
> considered to be the primary "hit men" in that city, Thomas
> Tarrants and Danny Joe Hawkins. They introduced the idea
> of getting the Roberts brothers, now firmly committed to
> conspiring with the FBI, to set up a trap wherein Tarrants
> and Hawkins would, it was expected, be killed by officers
> while staging a Klan bombing.[89]

The plan worked only in part. Tarrants arrived at the scene
of the projected bombing, the home of a Jewish business-
man, on June 29, 1968, not with Hawkins, but with a woman
member of the White Knights, Kathy Ainsworth. In the

ensuing gun battle, Miss Ainsworth was killed and Tarrants seriously wounded.

This is a strange sort of *agent provocateur* activity, because the aim was not a show trial, not a propaganda justification for the government. It was simply to eliminate individual terrorists, whom it was difficult to catch in a legal way. As Dunbar tells us, it is a measure of the hatred and contempt in which the White Knights were held by the business people of Meridian, because of the injury they did to Mississippi's commercial life, and by the federal and local law-enforcement officers, not to speak of the Jews, that this extreme solution could be approved. Ironically, the "deal" worked out between the Robertses and the police and FBI might have constituted a strong defense for Tarrants if he had been able to bring it out at his trial, because the federal circuit court had already held it to be a denial of due process of law to a defendant for law-enforcement officers to pay a fee, not simply for information, but contingent on the proof of commission of a crime by the defendant.[90] The police-FBI action, however, was not concerned with a trial but with liquidation, and in fact, the ambush had little propaganda value, because newspaper reporters, with the exception of Jack Nelson, could not be bothered with an obscure shoot-out.

A similar case occurred in Seattle during the period of violence in the spring of 1970. It resulted from FBI-police cooperation, at a time when the authorities were under pressure to come up with a solution to a wave of bombings which had afflicted Seattle for some years. According to Richard Cooper, also of the *Los Angeles Times*, Alfred Burnett, a black man charged with violating his parole for a felony, acted as an informer for the Seattle police intelligence unit and the FBI.[91] Burnett had apparently set up a bombing at a real estate office, and had informed the police. Being unable to locate his original choice to place the bomb, a former Black Panther, Burnett swore in an affidavit that he offered seventy-five dollars to Larry Ward, a young black man with a clean record and no previous connection to bombings. Ward agreed to do it, and after Burnett let him out of the car at the scene, the police closed in and Ward began to run. He was killed by shotgun fire, although he was apparently unarmed and surrounded by policemen. The majority of a coroner's jury ruled that the killing of Ward was not justifiable homicide, but the authorities have refused to prosecute.

Despite the slight public notice they have received, the action of the authorities in the Klan and the Ward cases is beyond the pale even of the provocative activities discussed earlier in this chapter. When the police use provocation as a means of eliminating their enemies by summary execution, we are truly on the verge of the breakdown of civil government.

The shadow of J. Edgar Hoover's chief policy—that of preserving his own prerogatives against his critics—has fallen across that conspiracy case in Harrisburg, Pennsylvania, against Reverend Daniel Berrigan and others. In 1970, Hoover came under strong attack in the press and the Congress because of political surveillance, and during the congressional hearings he in effect threatened his critics with doom if they did not continue to support him, by revealing a radical conspiracy to kidnap "a high government official." Father Berrigan and others, including Sister Elizabeth McAlister, were later indicted in Harrisburg for a conspiracy to kidnap presidential aide Henry Kissinger. It developed that there were letters between Berrigan and Sister McAlister concerning an inchoate scheme for a political hostage-taking, and letters had been carried by a supposedly confidential courier, Boyd Douglas.[92] It is worth noting that some letters would not have passed, the thoughts would not have been communicated, but for Douglas. Douglas apparently wrote a covering letter for one of Berrigan's letters to Sister McAlister, in which he said they would need a gun and offered to get one which could not be traced. He also tried to enlist other conspirators.[93] Of course, Boyd Douglas was an FBI agent; he was on parole from prison attending college, and like Thomas Tongyai and Wilbert Thomas, he sought power over women—always had a line for the girls.

Shades of Denis Healy and the Christian Front club! These things do tend to happen when Hoover needs congressional approval for his budget. This is not to say that the case suddenly happened, and Boyd Douglas suddenly appeared, because of Hoover's congressional problems; rather, the FBI took advantage of the thin but sensational facts it possessed at the time. It seems, from a prosecutorial point of view, that the case was actually unfinished at the time it was brought to public notice. No defendant, it appears, had yet performed an overt act by actually getting a weapon, or even making a firm agreement. Hoover may have pushed the government into action by exposing Douglas's actions before he could complete his provocations.

Where did Douglas mean to get that "untraceable" gun? The FBI is not unwilling to obtain weapons in a proper case, as Horace Parker's testimony shows. One of the FBI documents seized in the raids on the Media, Pennsylvania, office in 1970, and distributed by Resist, contains this matter-of-fact advice:

> . . . while our informants should be privy to everything going on and should rise to the maximum level of their ability in the New Left Movement, they should not become the person who carries the gun, throws the bomb, does the robbery or by some specific violative overt act becomes a deeply involved participant. This is a judgment area and any actions which seem to border on it should be discussed.

It is difficult to believe that in a case as important as the Kissinger kidnapping the central office would not have approved supplying a gun. It is painfully evident that the

FBI has approved advocacy of violence and even violence itself as a tool of infiltration in many cases.

All of the cases of the late 1960s, the campus provocations, the weapons and explosives cases, the White Knights case, and the Hoover allegations of conspiracy, have taken us away from New York and the Bureau of Special Services. We know from the Panther Thirteen trial and the New Dunston Hotel case that the New York police were not asleep at their "black militant" desk. There is one more New York case, decided by a jury within a day after the Panther Thirteen trial, which tells us as much as any case, old or new, about the methods of infiltrators, the connection between infiltration and provocation, and the interplay between the impulse to violence and the provocation. That is the so-called Harlem Five case, brought against five young black men, members of the Harlem Youth Federation, for conspiring to kill policemen—"to kill a cop a week," as the sensational headlines put it at the time of their arrest—and for possession of explosives. The infiltration was carried out and the arrest made shortly after the violence following the death of Martin Luther King, Jr., in April of 1968.

The case is important chiefly because of the completeness of the record. There are hours of tape recordings made by two black undercover police officers wearing microphones, together with dozens of pages of transcripts taken from the tapes, all entered as prosecution exhibits. The usual disputes about subtle questions of motivation as well as about out-and-out lies are minimized, and we can get close to the facts.

An early tape, made April 26, 1968, involves just one of the defendants, Preston Lay, and the two black police officers, Carrington and Hubbard.[94] At this point, Lay has a grandiose plan for seizing weapons from an armory, including even a detailed street map of the job. But it develops that none of the other people invited shows up at the meeting. Lay's plan is difficult to execute without a group, and

Hubbard tells him that they have to have a workable plan before Malcolm X's birthday on the weekend of May 19, because there is likely to be a riot then, and after that the repression will be heavier. Hubbard asks if Lay can get more men and more information before that date.

A second tape, made May 13, records a conversation between yet another lone defendant, Ebb Glenn, and Officer Carrington.[95] Glenn's ideas are a good deal less grandiose than Lay's. He is willing to kill a single cop, but, he says, Lay "wants nothing before the armory." A tape made the following day includes the two policemen and four defendants, Lay, Glenn, Wallace Marks, and Hannibal Thomas.[96] It confirms Glenn's conversation about Preston Lay. There is talk about the possibility of killing a single policeman, and Lay says that an attack on one policeman would make the assault on the armory more difficult because the police would "work overtime." There is some rational debate about radical tactics. Thomas opposes overt acts "before we are ready." Later, he adds, "we are talking about working on the terrorist level, before we even work on the political level." Carrington says, "We need gun power," but Marks and Glenn both say they are trying to make up their minds. Toward the end of the transcript, Preston Lay pronounces these sovereign words about the terrorist plan: "It's dumb." There is further discussion about the ways of performing an assassination, and Lay, who works for a machine company and has some technical knowledge, tells how bombs can be made from shotgun shells. At this point Officer Carrington asks, "When can you have the four bombs ready?" and Lay replies, "Thursday."

But even then, they do not stick to the point. Glenn is off on a plan to raise money by selling marijuana, until finally Hannibal Thomas says plaintively, "What we gonna do Thursday, please?" and Officer Hubbard adds, "Yeah, that's what I want to know." There is more discussion, until Officer Carrington says, "So, when are we gonna hit the first one, how we gonna hit it?" But Thomas raises a theoretical question about the idea of Che Guevara, and Officer Carrington inquires gloomily, "Che?" Thomas starts to talk to Lay about whether he can make a silencer for a gun, and Officer Hubbard says, "Wait a minute, what are we gonna do now? It's gonna be all of us now, in one group." Lay says he will bring the bombs, and they agree to meet again Thursday, two nights later.

Officer Hubbard asks, "Wait a minute, when are we gonna plan what we're gonna do?" It turns out that no one knows how or even whether the bombs will detonate, and Officer Carrington suggests that a board can be rigged as a detonater. Officer Hubbard asks, "Is this what we're going to do Thursday? This is the next time, right?" and Officer Carrington replies, "Yeah, the next time we do that." Officer Carrington summarizes the plan: "So Thursday when we meet here you'll have four bombs and the rifle with the silencer, 'cause Hannibal [Thomas] said he's got ammunition." But Officer Hubbard is still not satisfied with its definiteness. He asks, "What are we, we gonna off 'em? We're gonna off 'em, right?" and a few moments later, "When are we gonna plan this?" They agree again to meet, Glenn again introduces his marijuana scheme, and the following colloquy takes place:

HUBBARD. So [in] other words, starting with this week, it's gonna be a weekly thing like, more or less.
MARKS. Right, right, right . . .
CARRINGTON. So we'll be doing this once a week.

This conversation is the only place in which the subject of taking action once a week is discussed, and is apparently the source of the sensational news line "Kill a cop a week."

The next tape records a telephone conversation the next day, on May 15, between Ebb Glenn and Officer Carrington.[97] Glenn says he has been thinking about what Preston Lay and Hannibal Thomas said, and concludes, "I don't

think we are ready." Carrington does not specifically urge
him, but instead merely asks Glenn to make sure that Preston Lay brings "the stuff" with him the next day.

On Thursday, May 16, 1968, the two officers are the first
to show up at Hannibal Thomas's apartment.[98] The technical man, Preston Lay, arrives with two unfinished bombs
made from shotgun shells; he has not yet made the si-
lencers. There is a long wait for the others, during which
the two policemen talk of getting the friction tape to complete the bombs. Lay does not make a move. Thomas and
Marks drift in, and Marks is not ready. Thomas is proud of
having been put in charge of a bus taking demonstrators to
Washington, and he says he has to leave at one o'clock in
the morning. Carrington explodes, "Hey, wait a minute.
No, no, no, no, no, no, no, no, no. Wait a minute. We going
to do something tonight." Carrington asks Marks to go
home and get his gun because the bombs are inoperable.
Carrington tries to get the action going to have it completed
before one in the morning. Thomas says it cannot be done
that night. Later, there is this exchange:

CARRINGTON. When we gonna do our thing?
MARKS. Aw, man, I was hoping we could do it tonight or tomor-
    row, but ...
CARRINGTON. Tonight, tonight, tonight is sweet.
HUBBARD. Tomorrow, we won't be around in time.

Marks finally agrees that it might be done that night.

There is a knock at the door, the police burst in, and
Officer Carrington, actor to the end, says to the defendants,
"You know them?"

There is something terribly sad about the conversations
on these tapes. The defendants apparently subscribed at
least to parts of the Nation of Islam philosophy; they used
Muslim greetings and talked about "the devil"—the white
man. They had schemes, hopes of violence, unquestionably;

there is a plan to attack an armory, another to kill police-men, and still other plans. But those plans were hardly more than fantasies, the fruits of racial animosity. In the first major conversation, on May 14, the only one of the defend-ants who was initially in favor of an act of individual ter-rorism was Ebb Glenn; Lay wanted bigger things, and Marks and Thomas felt there were theoretical objections to the action. But every time they got off the subject of the terrorist act, the officers demanded to know the precise de-tails of a specific plan for a specific date. They finally all agreed that Lay would make some bombs by May 16.

Even on the appointed day, no one was eager. Lay made no move to finish his uncompleted bombs; he had, indeed, never wanted to use them and thought the plan "dumb." Hannibal Thomas had agreed to leave town, and Marks was not ready. Carrington had all he could do to keep them together. It is perfectly plain that setting a definite dead-line, May 19, and selecting a simple terrorist plan were essential elements of the case, and that they never would have happened without the police officers.

The quick answer usually given to the sort of analysis I have made here is that there was a real impulse to violence in the defendants, and that if the police had not channeled it, it would have found some other, uncontrolled outlet. In the first place, that is not any answer at all, because people are not usually punished for impulses, and there is in fact no compelling reason to suppose that violent impulses will find violent outlets. But even if there were such a reason, that would not justify the actions of the police officers in setting a deadline and constantly keeping the defendants to a plan they would not otherwise have adhered to, *pre-cisely because* those policemen were successful undercover agents who had the confidence of the defendants. If there were any real violent issue of the defendants' talk, without the active intervention of the police, the officers were in a

position to report it. In other words, once they had infiltrated the group, any supposed justification for their provocations was automatically destroyed.

The end of the Harlem Five prosecution reveals much
about the policy behind such a case. Between the arrest
and the trial, a period of nearly three years, some of the defendants were involved in community activities, and Liv-
ingston Wingate, head of the New York Urban League,
spoke up in their behalf. This emphasizes something which
should already be obvious from the transcripts of the tapes:
if the city authorities had spent as much time and money
drawing these young men into the life of the city as they
spent working them up to the point of a conspiracy, most
of their violence would have been dissipated. As in the New
Dunston Hotel case, the authorities are no longer willing to
do that.

The jury in the trial of the Harlem Five ultimately found
all the defendants not guilty of the conspiracy, but found
some of them guilty of unlawful possession of explosives.
When the time came for sentencing on that charge, the
judge put some defendants on probation, apparently because of the entrapment evidence and because they had
shown, in the traditional way, that they were "rehabilitated." It certainly would have been shocking if he had not
done so. Yet because of the then recent shootings of policemen, the police commissioner took the almost unprece-
dented action of publicly criticizing the judge for being
lenient with men who had been convicted of possessing
bombs "to be used for killing police."[99] I am charitable
enough to assume that the commissioner had never read or
even heard about the contents of the transcripts of the
tapes, and that he relied on the headlines or the advice of
someone in the Police Department. Whatever the source of
the opinion, it significantly illuminates the policy behind
the prosecution of the case. It was intended to prove that
there are black militants who menace the lives of police-

men, and to bring down repression on the heads of militants generally. Perhaps even more, as defense attorney William Kunstler said, the case, following as it did so closely on the riots after Martin Luther King's death, was intended to prove that the police are able to contain and control ghetto violence. Its political aims did not work out very well, and someone in the department was astonished and disappointed to find out that they had not worked.

The police work in the Harlem Five case is reminiscent in some respects of Wilbert Thomas's actions. A deadline is established; grandiose plans are reduced to one simple plan, and the means are found to execute it. The officers in the Harlem Five case did not go quite as far as Thomas; they did not themselves offer to supply the facilities to commit the crime nor draw a map of the project, but they did insist that the defendants make a plan and get the means to carry it out.

These cases in their turn are like the English cases of 1816 and 1817 discussed earlier in this chapter. The agents work with a genuine, though inchoate, radical impulse, and they make their subjects think that it is feasible to put the impulse into action, as William Oliver did before the Pentridge rising. They set a deadline, as Oliver did, and as Edwards did in the Cato Street Conspiracy. Finally, they hammer out, or demand that their subjects hammer out, a specific plan which is to be carried out by the deadline. At the deadline, everyone is arrested.

We know that the English cases of 1816–1817 were not merely the results of overzealousness by agents. They were actions of policy, carried out with the knowledge and approval of the authorities. Similarly, it is almost impossible for me to believe that New York cases like the Harlem Five case are not instruments of policy. It is hard to imagine the officers setting the deadline of the weekend of May 19, 1968, and working to make the arrest come off before that date, just because of overzealousness. They must at least

have had instructions to give their subjects a definite deadline and try to make them meet it, even if that particular
deadline was not chosen for them for political reasons.
There is no independent reason for an officer to pick a
deadline date, and push to meet it, unless he is working
within a schedule and a policy. What that policy most
likely is, we have already learned.

The teaching of history is that provocation in all countries at all times—in France, England, Russia, Germany,
and the United States—has been predominantly a matter
of policy. The "overzealous" agent in a political case is
largely a myth; his superiors generally know what he is
doing and approve of it, or approve of it after they find
out. The political secret agent is not usually an independent
contractor, and he is less so in the United States today than
he has been in other countries in the past.*

The thing that is puzzling at first glance about the present situation is the apparent sudden growth, within the last
few years, of political provocation in this country. It is
partly explained simply by the enormous growth in undercover police work, at both the local and the federal level.
This has been a poorly planned response to an unplanned
phenomenon, the upsurge of grass-roots radicalism on
campuses and in the streets, in styles of life and in politics.
The police and the FBI have generally been careless in
selecting their informers and infiltrators, using anyone who
comes to hand, without being able to gauge his reliability
any more than they could gauge the actions of those they
were infiltrating. We could now almost sketch a portrait of
the character of the *provocateur*, whether he is a policeman
or a mere informer. He entertains fantasies about and seeks
violence and control over other people, particularly women.

---

* As this goes to press, Robert Hardy, an informer in the "Camden
Twenty-eight" draft-board raid case, has confessed that he was a
provocateur, saying, "It is a case of manufacturing crimes to support
repressive policies and the political futures of persons in power." Donald
Janson, "FBI Is Accused of Aiding a Crime," *New York Times*, March
15, 1972, p. 1.

His longing for power makes him gravitate toward conspiracy.

At a deeper level, it seems that the pervasive atmosphere
and standards of foreign espionage have penetrated ever
more deeply into the consciousness of domestic agents.
Twenty years of cold-war intelligence work, including
years of brutal adventurism in Latin America and the Far
East, combined with the almost universal popularization of
its methods, in everything from James Bond novels to the
memoirs of CIA agents, have affected domestic undercover
agents. Some of them, such as Tongyai and Jarrett, actually
have such espionage work in their backgrounds. But all,
like Wilbert Thomas, feel that they are fighting an essentially foreign ideology, using the weapons of war. The FBI,
in particular, bears a heavy responsibility for introducing
the espionage ideology and encouraging its methods. The
methods of domestic espionage are actually quite civilized
compared with accepted tricks of foreign espionage, which
only begin with such provocations as black propaganda,
and extend over to manipulating weaker governments and
political assassination. To Jarrett, I am sure that the mere
delivery of hand grenades must have seemed a very mild
police action. The long-time fear of subversion and the
standards of foreign espionage have themselves invaded
domestic police work, and have destroyed whatever ethical
strictures it may have had in dealing with radicals.

Neither of these explanations, neither sloppy selection of
informers nor a corruption of standards by war, fully accounts for the policies operating behind the work that the
agents do. In every case, contemporary or otherwise, the
policy has been essentially the same. The provocation is intended to eliminate enemies, encourage further repression
from the authorities, and at the same time justify that repression to the public. In the campus cases, the provocation
was intended to smoke out and eliminate violent radicals, to
bring a greater police presence into the colleges and make
it seem necessary. Weapons were given to the Friends of

the Panthers to link them in the public mind with violence, to eliminate them and justify eliminating them. The Berrigan case is intended to frighten the Congress and the public into supporting the FBI. The Klan action in Meridian was intended, unfortunately, simply to liquidate some Klansmen.

And what policy did the Cain, De Leon, and West case advance? What policy did it advance to expend the efforts of an expensive agent on creating one tawdry little robbery? What policy did it advance to spend so many thousands of dollars, which could easily have been spent in Brownsville, trying to prove that the defendants really attempted that robbery? A very important policy from the point of view of Wilbert Thomas's superiors, I think. They wanted the public to think that Black Panthers, especially in Brooklyn, were not truly political at all, even in the violent sense, but simply "black gangsters." It was, in a deep sense, a racist policy intended to forge a direct link between the Black Panthers and a public fear of Negro crime in the streets. It was being pushed by elements in the police, but it was a policy exactly congruent with the views of the intransigent minority of the House Committee on Internal Security.

Earlier in this chapter, I had occasion to call official provocation a political act of desperation in a nation like the United States and a city like New York, because of the likelihood that the provocation will be exposed at a trial and thus undermine confidence in the government. Such desperation, I think, is reflected in the recent upsurge in political provocation. Law-enforcement agencies and other conservative authorities are desperate to have the public believe that really uncompromising forces for change, and especially those which oppose the police, are merely criminal. Unless they are stopped, these authorities must now take the next step in order to enforce their repression: that of limiting the protections of fair trial and free inquiry.

11

THE LAW:

REMEDIES AND FAILURES

The criminal trial process is not designed to control a social problem as serious and subtle as political provocation. The most that a trial could ever be expected to do is reveal the truth and do justice to defendants in particular cases; but under present law the trial does not even do that, except in a haphazard way.

The trial of Alfred Cain and his companions in the Brooklyn Black Panther Party for conspiracy to rob the New Dunston Hotel exposed, in a number of ways, both the strong points and weaknesses of the trial process in coming to grips with the political police.

The use of Wilbert Thomas's BOSS reports (the "René reports") proved to be one of the strong points for what are, I think, rather special reasons. The reports were not, apparently, intended for use in court; originally they were intended for the eyes of superior officers. Viewed in that light, they seem to show certain elements of sycophancy. At an early stage, Thomas reported that the Black Panthers were studying Marxism-Leninism—"Get it any way you can." Now, it is plain that no Black Panther used that phrase, so Wilbert Thomas must have used it, assuming that it would be greeted with approbation. Similarly, when he described the incident about being chased by a "pig on horseback," and provoked vituperation from the officer of the day, he must have expected approval. Thomas said repeatedly that he was allowed very little discretion in his actions. He told the jury and later Norma Sue Woodstone that he had to report constantly and follow detailed directions which left little room for "creative investigation." That seems to have been substantially accurate, and it suggests that the reports to a large extent reflected what his superiors wanted to read. We should think of them reading Patrolman Thomas's "suggestions" in the report of August 14 with approval.

The slant of the reports is a further confirmation that the "overzealous policeman" theory is not tenable for political provocation, and that a policeman may be intensely ambitious, as Thomas showed he was in his interview with Mrs. Woodstone, but the ambition is channeled and directed in such a way that superior officers—policy makers—must bear the responsibility for what is done and said in pursuit of advancement.

The René reports came to the defense under a rule, applicable in New York only since 1961, requiring that all background material of a prosecution witness be given to the defense after the witness completes his direct testimony. The rule figured in both of the Cain cases described in this book. In the misdemeanor trial, the court failed to order a policeman to produce his memoranda—clearly an error—but in the conspiracy case, the documents were produced. Before the New Dunston Hotel conspiracy trial, the rule had been applied only rarely to voluminous records of political infiltration like the René reports. The police, then, had not attuned themselves to look for the defenses which might arise out of the reports. The defense of entrapment, moreover, is new in New York State, having been in effect only since 1967, and it is even more unfamiliar in cases drawn up by the political police in New York City. It is to be expected that BOSS reports will become more and more colorless as time goes on. Wilbert Thomas himself testified in a way that varied from his written reports. In another, much smaller conspiracy case where political agents testified, I felt what may be a breeze blowing off the wave of the future. When I asked for all prior statements of the two agents who testified, the court ordered them to be produced, and after a short delay for a trip to headquarters, the prosecution produced a single sheet (suspiciously crisp, I thought) listing nothing but the names of the defendants, the charges, and the dates of arrest. That is ridiculous, of course, but it is possible to produce convincingly drab reports. Much of this book can unfortunately be used as a primer in what to leave out of a BOSS report. In short, one cannot expect the police to give out useful material for cross-examination forever, and lawyers in future cases may not be even as minimally fortunate as we were.

We were fortunate also that the prosecution was unable to gauge the temper of the times and the attitude of the jury. Wilbert Thomas entertained, and the prosecution supported, a set of iron assumptions that every piece of ferocious rhetoric proved a criminal intent, and that programs of serving the people were disguises for criminal conspiracies. All of that offended most of the jury and made them suspicious in our case, as it apparently did even more in the trial of the Panther Thirteen. The defense attorneys almost took it for granted that a "gangsters-in-black-berets" approach to the case would annoy many jurors, but the prosecution thought otherwise and even the defendants were not convinced. Reflecting upon the trial, I must say that it was not self-evident that the jury would be so sophisticated as to be offended. As recently as 1920, scarcely more than fifty years ago, a federal jury in Chicago took only an hour to convict a hundred members of the IWW of four counts of espionage.[1] Americans in large cities have imperceptibly become more suspicious of policemen than they were in 1920, or even in 1950.

Respect for the jury system has suffered vicissitudes in

the past hundred years, determined only partly by variations in public commitment to liberty.[2] Jerome Frank in the forties summed up the view of a whole generation that "trial by jury, as a method of determining facts, is antiquated and inherently absurd."[3] That view is not so widely shared any more; many of us would take it to be positively naive. Moreover, it is a surprising view for a legal realist like Frank, who recognized that judges are human beings who may have their views determined by economic or social prejudice. It could only have been justified for him on the assumption that juries are even more swayed by prejudice than judges, and that opinion, I believe, experience has shown to be generally wrong. Judges develop a kind of professional cynicism about legal cases and the sort of evidence which comes before them, which gradually kills their ability to see the freshness of facts and issues in the individual case. Increasingly, they tend to feel that they participate, as officials, in a process labeled "administration of justice" in which other officials, including policemen, participate. It creates a kind of "official bias" in favor of the testimony of public officials. Some judges, recognizing that they owe their jobs to the state, decide cases in such a way as to protect the state from claims of police abuse and from public criticism for official error. All these tendencies are strongest at the lowest level of the judiciary, because there the volume of cases is enormous and the pressures to create "assembly-line" justice are greatest.

The jury system has a number of characteristics which minimize these tendencies to stereotype cases and create institutional biases. Jurors, of course, are not professionals, and every case is new to them. Prejudice is brought into the open and reduced by the *voir dire* process. Most important, jurors owe nothing to the state. They are not paid regularly to be part of a "process," they have no sense of professional camaraderie with officials, and they have no desire to protect the state from criticism. The division of functions between judge and jury—the duty of the judge to explain the law, and of the jury to apply the law to the facts—in itself tends to reduce the possibility of unconscious or unspoken prejudice, because it requires everyone concerned to think through the facts and the law at least once. The kind of "gut-reaction" decision of which juries are often accused is actually quite difficult to carry out under a jury system. It is much easier for a judge acting alone, as law and fact-finder combined, to make such a snap decision.

A comparison between the misdemeanor trial of the Cain brothers in Chapter 2 and the conspiracy case casts all the contrasts I discuss here into high relief. The comparison is not a caricature, however; jury-justice is generally better than judge-justice. Although, of course, there are a few judges whose decisions are preferable to those of a jury, on the average and in the long run it has been my experience that the jury has to be the fairer deliberative body. The Supreme Court was clearly right in its decisions compelling the extension of the right to a jury trial to misdemeanor cases.

The advantages of the jury system now seem almost self-evident. In this day when "expertise" and "professionalism" are constantly under suspicion as mere covers for resistance to change, it is not surprising that an ancient institution for community decision-making should come into favor. Moreover, during any period when there is great grass-roots demand for change, with resistance and repression from above, the jury will seem comparatively free and liberal in its decisions. When the populace is relatively conservative, or uninterested in politics, the jury will seem less important. The jury seemed to be of inestimable value during periods of struggle for civil rights in England and the colonies against the Crown and to a lesser extent in cases growing out of labor disputes, and it has seemed valueless or worse under conditions of race prejudice or jingoistic nationalism.

The Black Panthers, chiefly through the trial of Huey

Newton, had attacked racism among white jurors in 1968 and 1969, and at the same time, cases like the Chicago Conspiracy case were coming to trial, in a manner which called into question the judgment of prosecutors and judges. The Panthers, the Chicago Seven defendants, and many others who insisted on calling their trials "political" and on bringing the issues in the trials constantly before the public, were excoriated for contributing to the destruction of neutral trial procedures. Actually, the contrary seems to have occurred; public concern coalesced around the issue of the fairness of the trial process, and trials perhaps became more fair. "Fair trial" was a slogan that radicals and liberals could agree about, and people who were interested in the issues from reading the newspapers, but who would never get involved in confrontation even to the extent of attending a peaceful demonstration, could make extremely conscientious jurors. It was not likely that trials would have become more fair and more free of racism if all defendants had sat quietly and insisted that they were fair; they could be improved only through defendants dramatically asserting the ways that their trials were unfair. An impartial jury has assumed paramount importance in political cases.

The right to a jury trial and the right to obtain background reports for cross-examination are institutional protections important to a defendant in any trial, and particularly so in a political case. They may vary in their effectiveness from time to time, but they are designed to be, and tend to be, genuine protections over the long run. In addition, in the New Dunston Hotel case, we were simply lucky about some elements of the trial process. The judges who presided over both trials and the attorneys who defended them were relatively able and fair. As other disastrous trials have shown, with biased judges or lazy counsel it could easily have been otherwise. The temper of the times may have loaded the dice just a little even here; the judges were determined to avoid every suggestion or suspicion of un-fairness. One of them had been particularly nettled by Kingman Brewster's pronouncement, then fresh in the news, and grumbled from time to time, "We'll see whether a black militant can get a fair trial."

TOWARD A BETTER TRIAL

The institutional protections against *agents provocateurs* were few in the New Dunston Hotel trial; they were rein-forced by luck and the public mood. Different laws, both of procedure and substance, would have made this trial a bet-ter one, and would make the trial process in similar cases better able to find the facts and do justice, and less at the mercy of the public mood.

CRIMES OF POSSESSION

One of the most serious legal problems in the case was presented in a provision of the New York Penal Law, local in its effects, but typical of the sort of statute which makes conviction in any complex criminal case extremely likely. All three defendants in the case were charged with possess-ing a sawed-off shotgun under a law which makes everyone riding in an automobile presumptively liable for any illegal weapon in the car unless it is in the possession of one indi-vidual.[4] Thus the jury could convict all three defendants of possessing the shotgun merely by finding that the gun was on the floor of the car. It was possible to convict the de-fendants of a serious felony simply because they got into a car, unquestionably supplied by the police department, in which a loaded shotgun of uncertain origin was present.

It is not clear that the members of the jury realized all this. Some apparently thought that Alfred Cain might have had possession of the gun, and others that he did not. In some general way, they thought all the defendants were responsible for the gun.

I conclude from this that the presumption making all those in an automobile liable for a weapon is confusing. The jury cannot tell what will rebut the presumption, and the statute opens an easy avenue of compromise by which everyone can be convicted, without assigning any clear criminal responsibility. That appears in fact to be one of the purposes of such a statute, and for that reason "presumptions" assigning collective or imputed responsibility ought to be dropped from the law. At the very least, when imputed responsibility is used, only the mildest penalty ought to be attached to the offense because of the likelihood of error. The possible seven-year sentence which attaches to possession of a loaded firearm should never be carried through, as it apparently was in the case of De Leon, to one who is merely *presumed* to possess the gun.

A change in the presumption in weapons crimes is only typical of a thousand changes which ought to be made in the substance of criminal law. There are, in addition, some systematic changes in criminal procedure which would particularly affect political conspiracy cases.

DISCLOSURE OF THE FACTS

The present rule which permits a defendant's lawyer to look at reports of the witnesses who testify for the prosecution is too restrictive, in cases which involve long-term, organized infiltration. The rule is relatively workable for crimes which involve a single act, or a series of simple acts, like the sale of contraband, in which one or two informants are involved. When the agent is part of a larger scheme of infiltration, it is just not enough to be able to look at his notes and not at those of the superiors who direct and analyze his work. Furthermore, the history of secret police practice shows that it is common to put more than one agent into an organization, as a check on reliability. It stands to reason that the reports of agents in the same organization will occasionally contradict one another, and defendants should have access to that information. As Conrad Lynn pointed out during the conspiracy trial, the reports of other agents and superiors are particularly necessary when the defense tries to prove entrapment, because the only proof of provocation, apart from the word of the defendants, is likely to be in the government reports. We were exceptionally lucky, in the New Dunston Hotel case, that there were independent witnesses to other acts of provocation.

In civil cases, it is not unusual for the parties to be able to obtain all sorts of memoranda in an effort to prove conspiracy. In antitrust cases, for example, the parties obtain bales of documents in an effort to find proof of a scheme to restrain trade, or to trace conspirators. In such cases, a report from an executive to his subordinate may be used as proof of intent; the entire apparatus of a corporation may be examined. There are restrictions against "fishing expeditions," but in practice, anything colorably related to the case may be investigated. Even in criminal cases involving commercial transactions, the government is usually able to get voluminous documents, at least from competitors and other possible witnesses. Defendants in criminal cases do not have any such powers in relation to the government, even when it is plain that the case being tried originated as part of a larger scheme of investigation.

The disparity in rights to examine background material is commonly justified in a number of ways. It is said that to open police files on a case will reveal the identity of agents and informants, which will destroy their usefulness and may endanger them personally. But the usefulness of agents that the government chooses to call upon as its own witnesses is impaired, and the danger, if there is any, runs against them as well. It is hard to see how the need to keep secret the names of one or two other agents can compare with the need for a fair trial and a thorough airing of the facts. If the government may choose to impair the usefulness of one agent, the defense should be able to call on others. Of course, records may contain evidence which is irrelevant to one case while it is valuable in another, but there are recognized methods by which a trial judge may sequester such material.

I think that the true basis for the rule which permits the government to dig into the files of a witness for evidence of conspiracy, while the criminal defendant has no similar power to subpoena the files of the government, is an unstated assumption that the likelihood of misconduct by government is much smaller than the likelihood of crime by private parties. There is no justification for looking in government files, the courts feel, because there is no great reason for supposing they contain evidence of wrongdoing. If the study of *agents provocateurs* in the previous chapter proves nothing else, it at least ought to suggest that that doctrine is dangerous.

There is a rule, now known as the *Brady* rule, which is intended, roughly, to cover the problem of full disclosure to the defense. The *Brady* case stated a general rule of fairness.

> [T]he suppression by the prosecution of evidence favorable to an accused upon request violates due process where the evidence is material either to guilt or to punishment, irrespective of the good faith or bad faith of the prosecution.[5]

Even presuming absolute good faith on the part of prosecutors, the rule is almost unworkable at the present time, because there is nothing but the occasional accident to reveal what the favorable evidence might be. No prosecutor can be expected to spend time looking for evidence to help the other side, and he may not recognize it if he sees it, because he may not know what his adversary's theory of the case is. A prime example occurred in the course of our conspiracy case. In the René reports, we read that Wilbert Thomas told Fat Man about a plan for a robbery, and that Fat Man said he did not want to hear about it. Now, did the prosecution reveal the existence of that report to Fat Man's lawyer? Certainly not. If trials are to begin to deal with political infiltration, the *Brady* rule must be expanded, at least in cases where there has been infiltration, to permit the defense to examine every document or report which is relevant to the case, and not merely those which relate to a particular witness, in order to make an intelligent search for exculpatory evidence. The present rules discriminate extraordinarily in favor of the state in a case in which there has been systematic infiltration.

This is a big step in criminal procedure, but it is not an impossible one for the courts to take; such a change was suggested by Abraham Goldstein of Yale Law School more than ten years ago.[6] The underlying rationale of the *Brady* case and similar cases seems to point in the same direction, because the requirement that the prosecution give exculpatory evidence to the defense cannot effectively be administered any other way.

JUDICIAL CONTROL OF SECRET AGENTS

Access to the records of what agents have done is only the most elementary of the checks upon the work of infiltrators that are needed by society and the courts. Much more important is some control over agents before they undertake their investigations. We had raised this issue too, in the New Dunston Hotel trials, without success.

A policeman, in uniform and representing himself to be a policeman, cannot get into a citizen's house to look at his private papers at all, unless the policeman has a warrant or obtains consent. But a policeman representing himself to be a friend can enter the citizen's house and talk to him all day long, obtaining the same information that is in the private papers. It is very likely that he can take the papers themselves and use them as evidence, if the citizen gives them to him as a friend.[7] It is said that the citizen "consents" by his very act of communicating with another person, even though he supposes him to be someone different. Despite this fiction, it seems that the similarities between infiltration and search are greater than the differences. A warrant is required for a search and seizure in order to protect the individual from intrusion by the state into his private affairs. The theory of the warrant requirement is that citizens should not feel that the authorities may come in on them arbitrarily and without just cause. There is, moreover, an element of freedom of speech and the press in many search cases, because the authorities are often looking for papers which are incriminating in connection with political crimes; the early English cases generally involved searches for political documents, and such searches are still common.[8] Citizens will hestitate to keep radical writings in their houses if they expect that the police will come in at any time. Infiltration by police agents creates a similar chilling effect, because the citizen never knows when to expect infiltration, has no protection against it, and cannot tell which of his loose pronouncements may be written down in a police report. A federal appeals court expressed the connection precisely.

> If the law places great risks of governmental intrusion on an individual's activity, especially in his private speech, he will be inhibited in the exercise of his first amendment rights, that is, the broader the scope of governmental searches and seizures which are determined to be consistent with the fourth amendment, the narrower the ambit of protected first amendment activity will become.[9]

Nevertheless, it has been the custom to permit infiltration of any group at the whim of the police, merely because the group is radical or in some other way piques the curiosity of the police; no prior judicial approval is required. It may be argued that a person need never fear infiltration the way he might fear a search, because he will never know about the infiltration unless he commits a crime. Once the use of infiltration becomes general, however, and a few arrests have been made, then everyone fears it even more than a search because he never knows when it is happening. In this respect, infiltration is like electronic surveillance. The use of an infiltrator, moreover, presents special problems that searches and even wiretapping do not present. The agent can construe one's words in a way they were not meant, or can lie about them. Finally, of course, the agent gets involved with those among whom he does his work, and may end up by entrapping them.

Based on these considerations alone, some judicial control over the use of informants is essential. Before introducing an infiltrator into a group, or making use of an agent who offers his services, the police should be obliged to make a showing to a judge that there is concrete evidence that a crime is being or has been planned or committed. If there is such evidence, an infiltration warrant may be issued. After this warrant has been issued, the police should make reports to the court at regular intervals, demonstrating that continued surveillance is needed.

Before the agent actually participates in a conspiracy or other crime, the judicial procedure for surveillance, the infiltration warrant, should be supplemented by a decoying warrant. Whether or not the agent has passed through a period of infiltration under a warrant, if he has time to make a report to his employers, they should report in turn to a judge. The court should have the power to disapprove the decoying warrant if the reports show substantial risk of entrapment, or if there is no reason to believe that a crime is being or will be committed.* In the New Dunston

---

* Of course, there will be instances when there is no time to get a decoying warrant, just as there are instances when there is no time to get a

Hotel case, for example, under the warrant procedures outlined here, the police would have had to obtain a warrant
to put Wilbert Thomas into the Black Panther Party, and
to justify the continuation of his surveillance work by
progress reports. In addition, at the time that the police
became convinced that an actual crime (conspiracy) was
in progress, they would have had to obtain judicial approval for Thomas to be a part of it.

This infiltration- and decoying-warrant plan for control
of agents is derived from existing law about electronic
eavesdropping and searches. In fact, the parallel is so compelling that variations of the plan, or parts of it, have been
proposed over and over again by legal scholars.[10] It is
quite as feasible as the present system of warrants for
electronic surveillance.[11] If the plan has a defect, it is not
that it is radical or impractical, but that it is not effective
enough. Judges will have a tendency to rubber-stamp the
applications of prosecutors for warrants, and the police
will tend to produce stereotype affidavits that will support
those applications. Nevertheless, a warrant system would
at least make everyone pause a little to be sure there is some
reason to use an infiltrator, if only because there is some
trouble involved in drawing the papers. More important,
it would tend to curtail the tailoring of reports to fit a particular case. If no reports are given to anyone other than the
police until the time of trial, they can be drawn in any
way that suits the case. If they have to be submitted to a
judge, they may be colored in such a way as to support an
application for an infiltration warrant, or for continued
surveillance, but they cannot be changed in the light of
later events. The applicants are obliged to adhere to their

search warrant. A subsequent showing that there was sufficient probable
cause, and absence of the risk of entrapment, to have justified a decoying
warrant will justify having offered the opportunity for a crime. It is hard
to imagine such an emergency in the case of infiltration over a period of
time, and surveillance (as distinguished from decoying) without a warrant should ordinarily be forbidden.

story, whatever it is. While their effects are very limited, then, the infiltration and decoying warrants have some virtues. They are logically a part of the protection of privacy, and they should be part of the law.

THE ENTRAPMENT DEFENSE

The entrapment defense must be carefully defined for conspiracy cases. Under present law, there are slightly varying definitions of this defense, which do not entirely comport with one another. The classic cases of entrapment in American law involve, not conspiracy, but crimes of sale and possession of contraband. In the most complete Supreme Court review of the problem, for example, the defendant was under the care of a doctor in order to be cured of drug addiction; the informant was a fellow patient.

> He asked petitioner [defendant] to supply him with a source because he was not responding to treatment. From the first, the petitioner tried to avoid the issue. Not until after a number of repetitions of the request, predicated on [the informant's] presumed suffering, did petitioner finally acquiesce....[12]

He was subsequently arrested and convicted of selling drugs. The Supreme Court reversed, and the majority reaffirmed the prevailing rule that entrapment occurs

> when the criminal design originates with the officials of the Government, and they implant in the mind of an innocent person the disposition to commit the alleged offense and induce its commission....[13]

Although it may be adequate for such cases as this, that rule does not work well in conspiracy cases. A conspiracy typically involves a number of elements and overt acts leading up to the planned crime. It is usually hard to say whether the plan "originated" in the minds of the defendants or in that of their co-conspirator, the agent. Under

the subjective or "predisposition" standard of the Supreme
Court, it is doubtful that the defense can be successful
unless the original idea for the entire plan comes from the
agent, a state of facts nearly impossible to prove. Much
more common, as the cases in Chapter 10 prove, is the
situation where many elements come from the defendants
but it is doubtful that they would have or could have
formed a complete plan without the agent. In that case,
one may feel there has been excessive provocation, but a
subjective test which looks into the defendants' minds
might find them "predisposed" and thus reject the defense.

Justice Felix Frankfurter advocated an objective rule;
in his formulation, the court should make a judgment about
whether the agent's actions create an undue risk of entrapping an innocent person.

> The crucial question . . . to which the court must direct itself
> is whether the police conduct revealed in the particular case
> falls below standards to which common feelings respond for
> the proper use of government power.[14]

He went on:

> No matter what the defendant's past record and present in-
> clinations to criminality or the depths to which he has sunk
> in the estimation of society, certain police conduct to ensnare
> him into further crime is not to be tolerated by an advanced
> society.[15]

One formulation of the objective standard has been
adopted in the New York statute: If the actions of the
policeman create a "substantial risk" that a person not
otherwise disposed to commit a crime would commit it,
then the defendant is entrapped within the meaning of the
law.[16] In conspiracy cases, the "substantial-risk" standard
inevitably works much better than the subjective standard.
Where there is a mixture of elements of the plan and of
overt acts coming from all parties, the jury will have to

decide whether the elements contributed by the agent were so essential that they created a substantial risk of entrapment. In the New Dunston Hotel case, the jury probably could never have resolved adequately the issues of "intent" on the part of individual defendants, but they were able to determine that the suggestions made by Wilbert Thomas on and before August 14 could not help but create an enormous risk of entrapment.

In his charge to the jury in the second trial, the judge combined both standards, quoting the statute, but adding that if the police planted the intent in an otherwise innocent defendant's mind, then the defense was available. My impression is that this was quite confusing and made it very hard for the jury to apply the defense. In the end they seem to have succeeded in applying a version of the objective test. As the forelady put it, "It was as if there were a fulcrum with proper police work on one side, and overstepping the bounds on the other." In the future, the courts should definitively restrict the entrapment defense to a "substantial-risk" test, so that it will be clear to juries that they are deciding about the quality of police work when they consider entrapment, and not about the quality of defendants.

The application of the defense of entrapment to crimes of possessing contraband, such as weapons, presents a special problem. The issue has not often arisen; almost all entrapment cases have dealt with a temptation offered by an agent to *sell* contraband which the defendant himself already possessed. When an agent does inveigle someone into possessing something, or gives him something to sell to another agent (although it is extremely rare that a defendant can prove such a set of facts), it is clear that the entrapment defense ought to apply. In the *Freed-Sutherland* hand-grenade case discussed in Chapter 10, the facts were clear, but the Supreme Court avoided the issue because it was properly a matter to be presented at trial. In the lower courts, the issue has come up only in recent years. In one case, where it was found that an informer had supplied the contraband sold by the defendant to a second agent, Federal Judge Constance Baker Motley outlined the only acceptable rule.

> [I]f the government were the source of the contraband, it seems clear defendant was entrapped *as a matter of law*.[17]

A similar defense ought to apply to the presumption which makes all persons riding in an automobile responsible for a weapon found in it, when the automobile comes from the police. If the presumption could be applied when the automobile comes from the police, all an infiltrator would have to do in order to obtain a conviction of everyone riding in his car would be to ask any person in the car who was armed to lay his weapon on the floor. In the New Dunston Hotel trial, I did request a charge consistent with Judge Motley's formulation, but it was rejected; such a case had never been reported in New York, and there was no law in the state on the point. It seems quite clear, however, that if the state supplies contraband, that should constitute a defense to a charge of possession or sale of the contraband, and if the state supplies a car, that should constitute a defense to the presumption about automobiles. The prosecutor in the *Freed* case, quoted in the preceding chapter, thought that it should make a difference whether the defendants were eager or reluctant to possess the contraband. This would be consistent with the traditional subjective formulation of entrapment, but it now seems inadequate. Supplying contraband or the essential elements of a presumption offers too much opportunity for framing defendants, and it is difficult to imagine a case where the public policy of a state would justify such an act. Considering the problem in the light of the objective test for entrapment, we may say that in a prosecution for possession or sale of contraband, if the contraband has been supplied by an agent, that automatically creates a substantial risk that innocent people will be entrapped.

This survey of recommendations for change in criminal procedure shows that it is at least possible for the law to exert some little control over the actions of secret agents. Broader disclosure to the defense would make it harder for the police to conceal provocation, the surveillance- and decoying-warrant procedure would afford judicial control over agents, and a "substantial-risk" rule for entrapment would help to set standards for police practice in conspiracy cases. Although I do not pretend that these changes would eliminate all the abuses of the secret police, it is important to realize that official provocation and its parent, surveillance, are not apocalyptic political problems beyond any practical remedy. That approach would tend to excuse and confirm courts and legislatures in their present policy of doing nothing at all about the problems of surveillance.

The objective standard for the defense of entrapment has been widely advocated, and occasionally adopted. It may yet become the accepted rule for the entrapment defense, but it is the least effective of all the protections needed against provocation. The two more important protections, those of broader disclosure and prior judicial control, are obstructed by major legal roadblocks.

DISCLOSURE OF THE FACTS

In the *Jencks* case,[18] arising out of a prosecution for the filing of an allegedly false non-Communist affidavit by a labor union official, the Supreme Court ruled that prior statements made to the FBI by witnesses, including the notoriously unreliable Harvey Matusow, had to be given to the defense for cross-examination. Even such disclosure, limited as it is to the earlier statements of witnesses who testify, which seems to be an essential part of the right to cross-examine one's accusers, came under attack from the FBI and congressmen. As the Supreme Court later put it:

> The day following our opinion [in Jencks], the House of Representatives was told that the decision in Jencks posed a serious problem of national security and that legislation would be introduced.[19]

Congress codified the decision in the Jencks Act,[20] which provided that "no statement or report in the possession of the United States which was made by a Government witness or prospective Government witness" should be supplied until after the witness testified. It is possible to interpret this statute so that it does not cover statements of agents who are never called as witnesses by the government, but in the light of the controversy preceding the legislation, the courts have tended to treat the Jencks Act as the *exclusive* means of obtaining statements of agents. Nothing but statements by witnesses who have already testified are available. The *Brady* rule, requiring disclosure of exculpatory evidence, is really ineffective against the strictures of the Jencks Act. The right of disclosure with regard to statements of agents has never expanded, and is not likely to do so in the foreseeable future.

JUDICIAL CONTROL OF SECRET AGENTS

At the present time the law is not developing in the direction of an infiltration warrant. Quite the contrary: control over secret agents is a problem which has fallen between that of electronic surveillance on the one hand and physical search on the other. The reasons are partly historical. The Fourth Amendment provides:

> The right of the people to be secure in their persons, houses, papers, and effects, against unreasonable searches and seizures, shall not be violated, and no warrants shall issue, but upon probable cause, supported by oath or affirmation,

and particularly describing the place to be searched, and the person or things to be seized.

Under present law, evidence seized in violation of this amendment is excluded from a criminal trial. The words of the amendment are designed to deal with a physical search as we know it, of a house or a person; in effect, they protect one particular aspect of a broader right of privacy. With the advent of sophisticated wiretapping and bugging equipment, a rather different invasion of privacy was assimilated to the ideas of "search" and "seizure." The law concerning bugging and wiretapping developed in such a way that it dealt with the entire field of electronic surveillance by a third party listening, whether through a wall or a wire, to the conversations of others. Judicial approval has been required for all electronic eavesdropping by third parties.[21] The notion of a physical "search" was almost abandoned for electronic surveillance, because everyone recognized that the problem was one of intrusion on privacy rather than upon some specific place.[22]

The requirement of a warrant for electronic surveillance, however, did not extend to recordings of conversations between two people when one of them, rather than a third party, was carrying the microphone, and no law, of course, reached as far as control of the actions of a person who reported his private conversations without the aid of a microphone and a tape recorder—the typical informer. Supreme Court justices who were concerned about the growth of surveillance techniques emphasized the sophistication of electronic equipment, and tended to recommend the extension of Fourth Amendment search-and-seizure standards to recordings by a party to a conversation. They ignored the problem of the informer pure and simple. Justice William J. Brennan, in advocating controls over electronic recordings of conversations, even by one of the parties, used the problem of the informer as a counterweight. In an opinion dissenting from the majority rule that one of two parties could make a legally admissible recording of a conversation, he had these words to say about informers:

> [T]here is a qualitative difference between electronic surveillance, whether the agents conceal the devices on their persons or in walls or under beds, and conventional police stratagems such as eavesdropping and disguise. The latter do not so seriously intrude upon the right of privacy. The risk of being overheard by an eavesdropper or betrayed by an informer or deceived as to the identity of one with whom one deals is probably inherent in the conditions of human society. It is the kind of risk we necessarily assume whenever we speak.[23]

The results of this position have been disastrous. The informer problem as a whole has been thrown away in pursuit of the solution to the problem of electronic surveillance. In 1967, when the Supreme Court was presented with the informer problem, no justice on the Court was in a position to say that the use of an informer, in the absence of electronic surveillance, gave rise to substantial problems of search and seizure.[24]

Conservative jurists recognized that the position of some judges who would accept the testimony of an informer merely because he relied only on his own memory, but would reject a recording of his conversations made without a warrant, was not strong. Finally, in the latest case dealing with a recording made by a party to the conversation, the majority said:

> If the conduct and revelations of an agent operating without electronic equipment do not invade the defendant's constitutionally justifiable expectations of privacy, neither does a simultaneous recording of the same conversations made by the agent to whom the defendant is talking and whose trustworthiness the defendant necessarily risks.[25]

In the end, in 1971, the law afforded no judicial control over informers, whether armed with microphones or mere notebooks.

Almost universally, judges and lawyers, like Justice Brennan in the words quoted above, have taken it to be a fact of life that police informers are beyond the control of prior judicial approval. It need not have been so. The words of Thomas Erskine May (quoted in the epigraph to Part Three), written as long ago as 1863 concerning the provocations under Sidmouth, contrast strikingly with the sentiments of Justice Brennan.[26] It is certainly possible for the strictures on search and seizure in the Fourth Amendment to be extended to information seized by means of an informer, just as they have been extended to information "seized" by means of a wiretap. The reason that they have never been so extended lies not only in the peculiar history of the law of search and seizure, but in the lack of a sense of danger from the use of "mere" informers. The words of Justice Brennan appear to contemplate the use of informers as an occasional practice, such as might occur when one genuine conspirator becomes a turncoat and informs on his companions. Under such circumstances, the use of an informer has been considered a legitimate police practice, and the courts have literally felt that they ought to encourage it. The possibility of a widespread system of infiltration has never been confronted, and jurists have not realized that such a thing could grow up—indeed, *had* to grow up—in the absence of controls. American jurists have been naive, at best, in accepting the police demand for total secrecy in detective work.

One hopeful sign is that courts have indicated that they may issue injunctions in cases brought against particular surveillance practices. Evidence which would be admissible if an informer presented it in a criminal case may be got at collaterally through a suit to prevent the surveillance before a criminal case develops, on the ground that the detriment to First Amendment rights is greater than the state's interest in gathering facts without probable cause to believe a crime is being committed. Yet these cases must depend upon the few occasions when someone accidentally finds out that surveillance is being conducted. They probably will be dismissed if they are brought "blind," upon mere suspicion of surveillance. Important as their function is, it is not likely that injunction actions can be relied on to do more than suggest the mass of secret surveillance.

In theory, the present state of the law in the Supreme Court still does not absolutely exclude the possibility of developing judicial controls through the courts. If the problem of the informer were to come to the Court in a political context, if the informer were a police agent in a political group, if he were to seize writings and base on them a case for criminal anarchy or some other political crime, protections might begin to develop. The duty of the courts to control informers would thus clearly be related to the First as well as the Fourth Amendment, through the need to prevent a system of surveillance which stifles by widespread suspicion the freedom of association and discussion. The practical prospects for judicial control of political infiltration by a system of warrants and an exclusionary rule, however, are dim. On one occasion when the use of informers came up in a political case, the idea of judicial control by prior approval was rejected.[27] In the light of the general acceptance of uncontrolled use of informers, epitomized in the latest decisions, it is now still more difficult to make a special distinction for political cases. Without an aroused public, howling for an end to abusive surveillance to the point where disorder threatens, such a change either by the courts or the legislature is almost inconceivable.

The possibility of developing greater protections for citizens against the political police is receding, in the final analysis, because of the policies of the government and the courts. If any special rule for political cases is likely to develop in the immediate future, it is that defendants will have fewer rights in such cases. Already the Justice Department has tried to dodge the requirement of judicial approval for electronic eavesdropping (the nearest analogue to an infiltration warrant) in cases affecting "the national security." One of the chief recommendations of the 1971 report of the House Internal Security Committee on the Black Panthers was that local police departments should receive funds from the federal Justice Department to finance political surveillance. The courts have been sadly willing, over the years, to accept the executive definition of a threat to security. In interpreting the *Jencks* rule, the courts were impressed by the public demand for "security" in FBI reports. They have always recognized a paramount need for secrecy in police work, and have never believed that there was any abuse in the use of informers so widespread as to call for legal change.

Under these conditions, the use of political provocation is likely to grow. There is an enormous desire in the executive branch to control political dissent and eliminate the annoyance of radicals. There is an equally great desire in the judiciary to ignore the fact that such a drive can only be carried out by systematic use of informers and *provocateurs*. For the foreseeable future, we are likely to be restricted to the protections we already have, and we are going to have to fight to keep those few intact, even down to the jury trial.

CONCLUSION

Legal and political problems—the conspiracy trial and its aftermath, the study of political provocation and its possible remedies—have taken us very far from the people in the streets, the people in this book.

It is time to come back to those people, because they were aware of a great many problems surrounding the New Dunston Hotel case which lay outside the theater of the trial. Alfred Cain recognized many of those problems, which previous chapters have only touched upon. The district attorney, acting through the grand jury, obtained an indictment of Alfred Cain, Ricardo De Leon, and Jerome West for a great mass of charges. Before the three defendants could get to work to show how questionable those charges actually were, they were being held in jail on enormously high bail. Alfred Cain knew that incarceration awaiting trial was part of their punishment, as well as that the number and complexity of the charges made a compromise conviction on some charge extremely likely. He perceived in a broad way something that the procedural limitations described in the foregoing chapter spell out: that the trial process was not designed to get behind the policeman's story to the truth.

If it is true that the trial of the three was more nearly fair than most, Alfred Cain, Jr., and the other defendants were simply not ready to be satisfied with the elements of fairness at the trial. If the stunning litany of charges in the indictment and a long detention in the Tombs had not soured them, their previous experience would have done so. After the outrage of their first misdemeanor trial, Alfred and Anthony Cain were not prepared to believe that they could get a fair trial. Their direct impression of criminal justice was shaped in the misdemeanor court, and whatever faith they retained that justice could be had, even against patent abuses, was destroyed there. Their experience is proof that it is of very little use to undertake an expensive, deliberative process in show trials and give slipshod, discriminatory justice in the general run of cases. Most people have their experience of the law in run-of-the-mill cases, and show trials cannot change the bitterness created by sloppy and prejudicial trial procedures.

It is no use to tell Alfred and Anthony Cain that a trial was fair "as trials go." It is too late for them and other people like them to compromise. That refusal to compromise, in fact, was their salient characteristic and that of other members of the Black Panther Party who have permitted me to set forth their memories and opinions in this book. They were formed, with some exceptions, by similar experiences—on the streets, in the schools, in the courts, in the army. Some were more tough-minded than others and some were physically tougher, but on the whole, so far from being the gangsters that the state would have them be, they were among the most committed and ablest people in their community. Some of them, including Alfred Cain, were as uncompromising in their demand for revolutionary change as for anything else. That stubbornness, that belief that the time has come to try for change at any cost, is where the tragedy lies in the confrontation between people and the state.

The Cain brothers do not expect the shortcomings in the trial process to be changed by reform any more than they expect it in the rest of society. For them, the defects of the trial reflect racism and the economic interests of the ruling class. Are they wrong about that? One way to think about this question is to consider the actual cost to the state in dollars and cents of the New Dunston Hotel conspiracy trial. I estimated that cost, including such items as the salaries of the judges, court officers, police witnesses, stenographers, and defense counsel and the cost of incarceration, at about a hundred thousand dollars. I asked Alfred Cain for his comments on that expense.

I'm glad that the state had to spend so much of their god [money] trying to hook us up: I feel this is an indication that we were doing something that was hurting these pigs who were oppressing us. We had been dealing with organizing, agitating, attempting to educate black people. Our actions were not as effective as they could have been had we taken the time to develop more of a foundation for basing our actions around at that time. But it was obvious because of the fact that the pigs had to spend so much of their money, we must be hurting them some kind of way. They must have felt that we were getting across to a certain amount of people if they went through the changes that they did to set us up and spend the money they did in the first place.

If we had the money to spend, right now I think it would have to be spent on weapons and other equipment necessary to defend the black community from the fascist aggression that is being committed against the people. Under different circumstances, it would be used to educate young black people who haven't acquired the technical skills necessary to rebuild our community. I don't know how many doctors could have been created with the use of those funds in a positive way, how many fucked-up houses in Brownsville or Bedford-Stuyvesant could have been rehabilitated with that money and made into decent housing so people could live without having to deal with rats and roaches and other inhumane conditions. We see that the priorities of the state are geared toward maintaining the interests of the state, not toward implementing any programs to elevate the people. That's the reason why the state spent the money that they did, because they felt as though we were trying to educate the people to their nature and therefore the money they spent—they figured they would be able to save a lot more to save that part of their regime that's left.

The case against the defendants in the New Dunston Hotel case had a great many weaknesses, particularly in its conspiracy sections. They were weaknesses that were fairly plain from the outset, on the face of the prosecution's case. An arrest could have been made for possession of weapons alone, which would have avoided most of the legal difficulties. It might even have resulted in a conviction, but it would not have proved anything for political purposes; it would have been one more unsurprising arrest of Black Panthers for violating the weapons laws. In this case, the political police were willing to take enormous risks, to expend manpower and money, on the chance that they might be able to convince the public that some Black Panthers were authentic gangsters. More generally, the police want to show some success in controlling crime in the streets, and they want to vindicate to the public their own opinion that the left, especially that part of it made up of black men, is bent on criminal violence. The political police are willing to take risks to make that story come true, so that repression will be justified.

The political police, and those who sponsor them, would prefer to spend society's wealth in the effort to construct a world where those who try for change are criminals, rather than spend it in an attempt to solve problems, even by such elementary means as education and medical assistance. Justifying social repression becomes more important than trying to solve social problems. The political police are confirming, in their own way, Alfred Cain's view that racism and class interests dictate the shape of criminal justice.

Viewed in this light, the authorities seem more desperate

than their adversaries. They are totally unwilling to compromise, to use means alternative to arrest and prosecution in dealing with the impulse to radicalism. It is not surprising that they chose as an agent a man like Wilbert Thomas. He is as determined as the Black Panthers, and if anything much more uncompromising in his views. He exhibits the same courage, the same willingness to take risks, to enforce his convictions. His views and his methods are, like theirs, in some ways the long-term results of war. He comes from the same people, but instead of aims of revolution he has adopted the aims of those who believe that demands for social change are criminal conspiracies. The New Dunston Hotel case, at the street level, was a tragic meeting between determined black men, on one side demanding social change at all costs, on the other resisting it at all costs. At the political level, it was a conflict between a force demanding change and a force resisting it by repression.

Fat Man continues to work at his job in the community. He was offered a "deal" on his stupendous indictment, whereby he might plead guilty to possessing a rifle without having registered it with the city—a most minor offense— to cover the whole indictment. He took that deal, and was given an "unconditional discharge"—no sentence at all. The misdemeanor to which he pleaded may well have been the only crime of which any defendant was truly guilty.

Jerome West and Ricardo De Leon are in jail serving their long sentences as this is written. The New Dunston Hotel case is on appeal, chiefly upon narrow grounds relating to the weapons charges. Ricardo De Leon has published in the *Village Voice* a series of eloquent articles on prison conditions, and has been indicted as a leader of the rebellion in the Tombs in October 1970.

Anthony Cain is in a civil service training program. Alfred Cain, Jr., is attending Brooklyn College, where he is a sophomore—he still sometimes wears his old army dress

coat with the little portrait of Mao in place of the marksmanship medal. His views have not changed very much.
Melvina Cain says:

> If I could give him to the army and then they send him some-
> where to kill somebody, I can say right on, go on, and better
> for your brothers, better for your sons. If he has to fight, he'd
> as well fight for what's right. I think this entanglement with
> the laws, certain things that happened to them I know were
> set for them, like traps and snares. So that I cannot say, well,
> stop then. If you are fighting for what you believe is right, go
> on, right on, fight for it. No use for me to slap you and cry. It's
> not going to do any good. Go on, fight. Get it out of your sys-
> tem. Because I've cried; crying doesn't do any good.

APPENDIX A

TELEPHONE CONVERSATION
BETWEEN RICARDO DE LEON AND WILBERT THOMAS, AUGUST 15, 1969

DE LEON. Hello. Power to the people. Hey listen, what the fuck do you mean by leaving me up there, man?

THOMAS. I tried to get you to leave.

DE LEON. Yeah, right, but I had to relate to some pussy, man, shit damn. Hey, dig it, I couldn't relate to it too tough because I was just trying to get there [*inaudible*] motherfucking meeting was over. I had to put up with that jive. The niggers he was relating to was up there on the stage talking some off-the-wall shit. You saw that big nigger that was talking all that off-the-wall shit.

THOMAS. Yeah.

DE LEON. The reason why I had to deal with all that shit because them Panthers over there is paper Panthers talking that shit, man.

THOMAS. Paper Panthers.

DE LEON. Yeah, right on, they up there talking all that off-the-wall shit and cutting me off and letting them niggers run all that madness. You dig it, like I needed some help, man, like what, you was scared or what?

THOMAS. No, I had to make it, I had to come home.

DE LEON. Yeah, well, did you relate to that other big fine bitch up there, man? Hey listen, I'm gonna run—give you a run-down on that, man.

309

THOMAS.   Right on.

DE LEON.   Now dig it, you got to play that for the money.

THOMAS.   Right, right, right.

DE LEON.   Dig it, that's where she's coming from, and when she gets kind of off the wall, just slap her down a few times—you dig it, that's all.

THOMAS.   Right.

DE LEON.   Hey, dig this, relate to the bitch quick, you know, because like she living there, we're going to be around there to deal with the situation.

THOMAS.   Right.

DE LEON.   You dig it, 'cause I just finished talking to Cain. I told him you still got the thing, you still got the paper, right?

THOMAS.   Right.

DE LEON.   Right on. OK, you know what, everything we talk—right?

THOMAS.   Right.

DE LEON.   Well, you relate it to Cain, don't relate it on the phone.

THOMAS.   Look here, about the car . . .

DE LEON.   Yeah.

THOMAS.   About that car . . .

DE LEON.   Yeah, you get it.

THOMAS.   Yeah.

DE LEON.   Right on, forget it.

THOMAS.   Right.

DE LEON.   You got it, you got it, yeah right, you got it, that's all.

THOMAS.   Right on, you dig it.

DE LEON.   Uh, so—like, uh—I'm going to see Cain in a few minutes, you know.

THOMAS.   Right—well, when will we get together, you know?

DE LEON.   I don't know. Cain gotta go see about his brother, man.

THOMAS.   I'll tell you what, let's just us [*inaudible*].

De Leon. Yeah, I'm gonna be around his house about twelve o'clock.

Thomas. Well, looka here, brother, why don't you get him and we can get together, and you know.

De Leon. Yeah, we gotta deal with something else, though—well—uh—right on, right on, right on.

Thomas. OK.

De Leon. OK, good enough.

Thomas. I'll have everything up tight when we get ready to get together.

De Leon. Yeah, right. You got any money?

Thomas. Yeah, I got a few dollars.

De Leon. I don't need nothing, though, that's all right 'bout now.

Thomas. I've got a few dollars.

De Leon. Yeah, I know, I know—uh—dig it—uh—I'm gonna, may need some this afternoon 'cause this crazy woman done vamped on my . . . hee, hee. Hey dig it, uh, she wanna go, she done made a whole lotta plans and shit, and relate to a whole lotta off-the-wall shit, and like, man, I ain't relating to it. I say, I got something to do, I got business to tend to, I got business, you know. Fuck all this entertainment shit, you know.

Thomas. I'll be able to, you know.

De Leon. She relate to all that fat pussy madness to me.

Thomas. Hee, hee, hee.

De Leon. Yeah, right on, blood.

Thomas. Right, so looka here, I got a few dollars to spend.

De Leon. Yeah, right on, blood, good.

Thomas. So we can go on and get our thing together and—

De Leon. Yeah, we'll do it, we'll get a couple of jugs of Bali Hai and sit around and rap.

Thomas. Right on.

De Leon. Right on. OK.

Thomas. All right.

DE LEON. Power.

THOMAS. Looka here—power—now I'll be looking for you to call me, now.

DE LEON. Yeah, right on, blood, I'll deal with it. Power to the people.

THOMAS. Right on.

APPENDIX B

INDICTMENT AGAINST ALFRED CAIN, RICARDO DE LEON, AND JEROME WEST

Supreme Court of the State of New York 4549/69
County of New York

The People of the State of New York

—against—

Alfred Cain, Ricardo De Leon and Jerome West,

Defendants.

The Grand Jury of the County of New York, by this indictment, accuse the defendants of the crime of conspiracy in violation of Section 105.10 of the Penal Law, committed as follows:

The defendants in the County of New York, from on or about July 31, 1969 continually to on or about August 16, 1969, with the intent to engage in conduct constituting the crime of robbery, agreed with each other and others to engage in and cause the performance of conduct constituting the crime of robbery.

During the course of the conspiracy the defendants were members of the Black Panther Party, a group which utilized a para-military structure and discipline in the pursuit of its objectives in the City of New York. The defendants' plan was to commit robberies so that they could obtain money to aid the Black Panther Party in accomplishing its objectives.

The defendants' plan was to, on August 16, 1969, forcibly take at gun point, from the landlord or superintendent of an apartment-hotel at 142 West 131 Street, New York County, money that he would have in his possession. Further, as part of the said conspiracy, the defendants agreed to use guns in the commission of the said robbery. In addition, the defendants agreed to use a chemical spray to narcotize and disable their victims.

Overt Acts

In furtherance of this conspiracy the defendants committed and caused to be committed the following overt acts:

1. On or about July 31, 1969, Alfred Cain told a certain person that he sought a gun to commit robberies.

2. On or about July 31, 1969, Ricardo De Leon told a certain person that he sought a gun to commit robberies.

3. On or about August 1, 1969, Alfred Cain asked another person to procure guns to be paid for by the Black Panther Party.

4. On August 8, 1969, Ricardo De Leon asked a certain person if he had guns for sale.

5. On or about August 13, 1969, Alfred Cain discussed plans for the robbery with a certain person.

6. On or about August 14, 1969, Ricardo De Leon and a certain person went to 142 West 131 Street, New York County.

7. On or about August 14, 1969, Ricardo De Leon and another entered the apartment-hotel dwelling premises at 142 West 131 Street, New York County.

8. On or about August 14, 1969, Ricardo De Leon pointed out the office of the hotel-dwelling premises at 142 West 131 Street, New York County, to another.

9. On or about August 15, 1969, the defendants examined a sawed-off shotgun.

10. On or about August 15, 1969, David Conyers discussed the intended robbery with a certain person.

11. On or about August 15, 1969, the defendants made arrangements to obtain a car.

12. On or about August 15, 1969, the defendant Cain received a drawing of the premises at 142 West 131 Street from a certain person.

13. On August 15, 1969, Ricardo De Leon issued rubber gloves to Alfred Cain, Jerome West and another person.

14. On or about August 15, 1969, Ricardo De Leon gave a knife to Alfred Cain.

15. On or about August 15, 1969, Ricardo De Leon and another met with David Conyers.

16. On or about August 15, 1969, David Conyers assembled a .30 calibre M-1 rifle and gave it to the defendants.

17. On or about August 16, 1969, Alfred Cain, Ricardo De Leon, Jerome West and another person rode in a car toward 142 West 131 Street, New York County.

SECOND COUNT:

AND THE GRAND JURY OF THE COUNTY OF NEW YORK, by this indictment further accuse the defendants of the crime of CONSPIRACY in violation of Section 105.15 of the Penal Law, committed as follows:

The defendants in the County of New York, on or about August 16, 1969, with the intent to engage in conduct constituting the crime of murder, agreed with each other and others to engage in and cause the performance of conduct constituting the crime of murder.

During the course of the conspiracy the defendants were members of the Black Panther Party, a group which utilized a para-military structure and discipline in the pursuit of its objectives in the City of New York. The defendants plan was to commit robberies so that they could obtain money to aid the Black Panther Party in accomplishing its objectives.

The defendants' plan was to forcibly, on August 16, 1969, take at gunpoint from the landlord or superintendent of an apartment-hotel at 142 West 131 Street, New York County, money that he would have in possession.

The defendants were armed with guns to use in the commission of the said robbery and it was agreed that they would shoot to kill anyone that would make a "funny move" during the commission of the robbery.

Overt Acts

In furtherance of this conspiracy the defendants committed and caused to be committed the following overt acts:

1. On or about August 16, 1969, the defendants possessed a sawed-off loaded shotgun, a loaded .30 calibre M-1 rifle, a knife and a canister of chemical spray.

2. On or about August 16, 1969, Alfred Cain, Ricardo De Leon, Jerome West and another person rode in a car toward 142 West 131 Street, New York County.

3. On or about August 16, 1969, in New York County, the defendants discussed plans to kill anyone that interfered with their planned robbery.

4. On or about August 16, 1969, in New York County, Alfred Cain aimed a loaded sawed-off shotgun at detective Alfred Halikias.

THIRD COUNT:

AND THE GRAND JURY OF THE COUNTY OF NEW YORK, by this indictment, further accuse the defendants of the crime of ATTEMPTED MURDER, committed as follows:

The defendants, in the County of New York, on or about August 16, 1969, with intent to cause the death of Alfred Halikias, attempted to cause his death by shooting him with a sawed-off shotgun.

FOURTH COUNT:

AND THE GRAND JURY OF THE COUNTY OF NEW YORK, by this indictment further accuse the defendants of the crime of ATTEMPTED ASSAULT IN THE FIRST DEGREE, committed as follows:

The defendants, in the County of New York, on or about August 16, 1969, with intent to cause serious physical injury to another person, attempted to cause such injury to Alfred Halikias by means of a deadly weapon, to wit, a loaded sawed-off shotgun.

FIFTH COUNT:

AND THE GRAND JURY AFORESAID, by this indictment, further accuse said defendants of the crime of ATTEMPTED ASSAULT IN THE SECOND DEGREE, committed as follows:

Said defendants, in the County of New York, on or about August 16, 1969, with intent to cause physical injury to another person, attempted to cause such injury to Alfred Halikias with a deadly weapon, to wit, a loaded sawed-off shotgun.

SIXTH COUNT:

AND THE GRAND JURY AFORESAID, by this indictment, further accuse said defendant of the crime of RECKLESS ENDANGERMENT IN THE FIRST DEGREE, committed as follows:

Said defendants, in the County of New York, on or about August 16, 1969, under circumstances evincing a depraved indifference to human life, recklessly engaged in conduct which created a grave risk of death to another person, to wit, Alfred Halikias.

SEVENTH COUNT:

AND THE GRAND JURY OF THE COUNTY OF NEW YORK, by this indictment further accuse the defendants of the crime of ATTEMPTED ROBBERY IN THE FIRST DEGREE, committed as follows:

The defendants, in the County of New York, on or about August

16, 1969, attempted to forcibly steal certain property from certain persons at 142 West 131 Street, New York County, and in the course of the attempted commission of the crime were armed with deadly weapons, to wit, a loaded sawed-off shotgun, a loaded .30 calibre M-1 rifle and a knife.

Eighth Count:

And the Grand Jury aforesaid, by this indictment, further accuse the defendants of the crime of ATTEMPTED ROBBERY IN THE SECOND DEGREE, committed as follows:

The defendants, in the County of New York, on or about August 16, 1969, being aided by other persons actually present, attempted to forcibly steal certain property from certain persons at 142 West 131 Street, New York City.

Ninth Count:

And the Grand Jury aforesaid, by this indictment, further accuse the defendants of the crime of ATTEMPTED GRAND LARCENY IN THE THIRD DEGREE, committed as follows:

The defendants, in the County of New York, on or about August 16, 1969, attempted to steal certain property from the person of another.

Tenth Count:

And the Grand Jury aforesaid, by this indictment, further accuse the defendants of the crime of POSSESSING A WEAPON, AS A FELONY, committed as follows:

The defendants, in the County of New York, on or about August 16, 1969, had in their possession a firearm, to wit, a sawed-off shotgun loaded with ammunition, said possession not being in the defendants' home or place of business.

Eleventh Count:

And the Grand Jury aforesaid, by this indictment, further accuse the defendants of the crime of DEFACEMENT OF A WEAPON, committed as follows:

Said defendants, in the County of New York, from on or about July 31, 1969 to on or about August 16, 1969, wilfully defaced a firearm, to wit, a sawed-off shotgun.

Twelfth Count:

And the Grand Jury aforesaid, by this indictment, further accuse the defendants of the crime of POSSESSION OF WEAPON, DANGEROUS INSTRUMENT AND APPLIANCE, committed as follows:

The defendants, in the County of New York, on or about August 16, 1969, had in their possession a loaded .30 calibre M-1 rifle with intent to use the same unlawfully against another.

THIRTEENTH COUNT:

AND THE GRAND JURY AFORESAID, by this indictment, further accuse the defendants of the crime of POSSESSION OF WEAPON, DANGEROUS INSTRUMENT AND APPLIANCE committed as follows.

The defendants, in the County of New York, on or about August 16, 1969, had in their possession a knife with intent to use the same unlawfully against another.

FOURTEENTH COUNT:

AND THE GRAND JURY AFORESAID, by this indictment, further accuse the defendants of the crime of POSSESSION OF A LACHRYMATING, ASPHYXIATING, INCAPACITATING AND DELETERIOUS GAS, LIQUID AND CHEMICAL in violation of Section 436-5.0 of the Administrative Code of the City of New York, committed as follows:

The defendants, in the County of New York, on or about August 16, 1969, without a permit, possessed a canister of lachrymating, asphyxiating, incapacitating and deleterious gas, liquid and chemical.

FRANK S. HOGAN
District Attorney

NOTES

CHAPTER 3. BLACK PANTHERS IN BROOKLYN

1. Gene Marine, *The Black Panthers* (New York: New American Library, Signet, 1969), p. 55; Bobby Seale, *Seize the Time* (New York: Random House, 1970), p. 125.

2. Marine, *Black Panthers*, p. 62; Seale, *Seize the Time*, pp. 153 ff.

3. Marine, *Black Panthers*, p. 180; Mark Abramson, "Preliminary Report on Black Panthers in New York City," mimeographed, New York, 1970, p. 7.

4. Seale, *Seize the Time*, p. 373.

5. *Ibid.*, p. 370.

CHAPTER 4. REVOLUTIONARY MEN AND REVOLUTIONARY HISTORY

1. Fred Hampton, "You Can Murder a Liberator, but You Can't Murder Liberation," in Philip Foner, *The Black Panthers Speak* (Philadelphia: J. B. Lippincott Co., 1970), p. 139.

2. Huey Newton, "The Correct Handling of a Revolution," in Foner, *The Panthers Speak*, pp. 41–42.

3. "Correcting Mistaken Ideas," *Black Panther*, October 26, 1968, quoted in Foner, *The Panthers Speak*, p. 22.

4. Bertram Wolfe, *Three Who Made a Revolution* (New York: Dell Publishing Co., 1964), p. 389; Ronald Hingley, *Russian Secret Police* (New York: Simon & Schuster, 1970), p. 100.

5. Wolfe, *Three Who Made a Revolution*, p. 387.

6. *Ibid.*, p. 380.

7. *Ibid.*, p. 375.

8. Eric Hobsbawm, *Bandits* (New York: Delacorte Press, 1969), pp. 95–96; Wolfe, *Three Who Made a Revolution*, p. 391; Edward Ellis Smith, *The Young Stalin* (New York: Farrar, Straus & Giroux, 1967), Chap. 9. It is said that Stalin was in charge of the operation.

9. Hobsbawm, *Bandits*, pp. 13–14, 15.

10. Hingley, *Russian Secret Police*, p. 100.

11. Neill Macaulay, *The Sandino Affair* (Chicago: Quadrangle Books, 1967), p. 112.

12. Carlos Nuñez, *The Tupamaros, Urban Guerrillas of Uruguay* (New York: Times Change Press, 1971).

13. "Former City Aide Sentenced to Jail," *New York Times*, September 22, 1971, p. 35.

14. James F. Clarity, "Rap Brown Wounded Here . . .," *New York Times*, October 17, 1971, p. 1.

15. Seale, *Seize the Time*, pp. 376–83; Marine, *Black Panthers*, pp. 201–7.

16. Seale, *Seize the Time*, pp. 377–78.

17. "Berkeley Pigs Murder Donald Charles Theard," *Black Panther*, February 6, 1971, p. 6. Stories such as this are written by local chapter people and not by national leaders, but if the opinions in such a story were very far from general party views, the story would be either changed or not printed.

18. House Committee on Internal Security, *Gun Barrel Politics: The Black Panther Party, 1966–1971*, House Report No. 92-470, 92nd Cong., 2nd Sess. (Washington: Government Printing Office, 1971).

19. One witness was arrested for a robbery. He subsequently appeared before the committee and testified that Black Panther Party leaders put him up to it, and then refused to pay his bail. *Ibid.*, p. 75.

20. *Ibid.*, p. 141.

CHAPTER 10. STATE AND REVOLUTION:
POLITICAL PROVOCATION IN EUROPE AND THE UNITED STATES

1. Edward Ellis Smith, *The Okhrana: A Bibliography* (Stanford, Cal.: Hoover Institution Press, 1967), Introduction.

2. Jean Galtier-Boissière, *Mysteries of the French Secret Police* (London: Stanley Paul & Co., 1938), pp. 107–10.

3. Vladimir Dedijer, "A Guide to Infiltrators," *New York Review of Books*, March 25, 1971, p. 31.

4. Paul Blackstock, *Agents of Deceit: Frauds, Forgeries and Political Intrigue Among Nations* (Chicago: Quadrangle Books, 1966), p. 57.

5. *Ibid.*, pp. 51–52.

6. The following account is largely drawn from Karl Bittel, *Kommunisten Prozess zu Köln 1852, im Spiegel der Zeitgenossischen*

Presse (East Berlin: 1955). The "memorandum" is my translation of the document reproduced at p. 16 thereof.

7. Richard Rowan, *The Story of Secret Service* (New York: Doubleday, Doran & Co., 1937), Chap. 45, especially p. 327.

8. Bittel, *Kommunisten Prozess*, p. 175.

9. *Ibid.*, p. 262, n. 1.

10. Now collected as Chap. 10 of Karl Marx, *Revolution and Counter-Revolution, or Germany in 1848* (London: George Allen & Unwin, 1920).

11. Galtier-Boissière, *French Secret Police*, p. 75.

12. The term "amalgam" is from Otto Kirchheimer, *Political Justice* (Princeton, N.J.: Princeton University Press, 1961), pp. 99, 196, 200.

13. Galtier-Boissière, *French Secret Police*, pp. 102, 93.

14. *Ibid.*, pp. 183–84.

15. *Ibid.*, pp. 191–93. The Canler quotation that follows appears on p. 193.

16. *Ibid.*, p. 230.

17. *Ibid.*, p. 216.

18. *Ibid.*, p. 234. Lagrange apparently betrayed Guérin, for the latter was convicted and sentenced.

19. *Ibid.*, p. 230.

20. *Ibid.*, p. 232.

21. Quoted in Kirchheimer, *Political Justice*, p. 118.

22. E. P. Thompson, *The Making of the English Working Class* (New York: Pantheon Books, 1964), p. 493.

23. *Ibid.*, p. 494.

24. *Ibid.*, p. 636.

25. *Ibid.*, pp. 632–36; *Fairburn's Edition of the Whole Proceedings on the Trial of James Watson, Sr. for High Treason* (London: Fairburn, 1817), *passim*, but see especially pp. 175–86 for Castle's cross-examination.

26. Thompson, *Making of English Working Class*, pp. 649–69.

27. *Ibid.*, p. 656.

28. *Ibid.*, pp. 700–706; John Stanhope, *Cato Street Conspiracy* (London: Jonathan Cape, 1962), *passim*.

29. Stanhope, *Cato Street Conspiracy*. The depositions are quoted from papers at the Home Office at pp. 163 ff.

30. Thompson, *Making of English Working Class*, p. 703.

31. *Ibid.*, p. 661.

32. *Ibid.*, p. 663.

33. Boris Nicolaevsky, *Aseff the Spy: Russian Terrorist and Police Stool* (New York: Doubleday, Doran & Co., 1934), pp. 18, 119.

34. Kyril Tidmarsh, "The Zubatov Idea," *American Slavic and East European Review*, Vol. 19, No. 3 (1960), p. 335; Wolfe, *Three Who Made a Revolution*, Chap. 16.

35. Tidmarsh, "The Zubatov Idea," p. 342.

36. *Ibid.*, p. 338.

37. Wolfe, *Three Who Made a Revolution*, pp. 283, 547.

38. The following account is largely drawn from Nicolaevsky, *Aseff the Spy, passim*. Also see Maurice Laporte, *Histoire de l'Okhrana* (Paris: Payot, 1935), pp. 77 ff.; Rowan, *Secret Service*, p. 700.

39. Theodore Dan, *Origins of Bolshevism* (New York: Harper & Row Publishers, 1964), p. 269 n.; Nicolaevsky concurs, *Aseff the Spy*, pp. 286–87. Disillusionment with political terror is discussed as doctrine in, e.g., Robert Hunter, *Violence and the Labor Movement* (New York: Macmillan Co., 1914), *passim*.

40. Nicolaevsky, *Aseff the Spy*, p. 277. It is possible to believe that Azev acted as the puppet of some ministerial, police, or palace intrigue. Lopuhin thought that Azev acted as Ratchkovsky's tool in killing Plehve (Nicolaevsky, p. 18). The opinion is adopted by Laporte, *Histoire de l'Okhrana*, p. 77. Nicolaevsky rejects it, and in any case, it would not make Azev any more an *agent provocateur*.

41. A. T. Vasilyev, *The Okhrana* (London: G. G. Harrap & Co., 1930), p. 71.

42. Quoted in Rowan, *Secret Service*, p. 700 n.

43. Wolfe, *Three Who Made a Revolution*, p. 547.

44. Wolfe's is the most complete account; *ibid.*, Chap. 31.

45. Vasilyev, *Okhrana*, p. 256.

46. See Ronald Radosh, *American Labor and United States Foreign Policy* (New York: Vintage Books, 1969), *passim*, especially Chap. 7.

47. Nicolaevsky, *Aseff the Spy*, pp. 39–40.

48. This is the entire thesis of Fritz Tobias, *The Reichstag Fire* (New York: G. P. Putnam's Sons, 1964).

49. *Ibid.*, pp. 185–86.

50. Ernst Kohn Bramstedt, *Dictatorship and Political Police: The Technique of Control by Fear* (New York: Oxford University Press, 1945), pp. 59 ff.

51. Because opinion, even thought, may be a crime, totalitarian regimes may use provocation just to bring out opinions. An example

—signing a petition for Spanish Loyalists in Nazi Germany—is cited in Bramstedt, *Dictatorship and Political Police*, p. 143.

52. Kirchheimer, *Political Justice*, p. 118.

53. Some years ago, when I surveyed the American cases, there were none reported dealing with "political" crimes, and only one or two with crimes of violence. (See Richard Donnelly, "Judicial Control of Informants, Spies, Stool Pigeons and Agents Provocateurs," *Yale Law Journal*, Vol. 60 [1951], p. 1091.) It should be noted that one possible reason for the paucity of evidence of political provocation in older American cases may be that the files have never been opened. The United States has never had a revolution since independence, and thus no succeeding regime has opened the files of an earlier one, as happened in France and Russia.

54. Complaints against provocation by private agents are collected in Hunter, *Violence and the Labor Movement*, Chap. 11. One such case is authenticated and reported as Koscak v. State, 160 Wis. 255, 152 N.W. 181 (Wisconsin 1915).

55. This case may be viewed more as a "frame" than as provocation. Curt Gentry, *Frame-up* (New York: W. W. Norton & Co., 1967), p. 58; Richard Frost, *The Mooney Case* (Stanford, Cal.: Stanford University Press, 1968), pp. 29–36.

56. Frost, *Mooney Case*, pp. 25–26. The Pennsylvania State Police are reported to have been physically rough, but little or no infiltration was discovered. Pennsylvania Federation of Labor, *The American Cossack* (Reading, 1915).

57. National Popular Government League, *To the American People: Report upon the Illegal Practices of the United States Department of Justice* (Washington, D.C., 1920).

58. Max Lowenthal, *Federal Bureau of Investigation* (New York: William Sloane Associates, 1950), p. 89.

59. Theodore Draper, *The Roots of Communism* (New York: Viking Press, 1957), p. 373.

60. Fred Cook, "The FBI," *Nation*, October 18, 1958, p. 266.

61. Quoted in Lowenthal, *Federal Bureau of Investigation*, p. 318.

62. Anthony Bouza, "The Operations of a Police Intelligence Unit," M.A. thesis, Baruch School, City College of New York, 1968, p. 18; Gerald E. G. Astor, *The New York Cops: An Informal History* (New York: Charles Scribner's Sons, 1971), p. 170.

63. Bouza, "Operations of a Police Intelligence Unit," p. 19.

64. David Burnham, "Thesis Provides Clues on Undercover Police," *New York Times*, March 8, 1971, p. 16.

65. Bouza, "Operations of a Police Intelligence Unit," pp. 60, 73.

66. *Ibid.*, pp. 66–67.

67. *Ibid.*, p. 69.

68. *Ibid.*, pp. 68, 69–70, 79–83; appendix in USA v. Walter Bowe et al., Docket No. 29881, Second Circuit Court of Appeals, Foley Square, New York, p. 97 b.

69. Transcript of Trial, People v. Herman Ferguson et al., Supreme Court, Queens County, N.Y., Indictment No. 468/68, pp. 226, 403.

70. Trial records are not often the best source of such information, of course, but other files are not open. The cases are recent, and reminiscences or discoveries outside the record are not available. We may briefly review the problems. The Statue of Liberty case is USA v. Walter Bowe, Robert Collier and Khaleel Sayyed, appendix to brief, Docket No. 29881, Second Circuit Court of Appeals, Foley Square, New York. In that case the defense offered, and the judge excluded, testimony to the effect that as early as 1964, at a rally in front of Manhattan Federal Court, Wood advocated blowing up the sewer system, and a woman angrily suggested to him blowing up the Statue of Liberty. This would have tended to show that the bombing was not the defendants' idea, but that Wood came into the group with the idea himself. Two defendants so testified. The problem is that the evidence did not really establish more than what *might* have happened. The most damaging fact for the defense is that the French Canadian courier, Michèle Duclos, testified for the prosecution, and in her account, Collier was plainly the leader. The decision of the district court was affirmed, 360 F.2d 1 (2nd Cir. 1966).

The second case is People v. Herman Ferguson et al., Supreme Court, Queens County, N.Y., Indictment No. 468/68. I am grateful to Elizabeth Holtzmann for lending me her copy of the transcript. As of this writing, not all aspects of the case are completed, since lesser charges against other defendants have not yet come to trial. One inconclusive but interesting point: Howlette testified that he wrote a speech, at the request of Ferguson, and his superiors approved it (transcript, p. 304). Shades of Roman Malinovsky!

71. *New York Times,* June 13, 1971, p. 25.

72. Burnham, "Thesis Provides Clues on Undercover Police"; Frank Donner, "Theory and Practice of American Political Intelligence," *New York Review of Books,* April 22, 1971, p. 29.

73. Donner, "American Political Intelligence," p. 28, n. 5.

74. Anthony Ripley, "Big Man on Campus: Police Undercover Agent," *New York Times,* March 28, 1971, p. 1.

75. The case of the so-called Panther Thirteen in New York City is not included because it would require a separate book, and because several other people are working on such a book.

76. "Hobart College Upset by Police Agent," *New York Times,* June 7, 1970; Ron Rosenbaum, "Run, Tommy, Run," *Esquire,* July 1971, p. 51; Frank Donner, "The Agent Provocateur as Folk Hero," *Civil Liberties,* September 1971.

77. Rosenbaum, "Run, Tommy, Run," p. 137. The secretary, not a defendant, tells the story.

78. *Ibid.,* p. 52; cf. Donner, "American Political Intelligence," p. 33.

79. Jack Nelson, "FBI Informant Accused of Violence on Campus," *Los Angeles Times,* September 11, 1970, Part I, p. 12; "Alleged Police Agitator Found in Minneapolis," *ibid.,* September 12, 1970; ACLU Southern Regional Office, Press Release of Attorneys Drake, Knowles and Dean, September 14, 1970, mimeographed.

80. ACLU Southern Regional Office, Press Release of Drake, Knowles and Dean, p. 6.

81. "Photos Indicate Ohio Patrolmen Had a Role in Student Disorders," *New York Times,* October 31, 1970, p. 26.

82. "Informer Says FBI Paid for Spray Paint," *New York Times,* December 8, 1970, p. 52; Richard Cooper, "Seattle 7 'Set for a Fight,'" *New York Post,* December 21, 1970, p. 33.

83. Bernard Weiner, "The Orderly Perversion of Justice," *The Nation,* February 1, 1971, p. 146. It has since developed that the Seattle office of the FBI used other odd individuals as informers in this case. John Kifner, "Seattle FBI Spy Tells of Actions," *New York Times,* June 13, 1971, p. 41, cites an affidavit of one David R. Sannes, a former army intelligence sergeant, who tried to convince radicals to commit a kidnapping and a bombing during 1970.

84. United States v. Donald Freed and Shirley Sutherland, 401 U.S. 601 (1971).

85. Donald Freed, "The CIA Comes Home (The Confessions of a Failed Liberal)," mimeographed, Los Angeles, 1970. Available from Box 3314, Beverly Hills, Cal.

86. United States v. Donald Freed and Shirley Sutherland, U.S. District Court, Central District of California, No. 4846-(WF)-CD, Remarks of Ferguson, J., February 16, 1970. Quoted in Appendix to Jurisdictional Statement, U.S. Supreme Court, October term, 1970, p. 27.

87. There is one incident in the famous case of the Black Panther Thirteen in Manhattan which may put it in the same class. The case, which charged a conspiracy to blow up public buildings, department stores, and police stations, and possession of weapons and explosives, has, as this is written, recently ended in a resounding acquittal. The pretrial motions and the trial consumed more than a year, amassing complex evidence about the practices of undercover agents; I cannot pretend even to summarize all of it adequately here. But I do want to recall one fact which is central to the entire framework of the case, appeared fleetingly in the pretrial hearings, was forgotten by most of us in the wash of other events, and never even came out before the jury: the dynamite which some of the defendants were supposed to have intended for bombings, and some of which they were supposed to have planted in a police station, was supplied by an FBI informer, Roland Hayes.

This matter was no secret after the pretrial hearings. A bill of sale for one hundred sticks of dynamite was attached to one of the affidavits applying to the court for an extension of time on an order to tap wires out in Brooklyn. Hayes was identified as an informer and as the source of the dynamite. In an interview in 1969 with some of the defendants, Hayes said that he had worked for the FBI since 1966, had infiltrated other radical organizations such as Youth Against War and Fascism, and had even made a trip to Cuba with other radicals, from which he had written foreign-intelligence reports. Hayes seems to have told the prosecution that he had obtained the dynamite without the knowledge of the authorities, and acting as a double agent; whether or not that is true, it does seem clear from his own statements that he got it without being specifically requested to get it by the defendants.

This fact was lost sight of because none of the police officers who testified at the trial admitted to having knowledge about it. The prosecution did not call Hayes, for obvious reasons, and the defense did not call him for a lot of reasons, one of which was that they were not sure what story he would tell, and they did not think that the judge would permit them to make him a "hostile" witness, subject to their cross-examination.

I have this information from Gerald Lefcourt, a defense attorney, and from Elizabeth Holtzmann, who heard a bit of it from one of the prosecutors. It is all relegated to a footnote because Hayes's motives are unclear.

88. Jack Nelson, "Police Arrange Trap: Klan Terror Is Target," *Los Angeles Times*, February 13, 1970.

89. Anthony Dunbar, "Conspiracy on Conspiracy," *Katallagete: Be Reconciled, Journal of the Committee of Southern Churchmen,* Vol. 3, No. 2 (Winter 1971), p. 35; Nelson, "Police Arrange Trap."

90. Williamson v. United States, 311 F.2d 411 (5th Cir. 1962). The detective who could have testified to the facts was carefully sent on vacation before Tarrants's trial.

91. Richard Cooper, "Killing Nags Consciences in Seattle," *Los Angeles Times,* May 2, 1971, p. 1.

92. John Kifner, "The Berrigan Affair: How It Evolved," *New York Times,* February 21, 1971, p. 1; Paul Cowan, "Intruder in a Gentle Community," *Village Voice,* April 15, 1971, p. 1.

93. Lee Lockwood, "How the 'Kidnap Conspiracy' Was Hatched," *Life,* May 21, 1971, p. 31.

94. People v. Preston Lay, et al., New York County Supreme Court, People's Exhibit 16A.

95. *Ibid.,* People's Exhibit 23.

96. *Ibid.,* People's Exhibit 25.

97. *Ibid.,* People's Exhibit 30.

98. *Ibid.,* People's Exhibit 41.

99. Lawrence Van Gelder, "Murphy Denounces Judge of 'Harlem 5,' " *New York Times,* June 11, 1971, p. 1.

CHAPTER 11. THE LAW: REMEDIES AND FAILURES

1. Melvin Dubofsky, *We Shall Be All* (Chicago: Quadrangle Press, 1969), p. 436.

2. Note, "The Changing Role of the Jury in the Nineteenth Century," *Yale Law Journal,* Vol. 74 (1964), p. 170.

3. Jerome Frank, *Courts on Trial* (Princeton, N.J.: Princeton University Press, 1949), p. 124.

4. New York Penal Law §265.15.

5. Brady v. Maryland, 373 U.S. 83, 87 (1963).

6. Abraham Goldstein, "The State and the Accused: Balance of Advantage in Criminal Procedure," *Yale Law Journal,* Vol. 69 (1960), pp. 1149, 1182.

7. See Hoffa v. United States, 385 U.S. 293 (1966).

8. E.g., Entick v. Carrington, 19 How. St. Tr. 1029 (1765); Dombrowski v. Pfister, 380 U.S. 479, 487 (1965).

9. United States v. White, 405 F.2d 838, 846, reversed 401 U.S. 745 (1971).

10. A version of the infiltration warrant is discussed favorably in Note, "Police Undercover Agents: New Threat to First Amendment Freedoms," *George Washington Law Review,* Vol. 76 (1969), p.

634; Comment, "Judicial Control of Secret Agents," *Yale Law Journal*, Vol. 76 (1967), p. 949; Comment, "Police Infiltration of Political Groups," *Harvard Civil Rights–Civil Liberties Law Review*, Vol. 4 (1969), p. 331. The decoying warrant was recommended in Britain by an official commission as long ago as 1928, *Report of the Royal Commission on Police Powers and Procedures*, Cmd. No. 3297, p. 42 (1928). It has been advocated frequently since then. Rotenberg, "The Police Detection Practice of Encouragement," *University of Virginia Law Review*, Vol. 49 (1963), p. 871; Note, "Entrapment," *Harvard Law Review*, Vol. 733 (1960), p. 1333.

11. See Berger v. New York, 388 U.S. 41 (1967), and resulting legislation. New York Criminal Procedure Law Art. 700 (1971).

12. Sherman v. United States, 356 U.S. 369 (1958).

13. *Ibid.*, p. 372, quoting Sorrells v. United States, 287 U.S. 435, 442 (1932).

14. *Ibid.*, p. 382.

15. *Ibid.*, p. 387.

16. New York Penal Law §40.05.

17. United States v. Dillett, 265 F. Supp. 980 (S.D.N.Y. 1966). See also United States v. Silva, 180 F Supp. 557 (S.D.N.Y. 1959); People v. Strong, 172 N.E. 2d 765 (Ill. 1951)

18. United States v. Jencks, 353 U.S. 657 (1957).

19. Palermo v. United States, 360 U.S. 343, 346 (1959).

20. Title 18 U.S.C. §35.00.

21. Berger v. New York, 388 U.S. 41 (1967).

22. Katz v. United States, 389 U.S. 347 (1967).

23. Lopez v. United States, 373 U.S. 427, 465 (1963).

24. Hoffa v. United States, 385 U.S. 293 (1966).

25. White v. United States, 401 U.S. 745, 751 (1971).

26. Thomas Erskine May, *Constitutional History of England* (New York: Armstrong, 1899), Vol. 2, p. 276.

27. The Smith Act case, United States v. Dennis, 183 F.2d 201, 224 (2nd Cir. 1950), affirmed 341 U.S. 494 (1951).

BIBLIOGRAPHY

The work which throws the most light upon all the problems raised in this book is:

Otto Kirchheimer, *Political Justice*. Princeton, N.J.: Princeton University Press, 1961.

Useful books about the Black Panthers are:

Gene Marine, *The Black Panthers*. New York: New American Library, Signet, 1969.

Philip Foner, ed., *The Black Panthers Speak*. Philadelphia: J. B. Lippincott Co., 1970.
A collection of documents.

Bobby Seale, *Seize the Time*. New York: Random House, 1970.

House Committee on Internal Security, *Gun Barrel Politics: The Black Panther Party, 1966–1971*. House Report No. 92–470, 92nd Cong., 2nd Sess. Washington: Government Printing Office, 1971.

Portions of the record in the New Dunston Hotel case, some of which are not in Chapter 10 of the present book, or are condensed there, can be found in:

Sara Blackburn, *White Justice*. New York: Harper & Row Publishers, 1971.
This book should also be read to get a feeling for the conduct of such trials generally.

The bible for *voir dire* of jurors in political cases, upon which many of the ideas in Chapter 9 are based, is:

Charles Garry, *Minimizing Racism in Jury Trials*. San Francisco: National Lawyers Guild, 1969.

AGENTS PROVOCATEURS

Works which purport to deal with agents in several nations are:

Richard Rowan, *The Story of Secret Service*. New York: Doubleday, Doran & Co., 1937.

329

This is a romantic account containing some interesting bits on secret police.

Paul Blackstock, *Agents of Deceit: Frauds, Forgeries and Political Intrigue Among Nations*. Chicago: Quadrangle Books, 1966.
This is somewhat off the point, but has some important theories.

Vladimir Dedijer, "A Guide to Infiltrators," *New York Review of Books*, March 25, 1971.

France

The material from France is rich, because the government has been overturned so often and incoming policemen have told scandals about their predecessors. Much of this is collected in:

Jean Galtier-Boissière, *Mysteries of the French Secret Police*. London: Stanley Paul & Co., 1938.
This is the essential book for France.

Ernst Kohn Bramstedt, *Dictatorship and Political Police: The Technique of Control by Fear*. New York: Oxford University Press, 1945.

Germany

Richard Rowan, *The Story of Secret Service*.

The Cologne scandal may be studied in:

Karl Bittel, *Kommunisten Prozess zu Köln 1852, im Spiegel der Zeitgenossischen Presse*. East Berlin, 1955.

Karl Marx, *Revolution and Counter-Revolution, or Germany in 1848*. London: George Allen & Unwin, 1920. Chap. 10.

The Reichstag fire is exhumed in:

Fritz Tobias, *The Reichstag Fire*. New York: G. P. Putnam's Sons, 1964.

Great Britain

The literature concerning the provocations under Sidmouth is reviewed brilliantly in:

E. P. Thompson, *The Making of the English Working Class*. New York: Pantheon Books, 1964.

See also:

John Stanhope, *Cato Street Conspiracy*. London: Jonathan Cape, 1962.

Fairburn's Edition of the Whole Proceedings on the Trial of James Watson, Sr. for High Treason. London: Fairburn, 1817.

Russia

The literature for provocation in Russia is a maze, but there are a handful of reliable works:

Boris Nicolaevsky, *Aseff the Spy: Russian Terrorist and Police Stool.* New York: Doubleday, Doran & Co., 1934.
This covers much more than just Azev himself.

Bertram Wolfe, *Three Who Made a Revolution.* New York: Dell Publishing Co., 1964.
This covers much material in great detail.

The history of the "Zubatov Idea" is exhaustively reviewed in:
Dimitri Pospielovsky, *Russian Police Trade Unionism.* London: George Weidenfeld & Nicolson, 1971.
This supersedes all other works, including:

Kyril Tidmarsh, "The Zubatov Idea," *American Slavic and East European Review,* Vol. 19, No. 3 (1960), p. 335.

Other works are:
A. T. Vasilyev, *The Okhrana.* London: G. G. Harrap & Co., 1930.
This memoir, by the last head of the organization, is unreliable, but important when considered in context.

Maurice Laporte, *Histoire de l'Okhrana.* Paris: Payot, 1935.
This appears largely to memorialize the opinions of Burtsev, and is as reliable as Burtsev.

Ronald Hingley, *Russian Secret Police.* New York: Simon & Schuster, 1970.
This is discouragingly sensational and derivative, but an important survey nevertheless.

Edward Ellis Smith, *The Young Stalin.* New York: Farrar, Straus & Giroux, 1967.
This book advances circumstantial evidence that Stalin was a police agent.

United States
Much of the material used for the United States consists of fugitive news reports and similar fragmentary accounts. The notes to Chapter 10 of the present book should be consulted. In addition, the following materials not cited in the notes are of value:

Senate Committee on Education and Labor, *Documents Relating to Intelligence Bureau on Red Squad of Los Angeles Police Department,* 76th Cong., 3rd Sess. Washington: Government Printing Office, 1940. Reprinted by Arno Press, New York, in 1971.
This contains some information on provocative tendencies.

Additional material on New York's BOSS (since renamed the Security and Investigation Section (SIS) has appeared in the papers in the case of *Handschuh v. SSD,* 71 Civ. 2203 Southern District of New York.

SOCIAL BANDITRY

The basic general work:

Eric Hobsbawm, *Bandits*. New York: Delacorte Press, 1969.

For Russia, see also:

Bertram Wolfe, *Three Who Made a Revolution*.
Ronald Hingley, *Russian Secret Police*.
Edward Ellis Smith, *The Young Stalin*.

For Latin America:

Neill Macaulay, *The Sandino Affair*. Chicago: Quadrangle Books, 1967.

Carlos Nuñez, *The Tupamaros, Urban Guerrillas of Uruguay*. New York: Times Change Press, 1970.